The Perfect

Gentleman

a Muslim boy meets the West

Imran Ahmad

Originally published as *Unimagined*

www.unimagined.co.uk

Published by New Generation Publishing in 2019

Originally published in the UK as *Unimagined* by Aurum Press, 2007
Published in Australia as *Unimagined* by Pier 9, an imprint of Murdoch Books, 2008
Published in the UK as *Unimagined* by PaperBooks, an imprint of Legend Press, 2010
Published in the United States as *The Perfect Gentleman* by Center Street, an imprint of Hachette Book Group, 2012
Published worldwide as *The Perfect Gentleman* by New Generation Publishing, an imprint of Legend Times Group, 2019

First Edition

ISBN: 978-1-78955-675-9

Translation rights available – contact author via website:
www.unimagined.co.uk

www.newgeneration-publishing.com
New Generation Publishing

Acclaim for
The Perfect Gentleman / Unimagined

The best books of the year – *The Independent*

Books of the year– *The Guardian*

The pick of the literary crop – *Sydney Morning Herald*

Best books of the year– *Belfast Telegraph*

Paperback of the week – *The Guardian*

Shortlisted for the *YoungMinds Book Award*

Best non-fiction read of the year– *dovegreyreader*

Number 1 Bestseller at *Byron Bay Writers' Festival*

Ranked number 11 at *Sydney Writers' Festival*

'Imran Ahmad came second in the Karachi Bonnie Baby competition. The photograph taken to commemorate his achievement is reproduced on the cover of this delightful book. "Smartly dressed, suave and handsome, I looked like James Bond, although I was somewhat unsteady on my feet." Imran was denied the first prize – the daughter of the organisers won. The judges were their friends. "I began my lifelong struggle against corruption and injustice." *Unimagined* is beautifully written, funny and endearing, and in its own quiet way, important.'
Sue Townsend – author of 'Adrian Mole' books

'… irresistible – a charming, laugh-out-loud-funny memoir of a Muslim Pakistani boy growing up in the western world. Full of surprises, hard to put down.'
John Berendt – author of *'Midnight in the Garden of Good and Evil'*

'It deserves all the praise it's had – it's very clearly and vividly written, it's funny and perceptive about schools and neighbours and friends and girls and especially about the narrator himself, with his continuing puzzlement about religion, his smartly pressed clothes, and his apparently naïve fixation with cars. It's very clever to have presented a character so original and unusual, and yet so warmly human and recognisable. The 'I' of the book is a real literary creation – a successful memoir depends just as much on art as a successful novel does.'
Philip Pullman – author of 'His Dark Materials' trilogy

'I cannot tell you how much I have enjoyed this book … Look, just go and buy it … What's not to like? Eh?'
Linda Grant – multiple-prize-winning novelist

'… endearing … unexpectedly subtle and touching …'
Nicholas Lezard – *The Guardian*

' … wonderfully funny, heart-warming, perceptive, enlightening and ironic … Reminiscent of *Adrian Mole*, with echoes of *White Teeth*, but it has its own unique voice … endearing, deadpan humour … Likely to be a word-of-mouth hit … has the makings of a slow-build bestseller …'
Publishing News

'A fascinating insight …'
Sydney Morning Herald

'… an amusing and highly accessible book which deals with a range of theological and cross-cultural issues …'
Canberra Times

'Forthright, wry, entirely enjoyable … A scrupulously well intentioned look at how Christians and Muslims might live respectfully side by side.'
Kirkus Reviews

'Occasionally, booksellers come upon a title which they believe is a defining moment in their trade.'
Clive Keeble – Bookseller, Langport, Somerset

'... exceptionally well-balanced ... a part-funny, part-serious book and it works like a dream ... had me enthralled ... very good indeed.'
Lynne Hatwell – *dovegreyreader*

'I don't normally consider unsolicited approaches, but I just loved *Unimagined* so much!'
Catherine Lockerbie – Director,
Edinburgh International Book Festival

'I read the first thirty pages just standing in front of the bookcase in the Edinburgh Festival bookshop. I knew there and then that it would make great television ...'
Barry Ryan – Creative Director, *Free@Last Television*

'Imran Ahmad, and his book *Unimagined*, came to my attention by pure chance on a rainy Edinburgh evening, when after hearing authors speak all day, I sought a moment of peace in the Writers' Yurt ... But it is impossible not to enjoy and be moved by Imran's book; his whimsical self-deprecating style is the spoonful of sugar that belies the importance of his work and the wisdom which informs it.'
Wendy Were – Creative Director,
Sydney Writers' Festival

'My team and I read *Unimagined* this weekend, and we all loved it. I learned more about Islam and the West from reading *Unimagined*, than I did from all the other books I've read, put together.'
Juliet Rogers – CEO, *Murdoch Books*, **Sydney**

'... had the audience in stitches ...'
Three Weeks, Edinburgh Festival Review

'I met Imran in Sydney and he gave me a copy of *Unimagined* to take home to Bali. I was short of time, so I gave it to my PA, Elizabeth Henzell, to read. I heard her laughing a lot as she read it, I asked her what it was like, and she replied, "It's wonderful!" I promptly took it from her.'
Janet DeNeefe – Director,
***Ubud Writers and Readers Festival* (Bali)**

'I met Imran at UWRF 2008 in Bali and invited him to Byron Bay; *Unimagined* was BBWF 2009's Number One Bestseller. Byron Bay hasn't seen the last of Imran!'
Jeni Caffin – Director,
***Byron Bay Writers Festival* (Australia)**

'I met Jeni Caffin at the Melbourne Writers Festival in September 2009. Jeni wrote and told me about Imran Ahmad ... Although our programme for Emirates Literary Festival 2010 was closed, I am so glad I went with my gut instinct ... copies of *Unimagined* sold out.'
Isobel F. Abulhoul – Director,
***Emirates Airline Festival of Literature* (Dubai)**

'The tender humour and intelligence of this memoir belies its political importance; through it, Muslims are humanised. Imran Ahmad, Pakistan-born and London-raised, writes beautifully of his life ... Just beautiful.'
Antonella Gambotto-Burke – author, journalist, campaigner

'In *Unimagined*, Imran Ahmad writes with warmth, humour and insight about the challenges and joys of growing up nerdy, dreamy and Muslim in Britain.'
Emily Maguire – writer, columnist

'My favourite book of 2007 is this memoir of a Muslim boy, born in Pakistan, who moves to London at the age of one in the 1960s. With his Islamic identity and desire to embrace the West, the book paints a beautiful picture of growing up in a strange culture ... the end result is unforgettable.'
Ann Widdecombe – former Member of Parliament, author, columnist, television presenter

'*Unimagined* is a funny, beguiling and insightful account of a young British Muslim boy growing up in 60s and 70s British society – his encounters early on in life with racism, and later with the material world of fashion, cars and girls. Above all, though, it's his struggle to find his religious identity that makes this timely book so important. Imran Ahmad takes us with him on his personal journey of discovery, gradually learning the meaning of Islam, measuring it alongside Christianity and working out where and how he fits in. I can't wait to read more.'
Sue Cook – broadcaster, writer

'This absorbing personal tale probably does more to help us understand each other in our multi-cultural society than one hundred Downing Street seminars. It's also very funny.'
John Pienaar – BBC Journalist and Editor

'Charming, informative and honest ... a childhood memoir in which the occasional bad thing happens, but is remembered and communicated without the melodrama or martyrdom of the form. The author has a photographic memory for all the important bits: mechanical failure in second-hand cars, dialogue and news stories glimpsed on television and precise exam scores. I enjoyed the book very much ... I read *Unimagined* in two days.'
Andrew Collins – broadcaster, writer, reviewer

'I was delightfully surprised to find a witty and incredibly relevant memoir which had me laughing out loud on more than one occasion. It reminded me of Nigel Slater's *Toast* with the short, pithy chapters which are both moving and funny at the same time ... What's more, he has the best author [cover] photo I have seen in years.'
Scott Pack – former Buying Manager, *Waterstones*; publisher, editor

'Compelling, revealing, and very easy to read. I liked the short chapters and the way the incidental observations added up to a bigger picture.'
Rosie Boycott – journalist, writer

'I consumed *Unimagined* as soon as I started it. I couldn't wait until the plane ride. It was an absolute joy to read. I loved every moment of it ...'
Randa Abdel-Fattah – writer, lawyer, social activist

'... style and a sense of humour ... what a change ... what a delightful change ... brilliant stories too about the joys and confusions of identity politics ...'
Yasmin Alibhai-Brown – broadcaster, journalist, author, columnist

'Engaging, an easy read and truly very funny. Most of all it is profound and revealing, giving the Western reader a deep insight into the Muslim psyche. In these days of incomprehensible suicide bombings and agonising military campaigns, when we live under the shadow of the 'Clash of Civilisations', this is a book that gives the world clarity and, perhaps, optimism.'
Hugh Fraser – writer, journalist, broadcaster

Book of the Week: 'I am jumping unashamedly onto this particular bandwagon as this is one of the best books I have read in ages. Clever, simple, funny and sad, the book describes the author's experience of growing up a Muslim in a newly multi-cultural Britain. Impossible to put down and equally impossible to forget.'
Clare Christian – former Managing Director, *The Friday Project*

'A charming, funny, heart-warming, unputdownable, disarmingly self-deprecating and true story of growing up as a Pakistani Muslim in Britain in the 70s and 80s. Imran Ahmad writes with an extremely light touch, but underneath there's a serious intention: to explode stereotypes, challenge bigotry with humour, and bring about a greater understanding of what it means to yearn to be James Bond.'
Professor Ruth Evans – Department of English, Saint Louis University

'... a wonderful book and Imran is a gracious, poignant, and engaging speaker. Everyone who came to hear him speak at Unity Temple was mesmerized by his stories, wit, and humility. Those who have read his book have greatly enjoyed his creatively written memoir. His personal mission of seeking to re-humanize both Christians and Muslims will surely lead him to an ever wider audience.'
Rev Alan C Taylor – Senior Minister, Unity Temple Unitarian Universalist Congregation, Chicago, Illinois

'I loved your book! I gave it to my mother, and she loved it. Then my sister read it and she loved it. Now my other sister is reading it. ... Of course you can have a late checkout.'
Mary Sitkowski – Manager of Chicago O'Hare Garden Hotel

'Imran, you bastard! I'm supposed to be revising for my Congress exam, and picked up your book for "just a bit." Now I've read the whole damn thing! ... We have so much in common, I might be your twin.'
Email from Lieut Greg Bowling, Texas National Guard

'My grandson (just turned 16) is not going through adolescence very gracefully so far and just spent 2 weeks in juvenile detention. We were able to take him books, so I ordered a copy of *Unimagined* for him, and he really, really enjoyed it.'
Email from Louise, Idaho

'Imran's book is so refreshing.'
[Addressing audience at Perth Writers' Festival, Australia]
James McBride – author of '*The Color of Water*'

'*Unimagined* is a delightful story ... gentle, very funny, and quietly assertive. It could not be more refreshing or timely.'
***Albion* magazine**

' ... a witty and often heart-warming account of growing up with two cultures, while his reflections on his Muslim identity make this a particularly topical memoir.'
The Good Book Guide

'There are topics for reading groups, however this book also makes a fantastic personal read being both thought-provoking and very funny.'
***New Books* magazine**

'... timely and most endearing ... a whimsical undertone ... describes a journey of self-discovery, integration and the challenges of coming of age in the West ... invites connection and familiarity with its readers ...'
***Emel* magazine**

'I do strongly recommend reading this, or even buying someone a copy as a Christmas present – it's a really great read!'
Being Mrs C

'… an ever present humor … funny and entertaining … incredibly 'readable' … I wanted to keep on reading it and find out what was going to happen next.'
Media and Islam, **San Francisco**

'This book was so crap. I can't believe anyone gave it anymore then one star. No redeeming features.'
Kevin Tanner, Sydney – Review on *Goodreads*

'Crap. No talent and does not come across as a good person. Can't believe people actually rate it.'
Kevin Tanner, Sydney – Another review on *Goodreads*

'How can anyone give this shite four stars!'
Kevin Tanner, Sydney – Comment on *Goodreads*

'A must read if you're looking for a book you won't be able to put down and are sad at the end because you wish it were a few hundred pages longer.'
The Baker Project

'[this] book is just so wonderful!'
Deborah Harper – *Psychjourney*

'… humorous and heartwarming … more remarkable is its authenticity.'
Austrolabe, **Australia**

'… [a] funny account of growing up as a Muslim …'
Panel Selection in *Bookseller's Choice*

'... a refreshing insight into the texture of life ...'
Saudi Gazette

'... poignant and often hilarious ... went down a storm at the Edinburgh International Book Festival ... will keep his audience in stitches.'
The Morley Observer

'... refreshingly upbeat ... vividly and with deadpan humour describes his struggles to find his place in [the] world ... often laugh-out-loud ... entertaining ... quietly significant ... insightful and occasionally thought provoking, it's a discreetly inspirational portrait of a boy determined to find the common ground between his roots and his desire to embrace the West.'
The Glasgow Herald

'... an insightful and humorous memoir. The author handles issues such as racism in deft prose and with deadpan humour ... paints a deeply emotional picture of a boy grappling with two different cultures and struggling to fit in. The reader can identify with the child's experiences, laugh at his *faux pas* and marvel at his honesty ... Ahmad keeps his writing style deliberately simple, and the self-deprecating humour in the book makes it an entertaining read.'
The Telegraph, India

'... doesn't contain any of the fighting radicals, extremists, fundamentalists and other nasty types who, if you believe what you read in the New York Post, are the only types of Muslims that exist.'
NewMatilda.com, Australia

'… a very readable book … I guarantee that *Unimagined* will make you laugh out aloud many times before you reach the end.'
Vinod Joseph – *Desicritics.org*

'... the mark of classic literature is that it goes straight to the heart – no matter the historical or class or ethno-cultural background of both writer and reader ... a wonderful book and the chance to reflect again on our shared humanity.'
Letter from Jim Kable – Australian living in Japan

'*Unimagined* is in my opinion one of the most important books I've read in the last couple of years. It's a quietly subversive masterpiece of militant moderation, and everyone should read it.'
Jonathan Pinnock – writer, blogger

'… a fluffy read of no real consequence.'
Alan Baxter – writer of dark horror fiction, Kung Fu instructor

'… extremely readable and thought-provoking … honest, direct, funny, sensitive … his writing showcases his personality and emotions. The prose is beautiful … Highly recommended.'
BOOK-A-HOLICS

'Its subtle imagery leaves a lasting imprint.'
Afrah Jamal – *Think Before You Ink*

'*The Perfect Gentleman* is a memoir worth reading, not only for its humour, but also because it makes one sit up and think.'
Newsline Magazine

'Packed with self-deprecating humor and charming witticisms … a poignantly honest and intimate memoir recounting his early struggles with race, religion, and relationships … heartfelt revelations about the nature of faith and individuality … an enjoyable and hilarious Bildungsroman.'*

Publishers Weekly

'I love that Ahmad is completely honest and doesn't shy away from writing about his doubts … This isn't a somber story of his tale of woe, mind you. Quite the opposite! The biggest reason why this book works is because of Imran Ahmad's personality. He comes across as incredibly down to earth and moral while still being funny and lighthearted. The reader can tell that even at a young age, Ahmad has always wanted to do the right thing and could see through any hypocrisy that he witnessed.'

Bushra Burney – *Caffeinated Muslim*

'Poignant and thought provoking – a roller-coaster ride of emotional consciousness.'

Autumn Blues Reviews

'The story of Imran Ahmad's journey to authorship is as hilariously entertaining as the book he penned … how remarkably honest, hilarious and heartstring-tugging the book is …'

***MPH Quill* magazine, Malaysia**

---

* I had to look this up: 'Bildungsroman' is a literary genre that focuses on the psychological, spiritual and moral growth of the protagonist from youth to adulthood, in which personal development is important and often features an on-going conflict between the main character and society. That's this whole book in one word.

'Kindness, gentleness, and good humor win the day in *The Perfect Gentleman*.'
Unitarian Universalist Examiner

'As a reader, I felt like I was witnessing my own growth … And that's one of the best things about this book. The reader – any reader – can relate to Ahmad's childhood, adolescence, and first steps into adulthood. With a unique voice, Ahmad speaks of universal feelings.'
The Mookse and the Gripes

'… a thought-provoking book which can be read on many levels … **10/10**'
The Review Girl

'…[a] delightful coming-of-age story that highlights the extraordinary depths of a most ordinary life … a dry, self-deprecating humour that layers every situation with multiple ironies and exploits fantastic comic potential in even the most sobering situations … weaving in the social, educational, political, economic and cultural ethos of a Britain that was coming of age with respect to its immigrant situation … a refreshingly upfront memoir … Ahmad's search for his identity is without guile and agenda. It is a rare read, both entertaining and educational, and hence qualifies as a memoir in the truest sense of the word.'
DNA India

'Just couldn't get interested in this fellow's life.'
Margaret Bryant – publishing industry expert

'May be one of the sweetest voices in non-fiction I've ever read.'
Jill Sevelow

'... one of the most interesting social commentaries in the guise of a memoir I've ever read ... His observations ... are fascinating ... very heavy material is explored within a mostly lightweight framework and it seamlessly flows in, out, and through more mundane and secular elements of everyday life ... effortlessly humorous, never breaking a sweat while revealing humor in everyday events and situations ... an amazingly easy read, yet is as thoughtful and provocative a book as I have read in recent memory.'
Bruce Cline

From: Kelder, Jeroen
To: Ahmad, Imran
Sent: Wednesday, April 18, 2007 5:41 PM
Subject: Your book
Amazing – I sat next to a gentleman in the plane and he was reading your book and laughing. Have to note that he was quintessentially British.
Sent from my BlackBerry Wireless Handheld

'Some of his writing shows a real sense of style.'

School report for Imran Ahmad – 1977
Martyn Payne
English Teacher
Hampton (Grammar) School

(Thank you, sir!)

For my father, who was always love and forgiveness.
I'll see you again, Dad, but there is absolutely no hurry.

Contents

ACKNOWLEDGEMENTS

This entire account is completely true. Some names (and other personal details) have been changed or lightly disguised, but most have not.

Acknowledgements is the most difficult part to write, for fear that I may inadvertently exclude someone. I am grateful to *everyone* mentioned in this book, whether family, friend, colleague, teacher, or perceived enemy. Without you there would be no story.

My deepest thanks to my most supportive and influential teachers, who were, *inter alia* (that's Latin for 'amongst others'): Pam Broadhurst, Steve Todd (recently I realised that *you* must have advocated strongly for me to be admitted to the grammar school), Jim Scouse, Crispin Pickles, Sarah Lyon, Martyn Payne, Colin Flood, Ken Rice, Geoff Salter, Martin Schrecker (oh no … this list goes on *ad infinitum* … I should not have tried to list them individually …).

To those dear friends who reviewed my early versions, and gave me their feedback and insight, my thanks and appreciation.

I am grateful to many people in the industry who have helped me on this path of publication: Scott Pack, Charlie Viney, Karen Ings, Nancy Northrop, Juliet Rogers, Colette Vella, Tom Chalmers, David Young, Kate Hartson, Rolf Zettersten, David Walshaw, Sam Rennie.

My joyful gratitude to everyone for supporting this narrative just as it was (more or less), and not demanding more sex and violence.

FOREWORD

Over the past five years, in the role of reviewer of non-fiction for the *Sydney Morning Herald*, I have read more than one thousand books. Inevitably, people query anyone's ability to read, absorb and evaluate so many books. Yet there are a couple of simple truths about such a frightening workload.

How do I read that many books? In two words: speed reading. But, more importantly, how does anyone confronted with such a daunting task know that their judgment is sound and their enthusiasms are correct?

A second simple truth: non-fiction falls into easily identifiable categories:

- Category A: books which would make a good magazine article and which some bright-eyed publisher has persuaded an author to flesh out to 80,000-100,000 words.
- Category B: books where the idea – be it a biography of a celebrity or an account of a widely publicised crime – is what the publisher wants, and, anyway, there's always a sub-editor waiting to turn tortured and tortuous prose into something approaching plain English.
- Category C: books where the writing is so beautiful, lucid, imaginative and worthwhile that they rise above the pile trailing clouds of glory and making the reviewer's heart sing. This last category, I can assure you, is very small.

After a while the overworked reviewer gets a 'nose' for Category C. The gems sit in the mountains of dross (don't get me started on the argument about too many books being published) in the Literary Editor's office shyly saying, 'Open me and you will be amazed.'

And so it was that, amongst another pile of books for review, I saw a photograph of a dapper child in a suit and said to myself: 'I wonder what that is about.'

Contrary to accepted wisdom, when you've read a thousand books you can identify a 'goodie' after a couple of paragraphs. And the wonder of a 'goodie' book is that it turns a speed reader with a deadline into a 'reading for enjoyment' lover of literature and, instantly, you are savouring every word, laughing at the happy moments, letting the life of another person wash over you and saturate your being, marvelling at the love of language and being swept along by the sheer power and beauty of a writer determined to tell his or her story.

I still remember my experience with *The Perfect Gentleman*. It filled an entire day. I could not put the book down. I laughed at Imran's memories of his childhood. I marvelled at his ability to look at his stumbles with such fearless honesty and I shared his gentle, wry irritation at the unfairness of the world.

The greatness of this book is easy to understand. Read it and you will come to know Imran Ahmad as though you have spent a lifetime growing up with him. You will warm to his wonderfully self-deprecating sense of humour and, almost incidentally, you will learn a lot about yourself and a vast amount about the complex multicultural confusion of growing up as an immigrant Pakistani Muslim in England. This is a wise and witty book about the new cultural reality of globalisation.

Bruce Elder
Literary Reviewer
Sydney Morning Herald

3

The Perfect Gentleman

THE PERFECT GENTLEMAN

Separation

1947-61

MY MOTHER'S FAMILY and my father's family were from the same village in India but, in the chaos and insanity of Partition*, they headed in different directions. I could describe those events and years of separation in heartrending, excruciating six-hundred-page detail, but this is not that kind of book. (This story will proceed mercifully briskly and you will not be tortured along the way.) Suffice to say that, eventually, both families ended up in Karachi, the capital of West Pakistan.

My father and mother were students together at Karachi University. My father took a liking to my mother and became fixated on the idea of marrying her. Of course, any form of romance was out of the question, so he took to visiting my mother's house, as a 'family friend', virtually every day for about five years. He could never seem to be there for the explicit purpose of seeing my mother, so he would busy himself with my mother's younger brother, who was a teenager. My father had a scooter and he would take my future uncle on rides around Karachi: perhaps to visit the beach; or to eat hot, fresh samosas; or to buy mangoes when they were in season. He had numerous traffic accidents in the process. Eventually, he was allowed

---

* On granting Independence to 'old' India in 1947, the British also partitioned the country into the predominantly Hindu 'new' India and the Muslim Pakistan – which was itself created in two separated fragments, West and East, on either side of India. This was a recipe for catastrophe. Millions of people had to migrate to their 'correct' new countries. Karachi was the original capital of West Pakistan, later superseded by Islamabad.

to marry my mother and he moved into the house of my mother's family. My father was a civil servant and my mother was a primary school teacher.

I didn't find out about any of this until my uncle told me, when he came to London from Texas, for my father's funeral.

Monsoon

1962-63

Age: 0

I WAS BORN DURING a particularly heavy and prolonged rainstorm, this being the last big splash of the monsoon season. The streets were flooded.

I was already two weeks late when my father, tired of waiting, had decided to go out for the evening. My mother went into labour and my grandfather had to run out in the heavy downpour to find a taxi to take my mother to the maternity clinic. My father returned home that night to find no one there except the servant.

Meanwhile, I took my time in arriving (a trait I still exhibit sometimes) and I emerged in the early hours of 13 September 1962, after an extremely difficult labour.

It is possibly a divine blessing that my father was not at home when my mother went into labour. Faced with the seemingly impossible task of finding a taxi in the middle of the deluge, it is possible that my father, in a state of panic and desperation, might have decided that the scooter was the only option.

THE PERFECT GENTLEMAN

Bond

1963-64

Age: 1

I CAME SECOND IN the Karachi 'Bonnie Baby' contest. I was wearing a black suit, white shirt and dark tie. Smartly dressed, suave and handsome, I looked like James Bond, although I was too young to see either of his movies. I was also somewhat unsteady on my feet. People were particularly impressed by my light skin.

First prize went to the child of the organiser. The judges were her friends. This is absolutely typical of third world, banana republic unfairness. In the West, the organiser's child would not be allowed to enter the contest. I was denied the title of 'Karachi's Bonniest Baby' by blatant nepotism. I began my lifelong struggle against corruption and injustice.

Life in Karachi was stable, but unpromising. The British government was encouraging Commonwealth migration to post-war Britain, due to acute labour shortages. Many people were going and my mother thought it was a good idea: an adventure with great promise that would break the stagnation of life. She persuaded my reluctant father, who enjoyed life in Karachi, that we should move to England.

If you knew someone who knew someone in England, then that person in England would be your first contact on arriving. My parents knew of someone in Manchester, so that was their first destination. Fortunately for me (as events would later reveal), they soon decided to move to London.

There was a nasty shock on arrival in England. The kinds of jobs that my parents had access to were not what they had expected. In England, they were not considered to be educated professionals. They were expected to be lower-class manual workers. Only if they accepted this could they get jobs. Accommodation was another problem as well.

When my parents first arrived in Manchester, they met a woman who offered to rent to them her unfurnished terraced house. They moved in and spent much of their precious money on furnishing the place. They breathed a sigh of relief that they had been able to settle down in England relatively painlessly. Three weeks later, a solicitor's letter arrived, advising them that they were not authorised to occupy the house. Their apparent landlady was really the tenant, who had sub-let the house to them; the true owner had discovered that Pakistanis now occupied the house and wanted them out. My parents had to leave the house and abandon the furniture they had bought.

1963-64
Age: 1

Bed-Sit

1964-65

Age: 2

ENGLAND AT THAT TIME had a very defined class system. I think that it could be analysed in great detail, worthy of a doctoral thesis, but a broad representation would be as follows:

1. Royalty
2. Aristocracy
3. Upper classes
4. Middle classes
5. White working classes
6. Irish
7. Coloureds

In this society, my parents, who were from the educated middle classes in Karachi, found themselves in a very hostile environment, at the mercy of uneducated, uncouth people in terms of jobs and accommodation. The latter, in the earliest days, was a series of bed-sits.

A *bed-sit*, for the benefit of my American readers, is a part of a house that is rented out, consisting of a bedroom and living room (which may be the same room), and use of a bathroom and kitchen (which may be shared with other bed-sits). The term 'apartment' is therefore too grand for this accommodation. If the bed-sit consisted of two proper rooms, then Pakistanis invariably ended up sub-letting one of the rooms to other Pakistanis.

This wasn't always due entirely just to lack of money. Accommodation was hard to come by for Pakistanis.

Although many people in London were renting out rooms, some had signs which read '*No Irish or Coloureds*'. The more liberal-minded ones had signs which read '*No Coloureds*'.

Even without the signs, some would make excuses to my parents, such as: 'We don't allow babies.' So, it was a very difficult time and it was in one such bed-sit, where my parents had rented a room from another family, that I formed my first permanent memory.

... My mother is standing precariously on top of a stool, facing a window in the kitchen. Something has happened to the old window – some part of it has dropped on my mother's hands, trapping them in the wooden frame. She is caught in a very awkward position on the stool, her hands stuck in the window frame, looking back down at me and trying to give me instructions. My father is out at work, I am two years old and my brother Rehan is a baby. Fortunately, the woman we sub-let the room from returns eventually and calls the fire brigade. I watch the fireman in his uniform, working on the window to free my mother ...

Our first bed-sit of our own in London was offered to my parents by a woman who was also a tenant in that house; she managed the place and collected the rent on behalf of the landlord. However, there was a condition. She told them that they must 'go to the park' every Friday morning, when the landlord came to get the rent from her, because he did not approve of children in his rental properties. It later emerged that there was a different reason why we had to be out whenever he came. The woman had not informed the landlord that this particular bed-sit was now occupied; she was pocketing the rent for herself. When, as was inevitable, the landlord eventually discovered the truth, this ended in acrimony for all parties and we had to leave the house.

1964-65
Age: 2

Forbidden

WE HAVE OUR OWN BED-SIT, at the top of a three-storey terraced house in Perham Road, Fulham. We have one big room and one small room. My father, mother, brother and I live in the big room. The small room is rented out to some other Pakistani man.

My parents buy me a tricycle. It is kept in the room and my father has to carry it downstairs for me when I want to ride it. I am allowed to ride it up and down the pavement* outside the house, with my father watching. The street is quiet, with only a few parked cars, and many children play here. The whitewashed houses are narrow and tall, each with two grand columns at the entrance. My father tells me that I can ride my tricycle to the end of the street, but then I must come back. I must not go around the corner; that is *forbidden.*

As I approach the end of the street, I imagine how much fun it would be to go around the corner, ride around the whole block and then surprise my father (who is chatting with a neighbour) by appearing from the other end of the street. This seems unbearably funny to me.

I reach the corner and suddenly launch into my scheme of playful disobedience; I lunge around the corner and pedal as fast as I can. The next corner is very close. (The block is very thin, being only the thickness of two back-to-

---

* Dear American readers: let's just clarify this right now. What you call 'the sidewalk', we call 'the pavement'. You say 'pavement' is what 'the sidewalk' is made of.

back terraced houses with very small backyards.) I conquer this side in no time and pedal furiously around the next corner. A shock awaits me; the block stretches as far as the eye can see. *What have I got myself into?*

I have no choice. I push on, pedalling the tricycle as fast as I can. It seems to take forever; the other end of the block comes closer excruciatingly slowly. I pedal and pedal, with a mounting sense of panic: I am alone and far away from home. I ignore the people that I pass, and they seem to ignore me. My legs are aching, but I dare not stop. Eventually, the corner comes and I turn around it. Now, I have just a short side of the block to overcome. I keep pushing the pedals and thankfully soon turn this corner.

The home side of the block stretches in front of me. There, in the distance, I can see my father; he seems a long way away. I pedal as fast as my weary legs can manage, and he comes closer, slowly closer.

When I reach my father, he does not seem to think my joke is funny. He is not angry, but he is disappointed. He tries to tell me that what I have done is foolish and bad in some way, but I don't really understand how.

1965-66
Age: 3

House

1966-67

Age: 4

MY PARENTS MANAGE TO BUY A HOUSE. This is through extreme hard work, careful saving and a first-time buyer's mortgage from the Greater London Council (GLC).

It is a two-storey terraced house in Weiss Road, Putney. It appears very narrow from the outside, but is quite deep. The front door is very close to the pavement; there is no driveway or private parking, which does not matter too much, as we do not have a car. There is a very small concrete backyard (not really a garden), which is rarely used.

For years, one or two of the rooms are rented out to a succession of other immigrants: Pakistanis, Chinese, Nigerians, Iranians. My parents, who for so long had lived at the whim of landlords, are now landlords themselves. But this is not about making lots of money; it is about trying to make ends meet.

In reality, I barely notice these other occupants. They keep to their own rooms, except when using the kitchen or bathroom. Our own parts of the house seem more than adequate, compared to the bed-sits in which we have been living.

There is a nice old lady named Mrs Rose who lives next door; she is a widow. She is very kind and friendly, never showing any resentment towards all these foreigners who've moved in. She has two budgies and she drinks a lot of tea; Brooke Bond PG Tips to be precise. The boxes of this tea periodically contain different series of collector's 'tea cards', which are about different subjects: 'Flags of the World', 'British Costumes', 'History of the Motorcar', 'Famous People', 'The Saga of Ships'. There are always fifty in a full set. Mrs Rose collects these, and then she gives them to me. Once in a while, she puts the latest collection in an envelope through our letterbox. It's always a nice surprise.

One day, my mother goes away to Putney hospital. My father goes there to visit and some family friends look after Rehan and me. When my mother returns, there are many people in the house and much excitement. She lays a baby down and I peer at him over the edge of the cot; he is my new brother, Rizwan.

We usually travel to places by bus. One evening we are hurrying towards a bus stop on Putney Bridge. A traditional red London double-decker, open at the back, is at the bus stop. I am in front, my father is right behind me, carrying Rehan, and behind them is my mother, with Rizwan in a pram. I will be the first from my family to board the stationary bus. My right foot is lifted and hovering above the edge of the deck ... when suddenly the bus lurches away. My foot comes down on empty space.

My parents are in no doubt as to why this happened. The conductor saw Pakistanis about to board the bus and hurriedly instructed the driver to pull away.

1966-67
Age: 4

18

Jesus

I START INFANT SCHOOL, at Hotham School in
Putney.[1] It is a big, redbrick Victorian school, with two
concrete playgrounds. The ground floor is the infant
school, the first floor is the junior school, and the second
floor is mysterious. Inside, there is wooden parquet
flooring and the classrooms are bright and colourful. My
teacher is Mrs Sikora, a slim, sprightly Scottish lady. The
activities are fun; I am part of the crowd. I am
unremarkable and my reading progress is average.

Every day we have Assembly. Every day I hear a story
about Jesus, who lived a long time ago. Jesus was a very
good man and told everyone to be nice to people. That
seems fair to me.

One day we hear the story of the Prodigal Son. I am
sitting on the floor with the other children, listening to this.
We are told that the Prodigal Son left his father's house to
go to a faraway land, because he thought that he could find
a better life. Instead, he fell upon hard times, had to work
as a swineherd, and was reduced to eating the same food as
the pigs. I try to imagine what this must be like. But there's
one thing that I don't understand. If he was herding pigs,
why didn't he just eat the food *from* the pigs? This, I know,
is Spam, which we are fed at school. I know that eggs come
from chickens and milk comes from cows, so I have
logically deduced that slices of Spam emerge from live pigs
in the same way.

It appears that I have little talent in the field of Art. One day, I draw 'some sticks falling from a tree'. This is what I tell my neighbouring classmates, when they ask me what on earth this picture is supposed to be. When she comes around to examine my work, Mrs Sikora (who is normally very nice and kind) does not interpret the crisscross of brown crayon lines in quite the same way as I do; she is quite scathing about the quality of my masterpiece.

On another occasion, the ball that I have drawn in the middle of an otherwise empty page, painstakingly filling in the small circle with a black crayon, causes her such consternation that she holds it up to show the class and calls it 'just a dirty black ball'.

I do have a growing awareness of being different: both foreign and not Christian. I learn a lot about Jesus in school, but I think that I'm not supposed to believe in him.

In the holidays and at weekends, I play in the street with the other children. They are of all ages and races. We wander around the neighbourhood with impunity, although my parents prefer that I stay within the immediate vicinity of Weiss Road. There is a sweet shop around the corner from our house. Whenever I get a ha'penny or two, I go immediately to the sweet shop to spend the money.

Our latest fashion is 'Tarzan' cards. They come in packets: four cards with a stick of bubble gum. Each card shows a scene from a cartoon Tarzan story. I really don't like bubble gum, but I like collecting the cards. I carry my thick wad of cards around with me in the street.

One day, two older boys, whom I know by sight, approach me. One is black and one is white. The white boy also has a stack of Tarzan cards. The black boy says that we can play a game in which we will win Tarzan cards from each other. He knows the rules and will show me how to play.

1967-68
Age: 5

We squat on the pavement outside my house and play the game. The black boy is orchestrating the game; the white boy is the other contestant. I don't really understand the game at all. Each time I pull one of the cards from my pile, the other boy also pulls a card from his pile. The black boy examines the two cards and then declares the winner. The white boy keeps winning and also gets to keep both of the cards each time. I don't understand how this works, but I keep playing, in the hope of winning my cards back.

In a very short space of time, I lose all of my precious Tarzan cards. This is a horrible, unbelievable thing that has happened. I am frantic and miserable as I realise that, because I have no more cards, I can't play anymore, so there's no chance to win my cards back. I notice that the black boy has a very cunning smile, as the two of them walk away with all of my Tarzan cards.

I run inside to tell my mother. She is dressed like a cleaning woman: rubber gloves, apron, scarf over her hair. She seems always to be cleaning the house. Very upset, I tell her what happened, hoping that she can make it right. She looks very tired.

At the end of the school year, my mother takes my two brothers and me with her to Pakistan and we live at my grandparents' big house for the entire summer vacation. My father continues to work in London; he has no choice. My mother is highly stressed by the misery, humiliation and poverty of life in England (not to mention the cold and the rain), and is possibly having a nervous breakdown. She is seriously considering moving us back to Pakistan permanently.

My grandfather is a tall, distinguished man with a bald head. One day he takes me to work with him; he is the Manager of the railway station. He wears a white short-sleeved shirt and dark trousers, and carries a leather satchel. We travel to the railway station in a motor rickshaw. His

1967-68
Age: 5

office has many open windows which look out onto the tracks and let in the blazing sunshine, and a fan blows across the room, oscillating steadily throughout the day, marking time like a clock. There are several essential paperweights on his desk: smooth, glass orbs with colourful trinkets embedded inside them. Many men come to see my grandfather, talking about important matters to do with trains, and he reads and signs endless papers. He introduces me as his grandson who lives in London; I try not to fidget too much.

My mother explores the idea of us attending school in Pakistan, but eventually she decides to give England another try and we arrive back in London. I can see my father through the glass wall at Heathrow Airport, waiting for us. It is good to see him again.

1967-68
Age: 5

Spam

1968-69

Age: 6

I RETURN TO SCHOOL and enter the next class. Somehow, and I'm not sure how, I acquire a reputation with Miss Waterford for being disobedient and not paying attention, chattering too much to my classmates. Academically I am somewhat dull – nothing special.

One day at school lunch, I notice that my classmate Stephen MacNamara has an interesting way of eating Spam. He cuts the slice into precise little squares. I wish that I had done the same. I look forward to the next time that we eat Spam. (Due to the unhealthy nature and repetition of school meals, I do not have long to wait.) When I next eat Spam, I remember to cut it into little squares, which is fun.

I tell my parents about it in the evening. They confer together, then issue a commandment: 'We don't eat pork.'

I am disappointed, but I obey them. From now on, I don't eat pork. I don't know *why*, but I don't do it.

We have an oil-fired central heating boiler installed in our house. There is an oil tank in the backyard, which must occasionally be refilled by a visit from a tanker. Since we live in a narrow street of terraced houses, the tanker has to parallel park outside, in front of the house.

One day, there is a relatively small space outside the house, when the oil tanker comes. My father is giving the Irish driver parking directions, trying to guide him as he attempts to reverse into the space. Unfortunately, communication between them is not very good, and they disagree on whether there really is enough space for the tanker to park. There is a heated exchange, they both get angry, and the tanker drives away.

My father gets on the phone to the company immediately. He is furious. He tells them to send another tanker, and 'not another Irishman'. I know that this is wrong. My father – who is basically a good man, decent and well-intentioned – has allowed himself to be influenced by the prevailing racism of our times, buying into it insofar as it is not directed against *him*. The irony of this is apparent to me, even at this age.

Doctor Who[2] is a very important television programme for all of my school friends and me. Some of my classmates say that they watch it 'from behind the sofa', because of the scary monsters. I can't say the same, because our television is kept in my parents' bedroom, so there's no sofa to watch it from behind.

Due to some Pakistani gathering one Saturday evening, to which my parents insist on taking us, I miss the *Doctor Who* episode in which the dark-haired Doctor changes into a new Doctor, a light-haired one. I am very upset with my parents; they have no idea about what is really important.

My friend Roger Maxwell explains to me what happened when we confer in the playground on Monday. It sounds very exciting. I'm upset that I missed it.

My parents receive *Life* magazine in the mail. In one edition there is an article entitled 'One Week's Dead'. I count eleven pages of small photos of American soldiers killed in a war that is happening somewhere. I never realised that so many Americans are black; I thought it was just a few. On American television programmes, we just see the occasional black person here and there.

Several editions of *Life* show photos of men going to the moon. I stare at them, enthralled. The pictures are

1968-69
Age: 6

amazing. They show the astronauts at every stage of the journey: going over the plan at the dining table in one of their big houses (while their wives make snacks in the kitchen); blasting off in a huge rocket; landing on the moon; planting the American flag and collecting rocks; coming back to Earth; splashing into the sea. These men are all white, unlike the ones killed in the war.

1968-69
Age: 6

Muhammad

1969-70

Age: 7

I AM AN UNREMARKABLE SCHOOLCHILD. Miss Rigby does not think much of me. She tells my mother that I am average. My parents always make a point of coming into the school at least a couple of times a year and asking my teacher how I'm doing. I find it extremely embarrassing that they come to the classroom to speak with the teacher; no one else's parents ever do such a thing.

There is some problem with one of the *Apollo* missions to the moon. My mother insists on watching the return to Earth, instead of letting me watch *The Flintstones* on the other channel. We don't often argue over which of the two channels to watch. There is a third channel, called BBC2, but hardly anyone watches it, because the picture is very bad and you need a new kind of television and a special aerial installed on the roof of your house to receive it properly.

My father buys a car. *Hooray!* It is an old British one, a Morris. It is sitting outside the house when we come home from school one day. The next morning, my father is going to take us to school in it, which is exciting, although Hotham School is barely five minutes' walk away. He turns the key, the car makes the starting noise, but it doesn't start. He tries again … and again … and again. The car refuses to start. We sit here for what seems like forever, with my father repeatedly trying to start the car, which it stubbornly refuses to do.

We walk to school and when we return at the end of the day, the car is gone. We never see it again.

Miss Rigby has noticed that I squint a lot. She tells me to tell my mother that I must get my eyes tested. Dutifully, I do so. My mother conducts a rough-and-ready eye test, asking me if I can read the numbers on a calendar across the room. I can't read any of them; they are a complete blur. But I'm afraid that my parents will be angry with me if I am found to be short-sighted and they have to pay for glasses, so I lie and say that I can read them all. My mother never figures out the truth and the matter is not discussed again.

There is a television programme about different religions and one day my mother makes me watch it, because this episode is about Islam. Okay, so now I know that I'm a *Muslim* and we believe in someone called *Muhammad*. Well, I bet that Muhammad could beat up Jesus in a fight. Oh, but they wouldn't fight; they would make peace, because that's what they're like. Damn.

How do we know Muhammad didn't just make it all up? There are so many religions with different beliefs. Only one can be true. How do I know it's this one? Anyone could just make up a religion. What happens to people who believe in one of the wrong religions? Hey, I'm only seven. I shouldn't have to worry like this.

My father buys another car, an old blue VW Beetle. It works fine. Finally, we are a mobile family. We visit other Pakistani families a lot.

We exist in a community that maintains its own, separate existence within the greater white English community. I lead a dual existence, belonging to English society (for the most part) at school, and being Pakistani outside school. My parents are friendly with the white neighbours, but it is no more than that. They have no white friends who come to visit our house.

I am a pirate in a class play, which is to be performed for the rest of the school. It is a speaking part: I have one line. The day of the performance will be on Eid, a key Muslim celebration. I tell Miss Rigby that I will not be in school in the morning, because I have to go to the mosque with my family, as is the tradition, but I will be back for the afternoon, when we are performing the play. She acknowledges that this is okay.

Eid goes as planned. My father, Rehan and I assemble with our fellow Muslims in improvised marquees in the grounds of Woking Mosque, for the sombre and incomprehensible ritual. We are back home for lunch, but I am anxious to get to school on time for the afternoon session.

Back at school, Miss Rigby seems surprised to see me. Having completely forgotten what I had told her, she has assigned someone else (Anne) to my part. I am here now, so I will be in the play, but Anne (who has already been made up) will also be in the band of pirates. The crucial moment comes and I deliver my key line – and so does Anne. Miss Rigby had not thought to instruct one of us not to say that line.

There is a girl in my class named Patricia Bastin. I like her a lot. In fact, I am in love with her. This means that I must marry her someday. I hope that my being a foreigner won't be an issue, but it does give me a sense of disadvantage, of inadequacy. I'm not sure how this process works, but I imagine that Patricia and I *will* get married one day.

My friend Andrew Baker senses my affection for Patricia. One day he tells me that *he* and Patricia have decided to get married, and have been discussing which *church* to get married in. I am heartbroken. How could I

1969-70
Age: 7

have been so stupid as to think that Patricia would marry *me*? I am different, a foreigner, and I don't go to church.

We have a new headmaster, Mr Campbell. He has a soft, dignified manner, a scholarly face and horn-rimmed glasses. He is very fond of classical music. Every morning in Assembly, he tells us some profoundly important moral story, often from the Bible, but not always so. I learn my basic morality from him: kindness, honesty, good deeds, helping others. Every morning he leads us in a prayer, and we pray to God to help us to be good and for nice things for everybody. I know that we Muslims believe in God, so although this prayer in Assembly is a different style from the one that we do in the mosque, I am not uncomfortable about it.

My father gets a new job. He now works for Pakistan International Airlines (PIA) and is based at Heathrow Airport. (He never changes job again.) He looks so smart in his uniform and he's really proud of it: it looks just like a pilot's uniform, but with only one white stripe around the wrists, not four gold stripes like a captain. (Over the years to come, the stripes become more numerous and gradually transmute from white to gold.) The most significant aspect of this job, which shapes my life forever, is that we will get cheap tickets on PIA and partner airlines (but always have to travel 'standby'). Also, I come to love airports and airplanes; the bustle, the noise, the anticipation of going somewhere, I relish these always.

Perhaps to celebrate his new job, my father trades in the Beetle for a VW Fastback, a coupé that always seems to be quite rare. We hardly ever see another one.

One night I have a dream. Jesus is in the playground, at the far end, and all the children are running excitedly to gather around him. Except for me. I'm hiding around a corner,

1969-70
Age: 7

taking a peek now and then at what's going on, but I'm keeping away, because I'm not supposed to be part of this. I feel awkward and afraid.

Being different is troublesome sometimes. Why couldn't I just have been 'normal' (i.e. white, English, Christian)? Then I would have just fitted in with everyone, and I wouldn't have to be afraid of Jesus.

One day at school, fish and chips *(everyone's favourite!)* is being served for lunch. The smell and the anticipation are delightful. Michael Swallow, who is from my class and seems a bit of a harmless rogue, decides to push into the queue in front of me when I am nearly at the counter. I am outraged, but – in a supreme moment of forgiveness, of which both Jesus and Mr Campbell would approve – I decide to let him go ahead, to not worry about it. I calmly deduce that this will result in nothing more than me getting my fish and chips just a few seconds later. Michael Swallow reaches the front and has to specify his choice: *fish and chips, or cheese and egg flan?* It's a mere formality.

I reach the counter and the hideous truth is revealed to me when my meal preference is not requested by the dinner lady.[3] There are *no more* trays of fish and chips. Michael Swallow got the last fish and chips! Those should have been *my* fish and chips. He and I realise this at the same instant. He is just walking past me with his tray of ill-gotten gains when his eyes and mine lock together, and I can see a hint of guilty acknowledgement in his face. But then he averts his gaze and hurries away. I am angry, furious; I feel bitter and cheated.

I look sullenly at what is put on my plate. A square of cheese and egg flan that looks like dry sick. A round dollop of implausibly white mashed potato, which I know from experience is utterly tasteless. A blob of some green mush that used to be vegetables, all appetising texture and goodness having been scrupulously boiled out of them. *This* is what kindness and forgiveness get you.

In the playground, Patricia asks me, 'What do you want to be when you grow up?'

I know the answer; I have thought about it a lot.

'I'd like to have my own television programme.'

'What, you mean like *The Imran Ahmad Show*?'

'No, I mean like …' but my voice trails off. I can't explain this; it will sound ridiculous.

What I *really want* is to be an actor who plays a character like Simon Templar in *The Saint*; a brave hero who helps good people and punches bad people and drives a sports car called a Volvo. But I know that this is a wild, impossible dream for two reasons. First, no one can imagine a television programme with a Pakistani man as the hero – that will never happen. Second, as a television hero I would probably have to kiss women – *on the lips!* – and Pakistanis don't do that. I cringe with embarrassment at what my parents would think if they saw me on the television, kissing women, like the Saint does.

In the summer holiday, my brothers and I visit Pakistan again, with our mother. My father calls the PIA office and tells them to give us good seats (if we get seats, of course, being standby). The captain tells us when we land that the temperature outside is 91 degrees. When I step out of the aircraft onto the top of the staircase, into the overwhelming, oppressive brightness, I immediately gain an understanding of what 91 degrees feels like, one which I remember forever. I feel my clothes sticking to me suddenly from the instant perspiration.

My grandfather comes to meet us with an array of relatives, taxis and a hired minibus. Karachi is as I remember it: hot, bright, colourful, frantic. My grandfather's house is big by London standards. It is

1969-70
Age: 7

detached, with iron gates and a driveway. It actually has several entrances, as it is organised into four separate units; two of them are rented out at this time. There is also a big flat roof, which has a couple of rooms built on it (where we usually sleep) and a large open area, with many clay plant pots. Every morning, when we wake up, my grandfather is watering the plants on the roof.

THE PERFECT GENTLEMAN

War

BACK IN ENGLAND, my new teacher, Mr Ford, surprises me in class by calling me to the front and asking me to talk about my trip to Pakistan. This is quite a shock, as it is the first time that I have addressed an audience, but I have plenty of material to talk about and my enthusiasm carries me through. I start with the story of the journey on a Boeing 707, which is thrilling, because most of my classmates have never flown.

There are questions throughout my talk and one person asks what they wear in Pakistan. 'Rags,' mumbles Mario. Mr Ford silences him with a severe look.

I answer from my fresh recollection. 'The women wear saris or brightly coloured loose trousers and matching shirts called *shalwar kameez*, and the men wear trousers and short-sleeved shirts.'

Every morning we have breakfast in the kitchen, before going to school. The radio is always tuned to BBC Radio 4, for the *Today* programme. One morning what we hear is particularly bleak.

'*This is the BBC News. India and Pakistan have declared war.*' My mother looks very upset. I know what happens in wars. I imagine Indian planes dropping bombs on my grandfather's house. I am very worried. Life goes on as normal for us in England, but everyone is tuned into the news all the time.

On the television news one evening, we see that the reality is as horrible as we imagine. The BBC reporter shows how Indian planes bombed an orphanage in Pakistan. *They bombed an orphanage!* Most of the children were killed. There is a nearby railway line, which was the intended target, apparently. (The BBC reporter makes this clear, but it is easy to ignore.)

So now I have something to hate: *India.*

Hatred is a delicious feeling – it comes so easily and makes me feel good about myself … superior to someone else.

Many evenings, Pakistanis gather together at someone's house or other, all talking about the war. (I imagine that Indians do the same.) This is a delight for armchair strategists. We children, who are invisible, play or sit and listen. *'If we can just win Kashmir, then this will all be over.'* I listen, think and nod with agreement. It all seems very simple. If we can take control of Kashmir, then we will win the war.* Apparently, Kashmir should have been given to Pakistan at Partition, because it is mostly Muslim, but India wants to keep it. *How evil and unreasonable!* Anyway, God will surely help Pakistan to win, because God is Muslim.

There are other things happening. *Horrible, horrible things.* Words I don't understand: *mass rape.* Words I do understand: *torture, massacres.* I see a Pakistani newspaper that shows a sequence of photographs. A man has been captured by soldiers and is tied up. They burn him with cigarettes. He pleads for mercy. Then they shoot him. I don't understand who is doing this to whom. *How can this be? Don't these people worry about what God will think?*

Not only does Pakistan fail to win the war, but also East Pakistan breaks away and declares its independence, as Bangladesh, with India's help. This is incomprehensible. It is treachery. My parents have some East Pakistani friends, a

---

* This particular war wasn't ostensibly about Kashmir, but people still spoke as if it was.

couple and their two daughters, whom we used to meet with quite often. I remember going to Windsor Castle with them. My parents don't phone them anymore and we never see them ever again.

We are doing a history project about the Romans at school. I have an encyclopaedia of History, which I bring to school one day to consult for the project. Mr Ford runs into me outside the school this morning and notices the book I am carrying. I tell him it is for the project.

At the end of the school day, as we file out of the classroom, Mr Ford again notices the book I am carrying, now being taken home.

'Is that yours?' he demands.

'Yes,' I reply.

'Are you *sure*?' he asks incredulously.

He thinks that I am completely dim and couldn't possibly own such a book. But he saw me bring it in the morning! I can't understand how teachers can be so forgetful.

One day, Mr Ford, for reasons best known to himself, decides to tell us about secondary schools. He says that we don't appreciate how lucky we are in school right now. Secondary school is a horrible place. The teachers are mean and will make our lives miserable. They will be nasty, unfriendly and will give us lots of homework. If we put a foot wrong, the punishments will be severe.

There is silence in the room; we look at each other with fear in our eyes. We all know that one day we must go to secondary school, which is frightening now, but at least it is a long way in the future. The anticipation and fear that he has instilled in me remain.

There is a problem that I always have with Eid, which comes twice a year. It is nice to get some presents

1970-71
Age: 8

(although these are not as extravagant or numerous as the ones that my classmates get for Christmas), but Eid means having to go to the prayer gathering in smart (generally new) clothes and this for me means 'rough' trousers. By 'rough' I mean that the fabric of formal trousers sets my sensitive skin on fire; the itching and irritation are unbearable. To prevent this, my mother allows me to wear cotton pyjama bottoms under my trousers, which keep the 'rough' material from touching my skin. The bottoms of the pyjamas are tucked into my socks.

Every Friday afternoon in the junior department we have 'Friday Concert', which is like a special Assembly; children from the different classes showcase their work, read stories, perform short dramas and so on. We all sit on the floor in a huge circle around the perimeter of the hall. One week, my class is to perform a short play and Mr Ford chooses me for a leading role, the Chief of the Blackfoot tribe. We rehearse the play a few times and perform it for Friday Concert. We are in our underwear and have some face paint on our cheeks to show that we are 'Red Indians'.*

Adam Smith, the Chief of the Whitefoot tribe, gathers his people for a meeting and, before them all, he snaps an arrow in two; *this means war!* He hands the broken arrow to a messenger, Michael Swallow, and orders him to take it to the Chief of the Blackfoot tribe (*that's me!*). Michael Swallow brings me the broken arrow and I hold it up before all my people, telling them, 'We are at war with the Whitefoot tribe!'

As for Michael Swallow, I order my men to 'Throw him to the dogs!'

---

* Nowadays I would, of course, say 'Native Americans' – but in those days this was the dreadful term in common use. We didn't know any better.

'No, no!' he pleads, pathetically, as he is dragged away.

Well, this serves him right for stealing my fish and chips, but I don't really understand what the dogs will do to him – lick him to death?

We go to war against the other tribe, many on both sides are killed and wounded, it is unbearable ... so eventually we decide to make peace, which is better than war. It makes good sense to me.

My friend Adam Smith invites me to his house after school for tea. Their house is semi-detached (there's a 'junk room' – a whole bedroom used just for storing old stuff, instead of being rented out) and has a big garden, and his mother is quite posh.

She calls us inside to eat and puts a plate of sausages and beans in front of each of us.

'Are these pork sausages?' I ask, in a serious, business-like manner. When Adam's mother confirms that they are, I respond automatically and somewhat abruptly, in a voice indicating strong concern, 'I don't eat pork.'

Adam's mother is the perfect host. 'Oh, of course you don't. How silly of me. I'll do you some fried eggs instead.' She pulls the plate away immediately.

'Why doesn't he eat pork, Mum?' queries Adam.

'Oh, it's religion, dear,' responds Adam's mother, in a distracted way, as she focuses on the frying of eggs.

Oh, so that's why I don't eat pork! It's because of my religion.

There's bad news about Jesus. Mr Ford tells us that the Romans killed him, by 'crucifixion'. He explains what this is, but I'm not sure that I understand. Apparently, if you hang for too long, you become too tired to breathe and so you die. This seems hard to believe. How could you ever be *so* tired that you couldn't manage another breath? Still, it sounds very horrible and we are all very subdued.

1970-71
Age: 8

But there was also a cruel trick the Romans used, Mr Ford tells us. They would put a little seat on the cross, so that the poor person could rest on it for periods of time. This made them less tired, so that they could breathe for longer, but then it took them three days to die. *Three days to die! How horrid.*

My father tends to get time off on Fridays, and in the school holidays he takes us to a mosque in Wimbledon for Friday prayers. The mosque is really a terraced house, devoid of furniture, white sheets spread over all the floors. The entrance hall is piled with pairs of shoes. My father sends us upstairs, which seems to be designated for boys, whilst he prays downstairs with the men. We sit on the floor in a room with other Pakistani boys, who all seem to know each other.

The formal congregational prayer is not too difficult. My brothers and I merely go along with all the bowing and kneeling and prostrating, along with everyone else. The problem is that after the official Friday prayer ritual is over, there seems to be some form of optional prayers which everyone does, but they do them separately, in their own time, not in a coordinated way. Not having a clue what to do and not wanting to stand out from the crowd, I always select someone in my line of sight and copy his every move, pretending to be muttering the Arabic prayers under my breath.

One day I am rumbled. A youth in my row stares at me, then calls to his friend, 'Hey Wajid, he's copying you.'

I carry on, pretending to be oblivious to this, as if I'm not really copying Wajid. He finishes and looks around at me. They both confront me.

'You don't know how to pray?' Wajid asks me in a critical way. 'Can you read Qur'an?' He is proud of the fact that he obviously can and I must be stupid. (He means

'*Can't* you read', but his English is not sophisticated enough for him to articulate this.)

I shake my head miserably. I'm a foreigner in white, English society and I don't seem to fit into Pakistani society either.

THE PERFECT GENTLEMAN

Narnia

1971-72

Age: 9

IN CLASS I sit next to a lovely honey blonde girl named Kim and she tells me about a book called *The Lion, the Witch and the Wardrobe*. When I see it in WHSmith, I persuade my mother to buy it for me and I am instantly absorbed in it. It is un-put-down-able. I devour it and then all the other books of the Narnia series, written by C. S. Lewis.

Each of these stories is a great read, but there is something that I'm very uncomfortable about. The enemies of Narnia are from a country called Calormen, and these people look unmistakably like Saracens, medieval Muslims; the Narnians themselves look like Crusaders. In wanting to identify with the characters, I am torn between a natural desire to be on the side of 'good', the white English children, and a feeling that I am condemned to be in the other camp, the Calormenes, the 'darkies' from Calormen (*coloured men?*) with their curved swords and spicy food and unmistakable Islamic cultural symbolism (their currency is called the Crescent). These thoughts cause me discomfort, but I still enjoy the stories.

One specific example troubles me deeply. Whenever Muslims mention the Prophet Muhammad, apparently they are supposed to proclaim 'Peace be upon him!' as a sign of respect. Whenever the Calormenes mention their leader, they always proclaim 'May he live forever!' in exactly the same tone. It seems to be a deliberate imitation of the Muslim custom.

The Narnia paperbacks which I acquire are published by Puffin. At the back of each book is a page inviting the reader to join the Puffin Club, the children's book club of

Penguin Books, for an annual subscription of fifty pence (payable by cheque or postal order). I do a sales pitch to my parents and I am able to procure the necessary financial instrument. I love being a member of the Puffin Club and look forward anxiously to the arrival of the *Puffin Post* magazine every three months. I always read it avidly from cover to cover. It is filled with information about endless numbers of exciting books to buy and read.

Every time I get any money from any relatives, I spend it on paperback books from the local WHSmith. If I don't have any money, I try to persuade my mother to buy me a book whenever we go to Putney High Street[4] together. (She usually goes to the furniture store on Saturday morning to make the weekly payment for the new sofas.) I am now hooked on reading and always have my head in a book. I read fiction at home and mostly non-fiction books at school, including a set of American science textbooks that take me deep inside the Earth and around the Solar System.

Also I discover a series of novels about an American boy called Danny Dunn. He knows a scientist (Professor Bullfinch) who is always inventing things, resulting in Danny Dunn and his friends having amazing adventures: time travel, space travel, being shrunk to the size of ants, travelling to the bottom of the sea, being trapped inside a fully automated house. (In one book, *Danny Dunn and the Automatic House*, an important visitor mentions that he doesn't drink tea, because: 'It's full of tannin – the stuff they use to tan leather. You can imagine what it does to the stomach.' I give up drinking tea immediately, switching to coffee as a healthier alternative.) America does seem like a good and exciting place; they have all the best inventions and adventures. (Only Americans get to go to the moon.)

My reading age finally shoots past my chronological age. Somehow, remarkably, I start to gain a reputation in class for being bright, especially in science.

On one of our many visits to the houses of other Pakistani families, my father is conversing with an old friend of his. In Urdu, he says something, which translates roughly as: *'When one hears the name of God, one's heart should tremble with fear.'*

This is not unusual for a Pakistani conversation amongst the older generation. We are certainly a *God-fearing* people who talk about God a lot, punctuating nearly every statement with *'insh'Allah'* ('if God is willing') and *'ma'sh'Allah'* (expressing thanks for the will of God).

I shudder to think of God. I have this deep-seated anxiety that I'm not going to make the grade and I'm worried about what happens to people who fail to please God.

Around Christmas, Miss Toyne is reading the Nativity story to us, going over it in some detail. The Romans were conducting a population census, and this required everyone 'to return to their place of birth in order to be counted'.

I can't get over the implications of this. *What a hassle it must have been, to return to one's place of birth, just to be counted.*

There are a couple of middle-aged ladies who are employed solely to patrol the playgrounds at lunchtime. They carry toilet rolls, as toilet paper is not supplied to the outside toilets. They dispense this to any child who requests it; the number of sheets given is at their own discretion. They are also responsible for authorising the movement of any child into the school building, for whatever reason. One of the ladies is very nice; the other is always miserable. Her face is implausibly white; it appears to be covered in talcum powder.

One lunchtime I begin to feel cold, as I am not wearing my coat, I am not engaged in any exertion and an icy winter wind is now blowing. I would like to get my coat from the cloakroom, but I need the permission of the dinner lady[5] to go inside the school (even though no one would notice me if I went inside just to the cloakroom).

Unfortunately, the miserable lady is patrolling my playground today. I approach her with absolute deference and respect.

'Please may I get my coat?'

She looks at me sternly, with undisguised disdain. I am standing in front of her, clearly shivering. She has complete and utter authority over me in this situation.

'Well, you seem to have managed without it this long. You don't need it now.'

She decides that I shall *not* have my coat. Rather than giving me the necessary permission to get my coat from the cloakroom – which is a mere formality in any case, since this process of getting the coat would not involve her at all – she decides that I should remain cold. This is how she uses her power over me.

I know that some people don't like coloured people and I think that this lady must be one of them. There's no other reason I can think of why anyone would be so nasty. I spend the rest of the lunchtime huddled by a wall of the playground, trying to keep warm as best I can.

Fortunately for me, I *never* have to ask her for toilet paper.

Every Saturday I watch an amazing television programme called *UFO*. It is set in the distant future – the 1980s. Aliens keep attacking Earth and a secret organisation called SHADO is set up to defend us. SHADO has a hidden underground headquarters; a moonbase; fleets of spacecraft, aircraft, submarines and armoured vehicles. And cool cars which have doors that swing open *upwards*.

What I really like is that lots of coloured people work for SHADO. The chief space pilot is a black man, and a young woman who looks Pakistani works at the headquarters. (She never says much, but she wears a big medallion and a very tight uniform.)

It's the same in *Star Trek*. It means that, one day in the future, coloured people won't be second class – we'll just be normal.

I know where babies come from. I understand the principles of reproduction; I have figured it out. Being 'married' induces a psychological change in the woman. Since the mind and body are closely linked, the mind triggers off a process in the woman's body, which causes the development and birth of a baby. I'm not sure where the baby comes out from, but it (usually) happens at the hospital. For example, Captain Kirk lost his memory and met an American Indian woman on another planet (it's complicated). He married her and took his shirt off … eventually she told him she was expecting a baby.

Mrs George (who used to be Miss Toyne) shows us slides of her visit to Morocco, which was her honeymoon. In one picture, there are some women in the street, dressed from head to foot in black robes, their faces veiled. Mrs George explains that these women are 'Moslems' and that is why they dress like this.

'*What?!*' I am shocked. I don't understand this at all. All the Muslim women I've ever seen dress in brightly coloured *shalwar kameez* and saris, both in England and in Pakistan. I've never seen anyone dress like this, covering themselves in black and veiling their faces, and I don't understand what it has to do with Islam.*

I know that a 'honeymoon' is a holiday that you go on after getting married; Mrs George is the second of my teachers to go on a honeymoon. It's such a funny word: *honey … moon.*

---

* In those days the *burkha* was much less apparent in Karachi than it is today.

One evening, at home with my mother, just for fun I ask her, 'What's a honeymoon?'

I am surprised and confused when my mother looks taken aback and answers, 'Oh … I don't know.'

She *must* know that a honeymoon is a holiday that you go on immediately after you get married – we've seen it on television so many times. (In *UFO*, Commander Straker and his wife were at Heathrow Airport about to fly to Greece on honeymoon, when two serious-looking men in dark suits told him he couldn't go, because General Henderson wanted to see him immediately.) Why wouldn't she just answer the question? *It doesn't make any sense.*

Mrs George moves away and for the summer term we have a new teacher, Mr Colling. He writes his name on the board, so that we get it right; not Collins, it's *Colling*.

Mr Colling introduces a new system to motivate us. He puts a chart on the wall with all of our names on it. He will give us a 'star' for every piece of good work that we do, and each week the recipients of the most stars will win a prize. In the first week, I come first with four stars. The prize is a picture postcard, which I choose from a selection (I opt for a picture of the Concorde) and Mr Colling writes on the back of it a formal statement to commemorate my achievement.

I win the next couple of weeks as well, but the competition soon heats up. People start doing extra work, unsolicited work, to present it to Mr Colling so that he will award them stars. The number of stars required to win goes up and up. In no time at all, four stars becomes a risible amount; the winner needs 10, 15, then 20 stars to win. Sometimes I win and sometimes I don't.

A new girl joins Hotham School, in a class adjacent to mine; she's called Beth Schwartz and she's from America. This is very exciting; I've never met a real American before!

1971-72
Age: 9   48

Her father is a famous musician and he is working in London for a while. Beth reads out one of her essays at our weekly Friday Concert; it's about her move to England. I love her accent – it's so exotic. In the essay she explains at great length that the 'first floor' of her hotel is called the 'ground floor' here in England, the 'second floor' is called the 'first floor', and so on. (Fortunately, there are only four floors in her hotel, so this laborious clarification does not go on for too long.)

One June evening, I am going for a bicycle ride around my neighbourhood, when I pass Beth Schwartz, who is standing outside her newly-rented house. She recognises me and waves, so I stop and we talk. *We have a great conversation!* She is such fun to chat with, and it's exciting to be conversing with an American (and a girl). I sit here on my stationary bike and she just hangs around with me.

An amazing thing happens – we have a connection. Beth says that she likes reading, I mention Danny Dunn books, and she says that she loves them. *I don't believe it!* I list the different Danny Dunn books I've read, and she says she's read them all. Then she mentions one that I haven't read: *Danny Dunn and the Homework Machine.* No, I'm sure I've never even heard of that one.

Eventually I set off on my bike again, but I feel a great exhilaration, a new excitement in my life. Beth Schwartz is my girlfriend! My girlfriend is Beth Schwartz! (*At least, I think she is.*)

In school, we are of course cool and detached with one another, as our relationship is a discreet one. I can't talk about it to my parents, brothers, friends or anyone – but it is wonderful to have her in my life.

I think about her a lot. I think about her last name: *Schwartz.* What an interesting name. *Sch-wart-zz.* Very exotic, special and unusual. I wonder what it must be like to have a father who is a famous musician (I've never heard of him, though).

1971-72
Age: 9

In the days and weeks that follow, I cycle many, many times up and down Beth's road, but I never see her there again. One Saturday, I do pass her and her mother, when I am walking with my mother towards Putney High Street, but of course we remain cool and barely acknowledge each other – that's the unspoken arrangement.

In class, the competition for the most stars has been extremely hot. For weeks, William Man (the Chinese boy) and I have been running neck and neck. Sometimes he wins, sometimes I win. I do an entire unsolicited project on space travel (which I research from the back of Brooke Bond PG Tips tea cards that Mrs Rose from next door gave me) to generate a large number of stars. Mr Colling receives work in a pile on his desk, he marks it and assigns stars. It takes over 30 stars to win now.

One day, after the lunch break, before Mr Colling has appeared in the classroom, Jimmy Rowland shows me something of which he is immensely proud. He has stuck several long, sharp pins, pointing upwards, into the soft seat of Mr Colling's chair. He thinks that this is unbearably funny. When Mr Colling sits down, he's going to get such a surprise.

I am horrified. I don't think that Jimmy has considered this very carefully. The pins are extremely long and when Mr Colling unsuspectingly puts his full weight upon the seat, they will penetrate deep into his backside. He will be subjected to extreme pain and severely injured. I know that this will not be funny; it will be very bad. I try to persuade Jimmy to remove the pins. He disagrees initially, but thankfully eventually he complies. He is sullen about it. He thinks that he's missing a great opportunity for a joke; I know he would be making a terrible mistake and I cannot allow it to happen. I am a 'good' boy, dedicated to truth and justice.

1971-72
Age: 9   50

In the last week of term, it is *imperative* that I win the contest for the most stars. I do masses of extra work, intending to leave it in Mr Colling's 'In' pile in good time to be marked for the end of the week.

William Man comes to see me at playtime. He is in a difficult situation. He has been offered five pounds (yes, *five pounds*, his father owns a restaurant) if he comes first at the end of term. This is such a huge sum of money; he considers it self-evident that I should let him win. He pleads with me to let him come first, because of what is at stake. I should be content to come second; it's only reasonable.

I am deeply tortured by this. I want to come first, but it would be rotten of me to deprive him of such a massive sum of money. I say that I'll think about it. He persists and finally I cave in to a certain extent; I say that we should agree to come *joint first*. We will somehow have to co-ordinate the submission of work, so that we achieve the same number of stars.

I make a huge effort to do extra work. I copy out poems from *Puffin Post* (properly credited) and write about submarines. There are several sheets of A4 paper; these are the valuable instruments that will get me to the winning position. I leave the work in Mr Colling's 'In' pile on Thursday morning.

It's Friday afternoon, the end of the competition is approaching and the class is buzzing with excitement and anticipation. Mr Colling is marking work, while the class is supposed to be reading books or engaging in some other worthy activities. I check the chart. William Man has 44 points, and I have … 40! *What?!* What is going on? I did more than enough work to be the winner. We agreed that we would monitor the score and one of us would make only a last-minute submission to keep us equal. How can I be four points behind?

1971-72
Age: 9

I look at Mr Colling's 'In' and 'Out' piles. There is nothing there from me. I ask him if he has marked my latest work – the submarine project, for example. He says that he has not seen any such work.

How can he not have seen it? I left it in the pile!

The horrible reality dawns on me. *Sabotage!* Someone removed my work! This is not fair. I am being cheated of my rightful prize by nefarious operatives. *Corruption and injustice.* It's the 'Bonnie Baby' contest all over again.

I start making a huge fuss. I tell Mr Colling that I did a massive amount of work and that some 'bad boy' has removed it. I enlist the help of my friends and we search the classroom. There is a great commotion; this would not be the best time for a school inspector to walk in through the door.

Suddenly, Mr Colling calls out, 'Imran, is this it?' He is holding up a few sheets of A4 paper.

I run over to him and examine the papers. It *is* the missing work. I am ecstatic. *Where was it?* He tells me that it just appeared on his desk. I look around. Harvey Robbins, the brilliant football player and friend of William Man, is looking towards Mr Colling and me. Something about his face tells me that he was involved in this, but there's nothing that I can put my finger on or prove.

I ask Mr Colling to mark the work, as it had been placed on his desk yesterday and *must* be included for this week's evaluation. Mr Colling dutifully starts going through the papers, periodically marking the pages with a star.

William Man comes up to me. He is very anxious and reminds me of our arrangement. I am ecstatic that my missing work has been found and I am feeling generous. I won't deprive him of the fortune, *unless* he was involved in the sabotage. But how can I ever know, one way or the other?

We count my score together as Mr Colling issues the stars: 40 ... 41 ... 42 ... It's going well. There is more than enough work to secure victory for me, if I want it. He reaches 43. A minute later, the vital star is issued ... 44.

1971-72

Age: 9

William Man and I are now first equal. But there are several more sheets left; many more potential stars are available to me.

This is the critical moment. I could win outright, with perhaps 46 or 47 stars. But I don't have the hardness of heart to deprive William of an unbelievable *five pounds*.

'That's enough, sir,' I say to Mr Colling, and quickly I pull the remaining unmarked papers from in front of him. Mr Colling is bemused, but does not argue.

I insist that William Man lets me choose a postcard first, and I pick a colourful one depicting a scene from Walt Disney's *Winnie the Pooh*. Mr Colling writes '*Joint First*' on both of our cards – the vital certification that William Man needs to collect the money. *What an incredible day!*

One thing has been troubling me. I know that I am a bit naïve sometimes and that other children are more cunning and streetwise than me. When I had reeled off all those Danny Dunn books to Beth, she had mentioned only one title, *Danny Dunn and the Homework Machine*, and I have never heard of this one. It worries me a lot; I wonder if she made it up. *Is she pulling my leg?* It sounds implausible and fake. It leaves me feeling uncertain of my relationship with Beth and of her honesty.

As it turns out, I never happen to see Beth outside school again, and I hardly ever converse with her in school. At the end of term, her family moves away somewhere else.*

We visit Pakistan again this summer; my mother's brother and sister are both getting married, in a double wedding. My grandfather's house is full of people, visiting from everywhere. So is the house next door, which belongs to

---

* Thirty-three years later, I discover that *Danny Dunn and the Homework Machine* is, in fact, a genuine book.

the family into which my uncle is marrying. That house is higher than my grandfather's, having a whole extra storey that was built without planning permission, apparently.

Days in Pakistan are a dreamy sequence of playing, reading, shopping, going to lunches and dinners. We kids just seem to be in the background everywhere, without any demands being made of us.

One day, my brothers and I are out walking with our father, coming back home from a nearby market. It is a bright, hot, slow afternoon. There are big houses, palm trees, sand instead of pavement, heat, flies, dust. The traffic noise is muted, as we are away from the busy main road. Just a short distance from home there is a parade of shops, with a large paved area in front of it. There is a dead child, a girl perhaps four years old, lying at one edge of this area. She is on her back, her eyes open, her mouth gaping, a hand on her navel, as if to say, '*I am hungry.*' She is dressed in brightly coloured clothes.

No one seems to notice or acknowledge her, not even my father. He walks past with forced indifference, nonchalantly eating a banana from the market. My brothers and I, wide-eyed and afraid, say nothing and follow awkwardly. It is not discussed. I am ashamed. I know from school Assembly the importance of doing good deeds to others. *Should we not do something? What would Mr Campbell say?* But it is never spoken of.*

---

* Years later, I understand. The 'authorities' in countries like Pakistan are the absolute embodiment of incompetence, injustice and corruption. To have any dealings with them is to invite injustice into your own life. If you call the police after someone is killed, you are most likely to be arrested for that death, regardless of how obviously innocent you are or even unconnected with the incident. My father was doing the right thing for all of us, by not getting involved.

Knight

1972-73

Age: 10

MISS BROADHURST, my beautiful dark-haired teacher, notices that I squint at the blackboard a lot. One day an unknown lady takes me from the classroom to the medical room, where she conducts a basic eye test. I have been found out. Miss Broadhurst has told on me. She can easily tell that I am short-sighted.

My parents are informed and a series of eye tests are carried out. We take the prescription to the opticians on Putney High Street. My new glasses will cost five pounds for the frame, and two pounds and forty pence for the lenses. I am worried that my parents will be very angry, but they seem okay about it.

I appear in the classroom wearing glasses, and the obvious insult *'Four eyes!'* is heard, but I am relieved to be able to see clearly. Also, the glasses make me look intelligent and scholarly.

I have two good friends in my class, Roger Maxwell and Andrew Baker. We are 'good' boys – meaning well-behaved, studious and intelligent. We walk around the playground discussing the books we've read. There are many 'bad' boys in the class; they are vicious, lazy and stupid. They sometimes threaten us, both verbally and physically. My new glasses cause them no end of merriment. I develop a deep-seated sense of righteousness, of always wanting justice for the good and punishment for the evil.

Miss Broadhurst is directing the Christmas pantomime.[6] It involves a dragon that is terrorising a village and three knights who arrive to fight it. She will hold auditions and there is one part that I desperately want: the Turkish knight. The other knights are African and English. I know that I am the right colour for the Turkish knight and I really want the role.

At the auditions, they mention that having a loud voice is key. I focus on that and put all of my energy into the role. I project my voice as loud as I can. There isn't much competition and Miss Broadhurst gives me the part.

Miss Broadhurst makes a fantastic papier mâché dragon's head, which goes over the upper body of the boy playing the role. He holds it in place with gloved hands. This boy is one of the class thugs; he doesn't have to speak, only fight, so I guess the role is quite appropriate for him.

For my role, I have a turban, a curly moustache, a vicious plastic scimitar, and shoes with upturned pointed toes. I definitely look like a Muslim warrior. *I'm going to kick some Crusader's arse! No, wait; the dragon is a more pressing issue.*

The play is exciting. The dragon has been frightening the villagers. The African knight arrives, fights the dragon, is wounded and retreats. The Turkish knight (*that's me!*) comes on stage and wields his curved sword. He declares in a loud, confident voice:

> *Here come I the Turkish knight,*
> *Come from the Turkish lands to fight,*
> *I'll fight this dragon who is our foe,*
> *He'll breathe his last before I go.*

He attacks the dragon and has a vicious fight with him, running all over the stage and making the appropriate noises, first yelling at the dragon, and then gasping in agony as he is wounded. He barely escapes with his life.

1972-73
Age: 10

The English knight comes. He fights the dragon, is wounded and retreats.

A doctor arrives and treats all three of the wounded knights, restoring them to fitness. The three knights confer and agree to unite and fight the dragon together. The three of them attack the dragon and, by working together, they are able to slay it. The villagers are grateful; they thank the knights and celebrate.

It's a very uplifting and fun play. I really enjoy it. We perform it on three evenings for parents and also once for the infant-school children. Their laughter is tremendous.

In *Doctor Who*, the Doctor has a new assistant, whose name is Sarah Jane Smith. She is *so* beautiful! She sneaks aboard his TARDIS and joins him in a fantastic adventure. They fight a really ugly and scary alien in a shiny space suit; his head looks like a baked potato. Saturday evenings become very special; I'm in love with Sarah Jane Smith.

If only Andrew, Roger and I had a TARDIS; we could travel around the universe having amazing adventures, during the school lunch break.

After the holiday, there's the usual January problem. Miss Broadhurst wants us to write about what we got for Christmas. Everyone else is writing with excitement and glee about the amazing things they received, all comparing notes. My brothers and I do not get Christmas presents from our parents, but I am able to write that Mrs Rose, the nice old lady who lives next door, gave us a tin of assorted fancy biscuits. This doesn't bother me, but some classmates get wind of what I have written and can't stop making fun of it: 'You got *biscuits* for Christmas!'

My parents are going to buy a house nearer to Heathrow Airport. We go to see one in a certain location, which I like. It has an open staircase and a row of bookcases on the

1972-73

landing. I become attached to this house and picture it as our future home. *(I wonder if they will leave behind the books.)*

Then, one day, my father announces that there is a brand new development in a different part of London, and we will buy a house there. I am in tears; I like that first house. *Why can't we live there?* My father seems taken aback at my distress, but his mind is made up.

There is a television quiz show I watch every Friday evening called *The Sky's the Limit*. One day, the presenter, Hughie Green, asks a male contestant, who is a London taxi driver, 'So, what do you think of women drivers?' I am outraged. *What a stupid thing to say! How can we make any generalisation about the driving ability of all women collectively? That's just like racism.* I imagine being asked the same question and giving a smart response. 'Are you asking about a *particular* woman, because why would women, *in general*, be any better or worse at driving than men?' *That would show him!*

We are moving to our new house at Easter. At the end of term, I say goodbye to my best friends Andrew Baker and Roger Maxwell, and we form a secret society called A.I.R. (after our first names), dedicated to global justice (just like in television programmes). We promise to keep in touch. I'm deeply sad to leave Miss Broadhurst, whom I find very attractive. She gives me the prize for the best project (mine's on 'Aviation'), declaring: 'Imran's was the best by miles.'

The new house is in Hampton, in the less crowded suburbs to the west of London. It is semi-detached, with front and back gardens, a driveway and a garage. (This becomes *home* to me. Regardless of where I live and the succession of properties that I own, or apartments that I rent, wherever in the world, this house will always be *home*.)

1972-73
Age: 10

We don't sell the old house in Putney; we rent it out to an Arab man named Ahmed Battal, who works for his country's embassy. Being a Muslim, he will of course be God-fearing and thus honest, trustworthy, honourable and morally upright.

Rehan and I are enrolled in our new school, Hampton Hill Junior, whilst our youngest brother Rizwan enters a nearby infant school. My new school has a more snobbish attitude than my previous one, being in a whiter suburb. They don't have much experience of darkies. My well-intentioned teacher immediately decides that I don't want to attend Assembly every day. (I'm not so sure about this; I quite like singing hymns like *'All Things Bright and Beautiful'*.) A strictly Catholic girl, a Jehovah's Witness and others wait with me outside Assembly each day, during the religious part of the gathering. We enter later for the secular communications.

My brother's teacher makes no such judgment, so Rehan *does* attend Assembly. This anomaly goes unnoticed by the school staff, although one day a pupil does ask me: 'Is it true that Ray-han is a Christian and you're not?'

Despite this managed separation, there are still certain occasions when I am present during prayers and hymn-singing. There is something strange about these, different from Hotham School. In the prayers, they pray to *Jesus*, rather than to *God*, and the hymns they sing are different as well; they also address Jesus instead of God. I find this strange and uncomfortable, and I don't understand it. There are some American books in the classroom which have this same sinister aspect. The characters pray to Jesus instead of to God, and their prayers are always miraculously answered.

My new teacher is Mrs Karanjia. She is an Englishwoman, but she has a strange name. I find out that she is married to an Indian man. I wonder how this could have come about.

1972-73
Age: 10   59

White people have 'love' marriages, whereas Indians and Pakistanis don't fall in love; they have arranged marriages. *(How do white people always manage to find the right person, by luck?)*

The headmaster of my new school is an elderly Welshman called Mr Hughes, who surely must be close to retirement. He is completely out of touch with my generation, and has strong opinions.

One day, early in the term, he calls an emergency meeting of all third-year boys, requiring us to sit on the floor in the hall while he addresses us. A sad-looking boy from the other class is standing with him. Mr Hughes explains that this boy had brought his wonderful badge collection into school today, badges which his grandfather had given to him. They had been on his coat, in the third-year boys' cloakroom, and they have been stolen – removed from the coat. Mr Hughes has deduced that a third-year boy must have done this. He is very disappointed, because nothing like this has *ever* happened before.

I listen to all of this sympathetically, staring into space, then smile at his last comment. If nothing like this has ever happened before, wouldn't it be funny if he thought that *I* (the *only* new third-year boy) had done it. The reason this is funny is that it is completely implausible, as I am a 'good' boy, dedicated to truth and justice.

'RAY-HAN, GET ON YOUR FEET!' yells Mr Hughes.

I am shocked out of my private contemplation by this sudden outburst of his. Why is he calling my brother's name? My brother isn't even here. I look up and around, startled. Mr Hughes is staring right at me.

'STAND UP, NOW!' he bellows.

'Are you talking to me?' I ask, completely confused.

'OF COURSE I'M TALKING TO YOU! DO YOU KNOW ANYONE ELSE CALLED RAY-HAN?'

1972-73
Age: 10

60

'Yes, my brother,' I reply feebly, as I lurch to my feet, nervous and terrified.

Mr Hughes is momentarily confused as to why two brothers would have the same 'Christian' name, but then launches undeterred into an attack on me.

'HOW DARE YOU SMILE? DO YOU THINK IT'S FUNNY, HAVING YOUR BADGES STOLEN?'

'No,' I answer feebly.

'NO, WHAT?'

'No, sir.'

This is a nightmare. I am a 'good' boy. Through no fault of my own, due to a moment of private musing, I have been mistaken for a 'bad' boy. Mr Hughes orders me to remain standing, then finishes his discussion of the heinous crime of badge theft. He dismisses the other boys, then comes over to deal with me. He reprimands me for my attitude (apparently smiling at the theft of someone else's badges), and my rudeness (not addressing him as 'sir'). I feel completely and utterly humiliated. This is such a miscarriage of justice. He dismisses me and I return to my class in a state of shock. My career at my new school has not got off to a very good start. I miss Mr Campbell, Miss Broadhurst, Roger Maxwell, Andrew Baker – they all know what I'm really like.

Mrs Karanjia hears about this incident and talks to me later. She asks me, in a very gentle voice, 'Did you mean to be rude to Mr Hughes?'

I explain the misunderstanding as best I can. She is sympathetic; she knows that I am a 'good' boy.

Mrs Karanjia takes a couple of weeks off to visit India. While she is away we have a different teacher, and one day this lady gives us a Science test, calling out the questions one at a time for us to write down the answers. I am good at Science, so I expect to do well.

1972-73
Age: 10   61

But there is one question that leaves me baffled. The question is: 'What do you get when something catches fire all at once?'

I repeat this question to myself. '*What do you get when something catches fire all at once?*' I don't have a clue what this is getting at. I shake my head in futility. All I can think of is *smoke*. You get smoke when something catches fire all at once.

At the end of the test, she tells us the answers and we mark our own papers. The answer to that question which stumped me is: '*An explosion*'. That was her definition of an explosion! Okay, I can't even begin to address the issues this raises, of scientific knowledge, teaching competence and communication skills. I am stunned.

My mother watches *Crossroads*, which is a television serial about a motel near Birmingham. I also watch it; it is very good. Unfortunately, it wrecks my theory of reproduction. A man and a woman who are *not* married go to bed together and, apparently as a result of this, she tells him later that she is pregnant. So, it's not the getting married that causes pregnancy – it's the going to bed together. As a result of this act, the mind must trigger off the physical process of pregnancy.

Mrs Karanjia returns and tells us of her trip to India, beginning with the journey. She mentions that the Air India plane had to fly over the Indian Ocean, to avoid Pakistan, 'because India and Pakistan aren't very friendly with each other'.

Everyone looks at me, as if it's my fault.

Although the standard of teaching is about the same as that of Hotham School, in this school they have exams in the summer term, something that I have never faced before. One afternoon, Mr Hughes is presiding over the exams,

1972-73
Age: 10

which are taking place in the school hall. He is giving instructions, treating us like imbeciles. It is the mathematics exam and he uses the first question as an example. It is about the number of sides a cuboid has.

He asks the question rhetorically: 'How many sides does the object have?' (It is hard to believe, but he thinks it is necessary to take us step by step through the process of reading and answering questions.)

Immediately, a girl shoots her hand up. I realise instantly that she has taken the question literally, not rhetorically. She is going to answer it. I also realise that Mr Hughes, when he acknowledges her, will not have a clue that this is the case. In this moment, I can see both sides of the situation, understand both parties' points of view – but there is nothing that I can do to avert what is about to happen.

'Yes?' responds Mr Hughes to the girl's raised hand.

'Six,' calls out the girl.

Mr Hughes is flabbergasted and outraged. He calls her something indicating stupidity, he tells everyone to ignore her answer, saying that it's probably incorrect anyway, and he makes the girl feel very upset, as if she's done something terribly wrong. She tries not to sob, in front of so many pupils.

The fact is that the poor girl merely misinterpreted Mr Hughes' ridiculously unnecessary articulation of the question and had no idea that she was doing something 'stupid'. Mr Hughes, for his part, should have realised what had happened when she thrust her hand into the air when she did. This was a tragic misunderstanding, a breakdown in communication. And I saw through it immediately.

Visiting my grandparents in Pakistan in the summer vacation, I find an ancient *English Translation of the Holy Qur'an, with Commentary* in an old bookcase. There are many volumes; they smell musty and the paper is faded to a yellow colour.

It is hard work to read. It seems to me that it's about 1 percent translation and 99 percent commentary. Somehow, in the commentary, the translator gets on to the subject of Hindus. He says that they believe in many gods (*how wicked*, he says) and that bad deeds are punished by coming back as a lowly animal (*how silly*, he says). With these beliefs, Hindus obviously must make the one true God very angry indeed.[*]

---

[*] Decades later, I learn that my 'understanding' of Hinduism is completely wrong.

1972-73

Age: 10

Islam

1973-74

Age: 11

I START GOING TO AN ISLAMIC SCHOOL on Sunday mornings (it's a regular junior school which is borrowed by Muslims at this time every week), and I actually learn something about Islam. So, Muslims believe that the Qur'an is the sacred and *absolutely infallible* word of God, and it was revealed in pieces to Muhammad by the Angel Gabriel. The first time that Gabriel appeared to him was when Muhammad was in a cave meditating, as was his habit. He lived in Mecca, in Arabia, in the seventh century AD.

The Arabs at that time were a savage, tribal people who worshipped countless false gods in the form of idols carved from wood and stone. They treated women very badly (it was common to dispose of unwanted newborn girls by burying them alive in the sand); they were constantly embroiled in violent tribal feuds; they were habitually drunk; they showed little in the way of morality. Muhammad was an anomaly amongst these people, with his quiet, thoughtful and compassionate manner. His mission from God, which he accepted only reluctantly, was to reform the Arabs, introducing them to the one true God, and to the concepts of human rights, justice and moral behaviour, and to send this light to the whole world. This was an extremely difficult and dangerous task; Muhammad's life was in danger for many years, but he succeeded in forging the Arab tribes into a single nation, which eventually became the mighty Islamic empire.

I learn more. Oh, *we do believe* in Jesus and Moses, Noah, Abraham and the other Bible characters. *I never knew that.*

Okay, I understand that there are some theological differences, especially about the nature of Jesus, but it's still good news. I don't have to mentally block out all these Bible stories that I hear in regular school.

I am never able to graduate from the lowest class of this Islamic school. The reason is that although they do have discussions about Islam, they place greater emphasis on teaching us how to *read* (not necessarily *understand*) Arabic. I am more interested in learning about Islam and not at all interested in devoting any of my brain capacity to learning to read Arabic (which is very hard work). I consider this unnecessary, as the Qur'an can be read in English. I want to learn *what* we believe, and *why* we believe it; what the *evidence* is that proves it to be true. This is the most important thing to me; since there are many religions, they can't all be true, and everyone just follows the religion they are born into. How do I know mine is the true one?

It troubles me. Islam is supposed to be a religion for the whole world, regardless of race, language or culture. It doesn't make sense that God would expect everyone in the whole world to learn to read Arabic, does it?

My father buys my mother a blue VW Beetle to drive to work, instead of her having to take the bus. We are now a two-car family! We just got a colour television as well (a Grundig 26-inch – *the biggest size there is!*). We must be rich.

In school, Mr Todd is reading to us extracts from *The Diary of Anne Frank*, a Jewish girl who hid from the Nazis in an attic in Amsterdam, along with her family. I listen with solemn attention, as does the rest of the class. I find it hard to believe that these events happened such a short time ago, in Europe, and it was white people doing this to other white people.

1973-74
Age: 11

Mr Todd never finishes reading this book to us, but I pick it up from his desk while I am waiting in line to have my exercise book marked, and I go straight to the end to see what happened. The notes say that Anne Frank died in a concentration camp at the age of fifteen. I feel utter horror as I absorb the details of this, and I imagine Anne Frank's family being my family. *They were just ordinary people!* I feel a lump in my throat and tears begin to well up in my eyes. I try to regain my composure before anyone notices.

I am selected (by a written test) to be a member of the team for the Panda* competition, a series of quiz contests between all the junior schools in the London area. The competition is run by the Metropolitan Police and the quiz is about road safety, the Highway Code and the history of the police. There are four of us in the team, plus one reserve. Every Tuesday mid-morning we depart from our classrooms and gather in a small meeting room. PC Rice, a pleasant police officer in his fifties without much hair, comes every week at this time to coach us for the Panda competition. These private sessions are interesting, fun, and feel somewhat exclusive; we are a sort of elite group within the school.

In one session, PC Rice mentions Customs and Immigration crime, and says that people who are foreign to Britain are called 'aliens'. We find this really funny; we've heard of 'aliens' before, but only in *Lost in Space* and *Star Trek*. In another lesson, he lets us examine his truncheon, which is made of very heavy wood. I tap it against my head. *Ow!* That really hurts.

We attend the first contest and win it convincingly against the other three schools. In every round, each

---

* Police cars were called 'panda' cars because of their dark and light colouring.

contestant has to answer a question specifically addressed to him or her. There are four rounds, so we each have to answer four questions, for a maximum of four marks each. Our team gets a perfect score: 64 out of a potential 64. This is a win-or-be-eliminated contest; the other three teams are knocked out of the Panda competition and we will proceed to the next round a few weeks later.

Mrs Alderson writes a detailed letter about our remarkable achievement to the local paper, the *Richmond and Twickenham Times*. The article appears and the spelling of my name is completely mutilated, but it's nice to be mentioned in the newspaper.

The younger children in my new school put on a Christmas pantomime. It appears to be the same one that I starred in at Hotham School a year ago, with three knights and a dragon. But the story takes a strange twist. The African knight comes to fight the dragon, and is killed. *I don't believe it.* The Turkish knight appears, fights the dragon, and is killed. *What is going on?* St George, the English knight, appears on the scene. He attacks the dragon, has an animated fight, and slays it. He is a hero; the villagers are delighted and grateful. The audience applauds uproariously. I clap because I'm supposed to, but I am deeply troubled by this turn of events.

This story is virtually the same as our pantomime, and yet has been changed in a quite vulgar way. The message is completely different. Instead of *unity*, it's about *separation*. Instead of *equality*, it's about *superiority*. There is something strange about this school; it is subtly different from Hotham in a sinister way.

After Christmas, when we return to school, Mr Todd asks us to write about what presents we received. In an awkward and embarrassed way, I say, 'We don't really celebrate Christmas, but I could talk about what I got for my

1973-74
Age: 11

birthday – a camera.' (My Kodak Instamatic, which cost three pounds and ten pence.)

He seems taken aback, both by my statement about 'not celebrating Christmas', and my hasty proposal of an alternative material acquisition to write about.

The next round of the Panda competition takes place and we win it. Again we get the maximum score and this time we win a trophy!

One day I am called out of my classroom and asked to go to the music room. A photographer from the *Richmond and Twickenham Times* has come to take a picture of the Panda team! He is an older man, in a grey suit, and he has quite a common accent. He wants the five of us to be huddled together on a table, for the picture. Rather than letting us manage this for ourselves, he acts with authority and goes to a great deal of effort to place us in a very precise way, deliberately and painstakingly arranging us into two rows. Richard, Catherine, Mark and Stephen are in the front row. I am the back row. My face peeks through a narrow gap between two of the other team members' heads. I am almost totally obscured. Stephen, the reserve team member (who's never even been in the contest), is in front of me, in a much more prominent position. It is obvious to me that the photographer has done this because I am coloured, but no one else seems to notice or say anything, and I just accept this as the way life is.

When the article comes out, I am just visible in the photo if you look closely and my name is misspelled, but it's nice to be in the newspaper.

Mrs Williams takes my class for one afternoon every week, to teach English. Over a period of a couple of weeks, she makes us complete a detailed English workbook which has one hundred questions in it, mainly comprehension, word meanings, sentence construction and so on. (*'Circle the correct*

1973-74
Age: 11

word: He was an imminent/eminent scientist.') We submit these workbooks to her and she never mentions them again, except to me one afternoon in an aside. I am standing at her desk, when she says to me in an offhand manner, 'You may be interested to know that you achieved the highest mark in the English workbook: 96 percent.' I am taken aback, but I don't know if I should show any pleasure or glee, because Mrs Williams' own attitude in conveying this news is so sombre, almost grudging.

My father needs to deal with something at our house in Putney, the one we've rented out, so we all go along with him. Mr Ahmed Battal is not in. My father has the key, so he goes in; we all follow to reminisce about our old house. Somewhat surprisingly, Ahmed Battal keeps a well-stocked bar in the living room; there are colourful bottles of all the different kinds of alcohol imaginable. *But he's Muslim!* I just don't understand it. (He has also powered his television by pushing its bare wires into the socket, without a plug.) I am very confused by his behaviour; I thought all Muslims knew the rules and would obey them without question. *Isn't he afraid that God will be angry with him?*

We attend the divisional final of the Panda Competition, held at Whitton Community Centre. Derek Fowlds, the presenter of *The Basil Brush Show*, is the quizmaster. *Wow!* This is getting serious, having a famous person involved.

We do it again. We win the contest hands down, getting the maximum score possible. We are now the Metropolitan Police 'T' Division champions!

My team is seated behind our table; Mark Williams (our team captain) is furthest away on my right and the gorgeous Catherine Folland is next to me on my right. Richard Bleakey is at my left, pushing himself against me in order to squeeze into the frame of the photograph. Derek Fowlds leans forward behind Catherine and me, as a photographer

1973-74
Age: 11

from the *Middlesex Chronicle* takes our picture, without trying to rearrange us first.

When the article appears, I am prominent, near the middle of the photo, and my name is spelled correctly. I think I'm famous! (More famous than when I was cheated out of the Karachi 'Bonnie Baby' title.)

Our new house is very near one of England's surviving boys' grammar schools, a government-funded secondary school providing a highly academic education and with selective admission by means of entrance exams. I walk past this school every day on the way to my junior school. It does look imposing; it has vast lawns and tennis courts, a very long driveway and seemingly hundreds of windows. I'm not sure that I'm good enough to get in.

There is no question about it – of course I will try for a place. It's a Saturday morning in February when I first enter Hampton Grammar School for the entrance exams. I feel very alone amongst the several hundred boys who are here for the same reason. We are taken in groups to separate classrooms, where we do the tests in English and Mathematics. I don't finish any of them in the time available.

I walk out of the school amidst a crowd of boys being collected by their parents. It is a sunny, breezy day. I am absolutely sure that I have failed. I walk home by myself. I am non-committal when my parents ask me about how it went.

The Panda team attends the next round of the competition, at Imber Court in Surrey, the Metropolitan Police horse-training establishment. We win the competition with a perfect score. (This is becoming a routine.) We are now in the top four remaining teams and are the champions of south-west London!

1973-74
Age: 11

THE PERFECT GENTLEMAN

Surprisingly, I do not fail the Hampton Grammar School entrance exam outright, unlike many of the boys in my class. I am called to an interview some weeks after the test. I have to take some schoolwork to the interview and I decide to take my project on 'Dinosaurs', which is in an exercise book. My father insists that I should also take the Panda competition newspaper articles, but I am embarrassed by the thought of showing off in this manner, especially as nothing like this has been requested. He insists, using his parental authority to the full, so reluctantly I slip the newspaper cuttings into the exercise book.

My mother drives me to the school in her Beetle and walks me in. I am interviewed by the Head of Lower School, the Reverend Glynn-Jones, and the Headmaster, Mr Alexander.

Reverend Glynn-Jones mentions that my English seems very good and he's surprised that I don't have one of those accents that Asian characters on television always have. (He demonstrates what he means, but I don't dare to say that I've never personally met anyone who actually speaks like this.) He goes over my exam papers with me. There is one answer that particularly puzzles him. It is a question about fictitious animals called *grice*. The question is: 'What is the singular of *grice*?' The idea is that one equates *grice* to *mice* and deduces that the singular is *grouse*. But I have written '*grie*', which is wrong. I am too shy to explain to him that I had equated *grice* to *dice*, and thus deduced the singular to be like *die*. (Not many people know that the singular of *dice* is *die*.) My convoluted intellect had deduced a perfectly valid alternative answer, which no one else had thought of – but my shyness and lack of confidence prevent me from explaining this to the Reverend.

Reverend Glynn-Jones does not seem very impressed so far, but he asks to see my schoolwork. I hand him the exercise book and, when he opens it, the newspaper cuttings slip out.

1973-74
Age: 11   72

'What's this?' he asks, surprised.

I am so embarrassed; I distance myself from this immodest act. I lay the blame squarely on my father.

'Oh, my dad said I should bring those,' I mumble, lamely and apologetically.

Reverend Glynn-Jones scrutinises the cuttings and then exclaims, surprised, 'Is that you?'

When I confirm that it is indeed me, he spends a few moments reading the articles intently. Strangely, he seems quite interested.

The interview with the Headmaster is also a sorry array of lost opportunities to impress. I seem to keep getting questions wrong. We do have a somewhat theological discussion, in which he asks me if I am a '*Mohammedan*' (I don't dare to correct him by explaining that this is a term Muslims do not accept, as it implies worship of Muhammad), and I also learn in this discussion that Christians don't just consider Jesus to be 'Son of God', but also 'God'. He is not preaching; we are discussing *The Lion, the Witch and the Wardrobe* and its parallels to Christian theology. I never saw this before; I just thought it was a great story.

I have no expectation that I have passed the selection process for Hampton Grammar School. One Friday in April at school, everyone else who was interviewed knows whether they are in or out, but I left home this morning before the mail came. No one in my class has succeeded. Mark Williams, who is in the other class, has made it, but Richard Bleakey, who is also in the Panda team, has failed (but his rejection letter mentions something about a reserve list). At the end of the day, it is warm and sunny when I run out to my mother's Beetle.

'Did I pass?' I cry out.

'Yes,' she replies joyfully.

1973-74
Age: 11

This is the single most important 'yes' of my life. *Thank God we moved to this house.*

The next day is our semi-final of the Panda competition, being held at New Scotland Yard. We are taken there with a coachload of supporters from our school. It is amazing to be going inside the famous police headquarters. They take our names at the front desk, due to 'security procedures'. (We are not criminals, we are 'good' people; celebrities even.) I've never seen so many police officers; this is their secret headquarters (well, the inside is secret, anyway). There is only one opposing team this time; they sit directly opposite us in this impressive auditorium. There is a jug of drinking water on our table; we each have a glass, behind the little signs with our names written on them. All around us are uniformed police officers; an Assistant Commissioner, his uniform plastered with insignia, is the quizmaster. The air is buzzing with solemn expectation. I am still ecstatic from getting into Hampton Grammar School yesterday; this excitement is almost more than I can bear, but Richard Bleakey seems very sullen.

We are the most amazing Panda competition team ever. We have never lost a point, *ever*. We are invincible. Catherine Folland and I are the only original team members, the only ones who have been in every contest. (I like her; she has intelligence and a dignified sense of humour.) Some people have dropped out, for various reasons (Mark Williams has gone to somewhere called the Seychelles on holiday with his family), and former reserves have become real team members. Richard Bleakey started out as a reserve, and only joined the team in the second contest. (I was hoping to be made captain, in Mark's absence, but PC Rice designated Catherine for this honour. Everyone laughed, because they knew I wanted it. I actually didn't mind: even in *Star Trek*, no darkie and no woman has ever been a ship's captain – so I guess that Catherine and I would be equally ground-breaking.)

This competition does not go like the others. I lose 2 points on one question, eventually scoring only 14 out of the maximum of 16 points. It is humiliating for me. We would still win, if my team mates achieve at least the same score, but it is not to be.

Richard Bleakey seems to be self-destructing, taking the team with him. He scores zero for three questions – a complete disaster. Catherine and I exchange concerned glances throughout; the contest rules keep us from conferring. The bizarre thing is that they are not difficult questions; Bleakey seems deliberately to be making up convoluted 'wrong' answers. It doesn't make sense. I know he's not happy about failing to get into the grammar school, but there's no logical reason to sabotage the Panda competition for us all. But there's nothing we can do, as we see our habitual victory vaporise before our eyes. *Beastly Bleakey!*

We lose the competition; we are given books about the Metropolitan Police (signed by the Commissioner himself, Sir Robert Mark); we receive a guided tour of New Scotland Yard (we notice big posters of naked women in some of the offices); we rejoin our supporters to enjoy a nice buffet lunch; we return to our school on the bus. It's all a blur. Failure is all I can think of. We have failed. We are failures. I stare out of the window of the bus at the passing buildings.

I continue at the Islamic Sunday school and come to understand the basics. This is Islamic belief, in a nutshell.

There is one, and *only one*, all-powerful God (known in Arabic as 'Allah', although 'God' and 'Allah' are interchangeable). He created everything, and the purpose of Man is to worship Him. God is omnipotent, omniscient and omnipresent. He knows everything (even our thoughts)

1973-74
Age: 11   75

and decides everything: life, death, accidents, disasters, failures, successes, wealth, poverty, health, illness, (exam results?) and so on. There will come a Day of Judgment, when everyone who has ever lived will be judged according to their deeds, and assigned to either Heaven ('Paradise') or Hell. Satan (in Arabic, '*Shaitan*') is one of the Jinn (non-physical entities who live in a parallel dimension); his job now is to lead people away from the 'Right Path', which he can only do if people are weak and willing to go astray. God will help to keep us on the Right Path, if we pray to him.

God sent many prophets to lead people to the Right Path. These include the Old Testament prophets, then Jesus, and finally Muhammad – the last prophet. The divergence from Christianity is over the nature and mission of Jesus. In Islam, he is a great prophet, meaning a servant and messenger of God (and born miraculously of the noble Mary, a virgin), but nonetheless a *man*, not the 'Son of God'. God is absolutely only One and could never have a son or partner in any way. God forgives sins directly, based on our worthiness, our deeds, and ultimately his Beneficence and Mercy. The death of Jesus was not an offering of sacrificial blood required for the redemption of Man. The Christians have got this wrong and the New Testament is a bit mixed up; Jesus was not really crucified to death and then resurrected. (But we seem a bit unsure about what actually *did* happen. Apparently the Qur'an says that Jesus did not die on the cross, it only appeared that way, and that people without specific knowledge of what actually happened fell into speculation, causing much confusion.)

The Bible is an unreliable document, having some divine input, but with considerable human tampering and addition. The Qur'an is the utterly infallible and absolute Word of God, unchanged, without addition or removal of a single monosyllable.

1973-74
Age: 11

Humans have a tendency towards idolatry, worshipping things – especially people, statues and images – which are not worthy of worship, because only God is worthy of worship and God is so magnificent that no image can represent him. Examples of Man's idolatrous nature are easy to find; even Moses' people, not satisfied with an invisible God, made the Golden Calf to worship when Moses was not there to lead them. Therefore, any attempt to represent God in an image is forbidden. This prohibition also extends to anything or anyone that people might be inclined to worship, including the Prophet Muhammad – whom we must constantly remind ourselves was only a messenger and a man, not someone to be prayed to. Respected, honoured and loved, *yes*, but worshipped, *never*. God considers idolatry to be the most offensive of sins; it is a direct insult to Him.

Jews and Christians are known as 'The People of the Book', meaning that they sprang from the same source of divine revelation and written guidance. They are our theological cousins; they've got the path a little wrong, but they are still heading in the right direction. (It is a matter of great discomfort for us that Christians believe that Jesus was the 'Son of God' and that they paint pictures of God and Jesus, showing reverence to such images.)

My problem is: *how do we know all of this to be true? We are relying entirely on the integrity of Muhammad in this belief system. But I should not be thinking like this. God can read my thoughts and will get angry.*

Mr Todd has been conducting reading tests on all of us, over the course of a few days. We each spend a few minutes standing beside him at his desk, reading aloud, in low tones, the lists of words he places in front of us.

One afternoon, the class is engaged in some quiet work while Mr Todd is concentrating on some administrative tasks at his desk. Suddenly, out of the blue and without looking up, he says aloud in an offhand manner, 'Imran, this is interesting. You are … eleven years old … but your reading age is …' His voice trails off, and only the silence is left. He doesn't look up or convey any indication about what he was going to say. I look at him: he is immersed in his work again, his head down, a pen in his hand.

I am wracked with doubt and insecurity. *What* was he going to say? I am eleven years old, but my reading age is … ten? Maybe … nine? Why did he even have to speak out loud and then not conclude the statement, leaving me beside myself with anxiety. *How cruel!*

Richard Bleakey has some news. He was on the waiting list for Hampton Grammar School, and now they are able to offer him a place. He *is* going there, after all. I suspect that he deliberately sabotaged the Panda competition for us, because he was not offered a place earlier, and I am still angry with him about this.

At the end of the summer term, we are clearing out our desks. We are instructed by Mr Todd to throw all of our exercise books into rubbish bags; we are *forbidden* to take any home. This is a direct order from Mr Hughes. He is worried lest the reputation of his school be tarnished by any exercise books (which have the school logo printed on the front) being found littering the nearby streets.

I am deeply upset by this. I have written a number of great stories in my English book (including one about how the world's scientists work together to foil a hostile Martian invasion). I want to keep them. I consider slipping the English book discreetly into my own bag, rather than into the rubbish. But I'm afraid: *what if I'm caught?* I am obedient and rule-abiding to the end. Reluctantly, I throw the priceless exercise book into the black bin bag.

Mr Hughes is a stubborn old man. He treats us like children.

1973-74
Age: 11

At the Sunday school, Islamic prayer becomes less mysterious as I learn how to do it; there is a system to it. The act is called '*salaat*' and the focus is on *worship* of God, rather than praying for things you want in your life. A unit of prayer is called a '*rakah*'. Each of the five daily prayers has a specified number of rakahs and a particular time slot in the day. The daily prayers are: *before sunrise* (two rakahs), *noon* (four rakahs), *mid-afternoon* (four rakahs), *after sunset* (three rakahs) and *night* (four rakahs).

In each rakah, you begin by standing to attention and reciting the opening chapter ('*surah*') of the Qur'an, which is known as the 'Lord's Prayer of Islam'; it praises God and asks for His guidance and mercy. Then you bow, then stand to attention briefly, then make two prostrations, all the time reciting '*Allahu akbar*' ('God is great') and other worshipful phrases.

At the end of the final rakah, you remain kneeling and recite some additional verses, then you say '*As-salaam alaikum*' ('Peace be upon you') to the person on your right and then to your left (even if there's no one there), and after that you can pray – as in asking for stuff.

I am able to master the regular prayers, but there remain all sorts of recommended and optional additional prayers, and I never quite understand the numbers of rakahs for these. I still have to copy someone else in the mosque, to fit in.

I know *how* to perform the daily prayers. This doesn't mean that I actually *do* perform them every day.

There is an additional complication. In order to perform a prayer, you have to be clean. There is a ritual ablution ('*wudu*') to ensure this. It involves washing the hands, mouth, face, nose, ears, neck, arms and feet. You don't have to perform this ablution every time you pray, if you are still clean from the last time.

The 'five pillars of Islam' are the things that we *must* do:

1. Declare a belief in the One and *only one* God, and that Muhammad is His prophet.
2. Prayer; *Salaat*.
3. Regular contributions to charity; *Zakat*.
4. Fasting during the month of *Ramadan*.
5. Performing the pilgrimage to Mecca once in your lifetime; *Hajj*.

The fasting is performed between sunrise and sunset each day during the thirty days of the month of Ramadan. During the fast, you abstain from food, drink and sex (which I know is kissing in bed with no clothes on; I've seen it on television).

The Islamic year consists of twelve lunar months, each one defined by the appearance of the new moon, so an Islamic year is about ten days shorter than a Christian year. This means that the month of Ramadan comes about ten days earlier in each successive Christian year. Ramadan is thus much easier when it falls in the middle of winter, than when it occurs in midsummer, because the days are shorter in winter.

There are two *Eids* or festivals, like Christmas and Easter. The 'small' Eid is to celebrate the end of the month of Ramadan. The 'big' Eid commemorates the fact that Prophet Abraham ('*Ibrahim*') showed willingness to sacrifice his only son, when asked to do so by God. (Fortunately, God was only testing Abraham's faith; He provided a sheep at the last moment to be the actual sacrifice.)

There's a long list of do's and don'ts. That which is forbidden is called '*haram*'. That which is permitted is called '*halal*'.

It's quite a lot to learn and follow. Christianity appears so much easier. You don't seem to have to do anything much except sing hymns.

1973-74
Age: 11

My mother's brothers live in Canada, and this summer we get to visit them in Toronto (the first of many such visits). For the first time ever, we fly somewhere that isn't Pakistan. Toronto is sunny, hot, exciting; everything seems very modern and larger than life. Even the sky seems bluer and deeper. *Isn't Canada just like America?* But a visit to *that* fabled country still remains elusive.

1973-74
Age: 11

THE PERFECT GENTLEMAN

Grammar

1974-75

Age: 12

IT IS SEPTEMBER and the time has finally come to enter Hampton Grammar School. I remember Mr Ford's dire warning about secondary schools and I am afraid. But I am also proud and excited to wear the uniform: black blazer and trousers; the school badge with rampant lions, sewn by my mother onto my breast pocket; white shirt and school tie.

This morning it is pouring heavily with rain and I sit at home reading the latest *Reader's Digest*; there is an article about bullying in schools. I am the last one to leave the house, as Hampton Grammar School is only a few minutes' walk away.

Finally, I head out towards the school with trepidation, carrying my attaché case, which my father has given me. A Prefect, standing outside in the downpour, directs the newcomers into the dining hall, where we sit bedraggled, wet, apprehensive and silent. Then we are herded into the main hall, to a very formal and solemn Assembly. A Prefect performs a reading from the Bible: the Parable of the Sower.

> *And as he sowed, some seeds fell along the path, and the birds came and devoured them. Other seeds fell on rocky ground, where they had not much soil, and immediately they sprang up, since they had no depth of soil, but when the sun rose they were scorched; and since they had no root they withered away. Other seeds fell upon thorns, and the thorns grew up and choked them. Other seeds fell on good soil and brought forth grain, some a hundredfold, some sixty, some thirty.*

The *seeds* – that's us, the new boys. Hampton Grammar School is a good place for us to grow. I know that in some schools, intellectuals and 'good' pupils are terrorised by ignorant thugs and cannot thrive.

Hampton Grammar School is indeed a very dignified and daunting place: polished wooden parquet flooring; cloisters; impressive artwork; Latin lessons. We are called by our last names, to emphasise that we are not children anymore. The lessons are serious, the teachers seem sombre, and the homework is a huge burden. Whatever homework is due in the following week, I always leave for the weekend. So, Sunday mornings become miserable. I wake up to face the prospect of homework in six, seven, maybe even eight subjects which needs to be done (after I come back from the Islamic school at lunchtime). I hate Sundays and that *homework feeling*.

It is understood that I will attend Religious Studies lessons in the first year, when the subject is the Old Testament, because Muslims believe in this (apparently). I am not expected to attend these classes in the second and third years, because then the subject is the New Testament and therein Islam and Christianity differ.

Reverend Moore teaches Religious Studies and he rationalises the Bible, putting stories into context. For example, if you lived in a valley and it was flooded, the water reaching in all directions as far as the eye could see, you might think that the whole world was flooded. In the absence of television, newspapers and communication, it would be *your whole world*. That's how a local flood became the Global Flood, according to Reverend Moore.

In another example, he questions whether Jesus *really* fed five thousand people miraculously with only those loaves and fishes, or, *by sharing his food openly*, did he compel others in the crowd to share whatever food they had with

1974-75
Age: 12

84

them, thereby ensuring that the entire crowd was fed? (He sometimes slips into the New Testament to illustrate a point, even though I might be offended by it.)

We read Genesis. It says that because Eve persuaded Adam to eat the forbidden fruit, God ordained that all women must suffer terrible pain in childbirth. This seems a horrible thing for God to do, just over a fruit-eating incident. *Am I supposed to believe this? I don't know. Muslims are supposed to believe the Old Testament, aren't they?* I'm scared to question it in my mind. God can read my thoughts and will get angry.

On one side of Hampton Grammar School is Rectory School, which is an ordinary secondary modern school. I have to walk past it on the way to my school. Some of the children from Rectory School seem common and uncouth; they loiter outside and their behaviour and language are both shabby. A few of them often abuse me verbally, either for being a 'Grammar' or a 'Paki', or both. I learn to walk fast and straight, not looking to either side.

On the other side of my school is Lady Eleanor Holles School, an exclusive and expensive private girls' school. We have little interaction with them either; they are too posh for us.

In junior school it was obvious that I was the cleverest kid in the class – there was no question about it. When I had to give the class talk, my chosen subject was 'Atoms and Molecules'. I explained the history of theories about matter, from the early Greeks to the present day. I explained that atoms were like mini 'solar systems', with electrons orbiting the nucleus of protons and neutrons. I explained the difference between elements and compounds. Mr Todd looked very impressed, but my classmates sat there looking blank-faced and dumbstruck. Afterwards, one of the more common girls said to me: 'I din nunderstand a word of wot you was sayin'.' It made me feel very smug inside, although I tried not to be too obvious about it.

But now, in Hampton Grammar School, I have no smugness – only a constant dread. I am in a sea of very clever boys, and struggling to keep my head above water. Every task is very hard, every subject is very demanding, and I feel only mediocre.

There are a few racist lowlifes even in my school. It's amazing that they could have passed the exam. They are racially abusive and bullying towards me, for being a Paki, the only one in the school at this time (there are a couple of Indians and one black boy). There is too much talk in the media and the gutter press about *immigrants*, who come over here and take people's jobs, or get unemployment benefits (or both). The lowlifes need to focus on the threat of *immigrants* in order to give themselves a feeling of superiority. So, they focus on me. The funny thing is, I can understand their point of view. From their perspective, why wouldn't they resent immigrants? They even have their own political party, the National Front, whose key policy is that all coloured immigrants should be repatriated, sent back *home*.

This causes me great concern. I imagine having to *live* in Pakistan, not just visit there. I can't read or write Urdu and I speak it clumsily, with an English accent. I don't see such an outcome as impossible. Something much worse happened in Germany not so long ago, so why couldn't such events happen here? And we darkies stick out a lot more than European Jews.

The worst example of the lowlifes is Peldman. He is in the year above me. He has long, untidy hair, and a sullen face with an ugly black mole. He wears his school uniform in a deliberately shabby way, the tie knotted carelessly, not reaching the bottom of his shirt.

Normally, I would have no interaction with a pupil in the year above. But Peldman decides to insert himself,

1974-75
Age: 12

uninvited, into my life. To him, I am a Paki who is not welcome in his country. I can never pass him in the corridors or the cloisters without him making this point and subjecting me to verbal abuse. This causes me always to have an element of tension as I walk around the school, and actual *fear* if I see him coming the other way. On one occasion he spits at me and a huge glob of his repulsive saliva lands on my head. I tamely wipe it off. I don't seem to have any other options. There's no question of complaining to a teacher; that would be pathetic. I assume that racial abuse *is* a normal part of life, as I *am* a foreigner and I *am* different.

This is the only thing that clouds my experience of this school.

The problem of sex weighs upon me. What exactly happens in sex and how does it result in the child getting some of the father's genes? Clues are given by all of the *Carry On* films which I watch on television. The jokes in them give a hint of the physical process of sex, of what it is a man does to a woman in bed that might get her pregnant.

One day, in Latin, it is my turn to translate out loud to the class. The next sentence in the Latin text is '*hastam emisit*'. I say the English translation out loud: 'He *froo* the spear.'

Mr Flood picks up on something immediately. 'Say that again.'

Puzzled, because I'm sure that I've got the translation right, I repeat, 'He *froo* the spear.'

'I think you mean, "He *throo* the spear",' says Mr Flood, inexplicably.

I say it again: 'He *froo* the spear.' I don't know what's wrong; I'm saying exactly the same as he is. There's no difference. I begin to panic. This is embarrassing. There is a definite ripple of amusement in the class.

Mr Flood is not being mean, but he is persistent. '*Throo*. He *throo* the spear.'

I try again, 'He *froo* the spear.'

Mr Flood shakes his head in bemused exasperation and lets it go. I feel hot with embarrassment; I'm sure my face is red.

I don't understand how what I said is different from what Mr Flood said.

Later, Ivan Hancock is sitting next to me in Mathematics and he explains it: 'If you raise your tongue up in front of your two front teeth, you make a "*th*" sound, instead of a "*f*" sound.'

I try it. '*Th*.' He's right. '*Th*.' '*Th*.' It's a different sound from '*f*.

All of these years I never knew this and no one ever told me that I don't talk proper.

I have settled into the life of the school, but very suddenly something seems to go wrong for me. I become an object of scorn amongst my own classmates. For Games and PE, we have been ordered by the stern and severe Mr Foster not to wear underpants under our shorts (to ensure adequate ventilation). When we change for these activities, the other boys notice that I have hair around my private parts. I'm not really sure when this hair appeared, but none of the others have any. It must be something odd about me. This causes them much merriment, and the moment of changing becomes an ordeal for me. Some of them call me things like 'chimpanzee' and 'monkey'.

On one such occasion, there is the usual tension and anticipation in the changing room, as the undressing process begins. This is the dreaded moment for me. As I remove my underpants, the room explodes into jeering and shouting, as everyone is staring and pointing at my private parts, the cause of much amusement and interest. Some are

1974-75
Age: 12

making monkey noises and strutting around, scratching their armpits like apes. 'Paddy' Maginn zooms in fast and low, and throws a crumpled crisp packet at me, aiming it at my groin. Everyone is laughing and shrieking, except me; I'm just trying to get my PE shorts on.

'SILENCE!' bellows Mr Foster. He has appeared out of thin air, drawn from his adjacent office by the commotion.

The silence is immediate and absolute, like a light being switched off suddenly. I am awkwardly hopping on one foot, trying to get my shorts on.

The PE lesson proceeds in a more subdued atmosphere, which extends to the changing room afterwards. *Thank you, Mr Foster.*

Mr Foster's severe reprimand buys me some relief from this torture, but another unpleasant development soon arises. People start saying that I smell. They say that I have that horrible thing called 'BO'. I just don't understand it. I am no less hygienic that I ever was before; why do I smell now? I become a virtual pariah. The desk next to me is often empty. Classmates make a great display of not wanting to sit next to me, even in front of the teachers. It is utterly humiliating. I am totally alone in every way: a foreigner, an outcast, a heathen. It is bad enough having to deal with the older boys, trash like Peldman, but to have my own classmates turn against me is unbearable.

I know that everyone gets called names for some reason or other. Stephen Allen is called 'Slim', because he isn't, and Duncan Chambers is called 'Phnom', because he used the word 'phenomena' enough for it to be noted, and Steven Maginn is called 'Paddy', because he's Irish. But somehow I don't feel that 'Smelly Paki' has the same affectionate nuance.

On top of this, the schoolwork at Hampton is difficult and challenging, and the homework is a heavy millstone. I don't have anyone to turn to for comfort and support. Life becomes miserable. *Mr Ford was right about secondary school.*

1974-75
Age: 12

However, I react rationally to the problem of smelling bad. There is a soap called Lifebuoy, and everyone knows from the television advertisements that '*Lifebuoy kills the bacteria that cause BO.*' I make sure that this is the soap that goes into the shopping trolley, when I go to the supermarket with my parents. I start taking a shower virtually every school night before going to bed, and use Lifebuoy all over, liberally and meticulously. My mother notices this sudden preoccupation with bathing, and asks me what has prompted it. I say, 'No reason. I just feel like it.'

With this diligence on my part, the problem of BO goes away. My embarrassing hair is eventually forgotten as well, when some of my classmates also develop these symptoms. Finally, my status as class leper comes to an end and I become one of the boys again.

There is a Religious Studies lesson in which Reverend Moore tells us about sex, although he doesn't tell us about sex. He explains that the man has 'seed', which fertilises the woman's egg, to create an embryo, and this explains how the child inherits the characteristics of both parents. Somehow, the man's seed reaches the woman's egg. He doesn't explain how this actually happens. The whole class listens in rapt attention.

One day in French, Mr Salter writes a list of French questions on the blackboard.

> *Quel temps fait-il?*
> *Quelle heure est-il?*
> *Qu'est-ce qu'il y a?*
> *Qu'est-ce que tu fais?*
> *Qu'est-ce que c'est?*
> *Qui est-ce?*

They look like complete gobbledygook to me. I have always found French pronunciation extremely difficult; I always mutilate the language as soon as I try to speak it. But my worst nightmare happens. Mr Salter asks *me* to stand up and demonstrate the correct pronunciation of these phrases to the class. That very thing which I cannot do, he has asked me to do! I am terrified; I am going to make a complete fool of myself, be humiliated. The class will be in hysterics; some of them are quite merciless.

I draw a breath to begin to articulate the first expression. Suddenly the school bell rings, indicating the end of the lesson.

'Saved by the bell,' declares Mr Salter.

I can't believe my luck. *Thank you, God!*

On television one evening, I watch a film called *The Wrecking Crew*. It stars Dean Martin as Matt Helm, a secret agent (it is a very inferior version of a James Bond film). There is a particularly beautiful woman in it. In one scene she appears in a stunning dress, cut very low to reveal her fulsome and tantalising breasts, with a long slit revealing her lovely legs.

My mother exclaims, 'Why does she bother to wear anything?' with utter contempt.

I pretend not to notice anything special, but in reality I am captivated by this woman (Elke Sommer) and cannot take my eyes off her when she is on the screen.

Lying in bed, I think about her for many nights. I imagine that I am a secret agent (James Bond, not Matt Helm). The woman and I are in scuba gear. The bad guys have captured us, tied us up together, facing each other, and have thrown us into the ocean. There we are, deep down in the clear blue water, tied up closely together, her breasts thrust against me, her legs entwined with mine, our faces close together behind our scuba masks. I can see her wide eyes inside her mask; her long blonde hair is streaming out. The water conveys a sense of danger; there's the possibility of drowning; but there's some other feeling as well, a powerful, overwhelming, tense exhilaration …

I have a shameful secret. Nobody knows about it; *what would they think of me if they knew?* I don't know how to knot my tie. I never learned. I hardly ever wore a tie before (the one at the 'Bonnie Baby' contest was on elastic). Since I started at Hampton Grammar School, I've been using the same knot (which my father tied for me), carefully loosening it and then retightening it.

One day, in the changing room before a PE lesson, I am carefully lifting my tie over my head as usual, when Graham Gunning notices this and comments that he has never seen me knot my tie. I feel a sense of panic and mumble something dismissive, but he can smell the fear; he knows he's onto something. I hang the still-knotted tie on the hook and continue to change.

After the session, we return to the changing room and I see that which I most feared has happened. The tie is still hanging on the hook, but it has been mysteriously un-knotted. *That bastard Graham Gunning did this!*

With a sense of impending doom, I get dressed. Finally, I must put on my tie. I imagine that if I just go through the right kind of motions, it will surely become knotted and no one will notice. I put the tie around my neck and make some knotting actions. It looks ridiculous and everyone can see. I am miserable.

'Slim' Allen takes pity on me and knots my tie for me. I feel humiliated, but it's better than stepping out of the changing room without a properly knotted tie and running into a teacher or, *God help me*, the Headmaster.

This weekend I insist on being taught how to knot a tie and I practise until I master it completely.

1974-75
Age: 12

One day, I suddenly get it! It just comes to me in a flash. All the *Carry On* films, all the jokes I've heard in the classroom and the changing room, when there's no teacher present, all the innuendos and so on. I have assimilated all the information from all these sources, and finally I get it. It all makes sense now.

Reverend Moore discusses Moses and the Ten Commandments. He runs through them all. There is a palpable tension in the classroom when he reaches: '*Thou shalt not commit adultery*'.

Matthew Taylor has the nerve to do it. 'What's adultery?' he asks, with feigned innocence.

A merry titter runs around the class. Of course he knows what adultery is; we all do. But we love it whenever sex is mentioned.

Reverend Moore is slightly bemused, but unfazed. He has been dealing with adolescent boys for decades. 'Adultery is making love to a woman that you are not married to,' he replies in a very matter-of-fact way.

'*Making love*' – *the very words are bittersweet, evocative of that unbearable longing that burns deep within.*

I dream that one day I will be a Prefect, but that can only be in the Sixth Form, and that is many years away. However, there is one position of responsibility which appears to be open to boys of all years, that of Librarian. I have noticed that a number of boys have Librarian badges; they perform various important-looking duties in the two libraries which the school has (one for fiction and one for non-fiction). There is a mysterious Librarian's room; I have no idea what they do in there.

Mr Scouse is our English teacher and he also appears to be in charge of the Librarians. One day, after class, I ask him how one becomes a Librarian, and he says, 'You just have to ask me.' So I ask him and he agrees to let me become a Librarian. I go to see him later to collect my Librarian's badge; this is the most important thing. When I rejoin my classmates for our next lesson, Mathematics, it takes only ten seconds before Malcolm McKay notices the badge on my blazer and draws the attention of the class to it. I am so proud; I have acquired a position in the establishment of the school.

I am assigned the Religion and Philosophy section of the Lower Library. It is my responsibility to ensure that the books are on the shelves in the correct order, according to the subject classification numbers on their spines. I perform this duty regularly and diligently.

Peldman and his friends often abuse me when I'm at work in the library; I try to ignore them.

There is another responsibility I have as a Librarian. Once a week, at lunchtime, it is my turn to be on 'library duty'. This means to be physically present in the library and ensure that all is well. What I'm supposed to do exactly, if things are not well, I'm not entirely sure. If Peldman and friends decide to throw books, to cause disruption, even to riot, I don't think that there is much that I could do to stop them. Nonetheless, I take 'library duty' very seriously.

We have a week's half-term holiday before the important end-of-year exams. My parents decide that I will take an extra week off school before half-term to join a family visit to the holy cities of Mecca and Medina in Saudi Arabia. We fly to Karachi, and from there we take a five-day trip to Saudi Arabia, staying in Jeddah with a friend of my father who is working there.

We are not performing the great pilgrimage, called the *Hajj*. That only takes place once a year, at the time of the great Eid festival. This is a lesser pilgrimage, called the *Umrah*, which can be performed at any time.

We arrive in Jeddah at night and my father has to negotiate with the Arab taxi drivers to take us to his

1974-75
Age: 12

friend's apartment. They stand around my father, all talking in animated tones and showing the price using their fingers. They are all asking for *five Saudi Rials* for this trip. My father disagrees and shows three fingers; *three Rials*. They persist in showing five fingers; *five Rials*. My father continues to show three fingers. Suddenly, en masse, they walk away. My father spends a few minutes looking for another taxi driver, with whom he agrees *eight Rials*. This driver leads us to his car, an enormous gas-guzzling American saloon (it's straight out of *Hawaii Five-O*).

When we get to our destination, my father's friend is not home, but his Egyptian neighbour very generously lets us wait in his apartment. His kindness and hospitality are overwhelming. It's funny that English is our common language. There are many foreign workers in Saudi Arabia, performing jobs at all levels from the most menial, to the most skilled and professional, as most native Saudis don't work, apparently.

A couple of days later, we travel to Mecca – an hour or so by car from Jeddah. I'm not sure what to expect. Here indeed is the Kaaba, the holiest shrine in Islam, the big cube shrouded in a black sheet. People revere it, and walk around it. It *represents* God, but it is *not* God. I am in awe too, but it seems to be an awe that is imposed on me. I don't know if this is all true or not. Deep within, I know that I shouldn't be having these thoughts, as God can read my mind and will be very angry.

We spend the day in the great mosque, watching the people come and go. A crippled man appears; he cannot stand upright at all. He shuffles slowly to the Kaaba low down on all fours, like an animal; his gaze is directed at the ground, as he cannot lift his head. His faith, and my questioning, make me feel ashamed.

Medina, when we get there, is more peaceful, more spiritual. This is the Prophet's last resting place. I thought that Muslims were not supposed to revere dead people, as only God alone is worthy of worship, so I'm a bit uncomfortable about how we are supposed to view the Prophet now. Why are we standing at his grave saying prayers?

We fly back to Pakistan. Due to flight-availability problems, we are not able to get seats to return to London until Sunday evening. My exams begin the next day; French in the morning and Mathematics in the afternoon. The subjects continue all week. On the first morning back at school, while we are standing in the cloisters waiting to go inside, Simon Alloway asks me how many *hours* revision did I do *each day*, during the half-term break? I evade the question awkwardly; I didn't do *any* revision while I was overseas. I feel a sense of impending doom.

Because of this trip to Arabia, my revision for each subject is brief and cursory, being limited to the evening or the lunchtime before each exam. Despite this, I get an A or B for each of the subjects.

I have learned an important lesson from visiting Mecca and Medina, which is that one doesn't need to study hard in advance for exams. A quick review the night before is all that is required.

Ahmed Battal has abandoned our old house, without paying his rent for a while and leaving behind an astronomical phone bill, for which my father is somehow liable. I really don't understand this. As a Muslim, doesn't Mr Battal know that God is watching? *Does not his heart tremble with fear at the thought of God's judgment?*

My father is disillusioned by this experience of being a landlord and decides to sell the old house in Putney. He had bought it for £5,000 and sells it for £13,000.

I've been continuing at the Islamic school on Sunday mornings; it seems quite a burden, on top of my regular

1974-75
Age: 12

school homework. Although they mostly want us to learn to read Arabic, we do have some interesting discussions occasionally.

What is 'Jihad'? Jihad means 'struggle' or 'striving', and there are two kinds of Jihad, it seems. The outer Jihad is the fight against oppression, against those who threaten society's well-being and peace. This can be an armed struggle, if necessary, but it must be defensive only, fighting for survival against aggressors and invaders, until they are willing to make peace or cease to be a threat. The idol-worshipping Arabs were always trying to eradicate the early Muslims, because of their threatening 'one God' concept.

The Prophet said that the 'greater Jihad' is the inner one. It is the internal struggle to be 'good', to overcome our negative sides and conduct ourselves with morality and self-discipline. In popular Christian imagery, it is depicted by having an angel on one shoulder and a devil on the other, both giving us advice. We know that we must discipline ourselves to listen only to the 'good' voice. That is Jihad; the eternal struggle to be a better person, the holy war against the dark side. Jesus' forty days in the wilderness, when he was tempted by Satan, was his personal Jihad.

There's a further complication about Islam that I learn about. Apparently there are two main sects in Islam; the Sunnis and the Shias. Immediately after the Prophet's death, there was a dispute over who was the correct successor to be the leader ('Caliph') of all the Muslims. This dispute caused a fragmentation into these two sects. The Sunnis are the overwhelming majority (about 90 percent) of Muslims. The Shias have a rigid and complicated system of clergy and additional rituals, much like the Roman Catholic Church. Even their *salaat* is slightly different. (Sunnis clasp their hands together in front of their navels during the standing part of the prayer, but Shias hold their arms straight by their sides, like soldiers standing to attention – this is quite a serious deviation.)

1974-75
Age: 12

Surely it's obvious that the majority Sunnis represent true Islam and the Shias are an embarrassing anomaly. *Why can't they just be reasonable and convert?*

Spock

1975-76
Age: 13

MARGARET THATCHER, the Secretary of State for Education and Science, is overseeing a period of major change in the country's education system. Hampton Grammar School is the latest one to get the axe. The school's board of governors faced a stark choice last year: eliminate selective admission and become a comprehensive, or go independent and lose government funding. They opted for the latter, and this year the school goes private. However, those pupils already in the school will finish their education at state expense. My year group becomes known as *'The Last of the Grammars'* and the name of the school changes to Hampton School.*

In the second year we start to have Biology lessons, with the bearded Dr Milman. These are in the amazing Biology laboratory, where the cabinets are filled with interesting exhibits: skeletons, stuffed animals, preserved plants. In the lab, you can always hear the sound of liquid bubbling somewhere, and smell strange things. There are always mysterious experiments being conducted by the daunting older boys, especially the awe-inspiring sixth formers.

---

* As a result of this, my brothers do not attend my school, as my parents cannot afford the fees. Instead, they go to a boys' state school in Teddington, and this results in a subtle distancing between them and me.

Dr Milman hands out to each of us the Biology textbook, which has a number of different chapters, each one devoted to a particular characteristic of living organisms: Respiration, Nutrition, Excretion, Growth and so on. Everyone turns immediately to the last chapter, Reproduction, and starts looking through it. The picture of the two rhinos engaged in intercourse is particularly fascinating. *How did he get up there?* I read this entire chapter in private, months before we reach this part of the syllabus (as does everyone else). Yes, my deductions were correct, but the book provides a lot of helpful clarification and detail.

As agreed previously with Reverend Glynn-Jones, the Head of Lower School, I will not attend Religious Studies classes this year, because the subject is the New Testament; Islam and Christianity have severe disagreements in this area (most notably that Jesus wasn't the Son of God, and that he wasn't killed by crucifixion). I ask Reverend Glynn-Jones what I should do while the rest of my class attend the weekly Religious Studies lesson. He points out a table in the entrance hall; he would like me to sit there and do work assigned by my Islamic Sunday school.

I am not at all happy about sitting in the entrance hall like this. Any visitors coming into the school through the front door automatically assume that I am a 'bad' boy who is being disciplined in some way. It feels humiliating. *Why can't I sit in the library?*

Nonetheless, I impress all teachers and pupils – going past in those frenetic two or three minutes that precede every lesson – by sitting at the desk, studiously transcribing Qur'anic verses in Arabic from one exercise book to another (making a half-hearted attempt to memorise the meanings of the individual words, but having no clue about the grammar and syntax). Even Mr Flood (a scholar of

Latin and Greek) pauses once, looks over my shoulder at the Arabic, and comments, 'That looks difficult.'

At the end of the forty minutes, I always go to wait outside the classroom where Reverend Moore is teaching my classmates, as the History lesson which will follow is in the same room. We always acknowledge each other politely when he comes out, although there is a great theological gulf between us.

The series called *Star Trek* is on television from time to time, and from it I identify my role model. It is Spock, the inscrutable Vulcan who always behaves 'logically'. He and I have much in common. We are both foreigners, existing in a community of 'regular' people. I am a Pakistani Muslim in a population of white, English Christians. Like Spock, I am calmer, quieter than everyone else, more reserved, verging on aloof. It is Islam that makes me so. No one else seems to be preoccupied with the critical issue of making sure that they go to Heaven and avoid Hell; instead they waste their energies on activities that seem irrelevant, and irreverent, to me: football, pop music, alcohol. I have a lot going on inside my head and view these popular pursuits as 'illogical'. Like Muslims and other Asians, Vulcans have arranged marriages, and are not given to displays of emotion in public. (I have never seen my parents, or *any* Asian couple, kiss each other, not even on the cheek.)

The subjects that I'm really good at, and enjoy, are English, French, Latin, History and so on. But Spock and Asian society approve only of Science. I can do well in Science, but it's an effort. With work, I can even come top now and then, but it really is a chore. However, I develop a deep-seated belief that Science *must be* superior to the Arts, even though Arts subjects are more interesting and enjoyable.

And so I decide to become a doctor, the ultimate use of Science and the most respectable of professions amongst

1975-76
Age: 13

Asians. My parents are delighted, so I never waiver from this path. (They had not been very supportive when previously I had expressed my desire to be a pilot, a police officer, and someone who works with computers.) When I think about some of the things that doctors actually have to do, I just put these to the back of my mind, assuming that it will all work out okay. (The truth is that I completely lack dexterity and it seems implausible that I could perform surgery or set a broken bone.)

Every weekday at 6 p.m. there is a television programme called *Today* on ITV, about current affairs in London. One day there is a news item about an elderly couple; the roof of their council house had collapsed and they had to be rescued from the rubble. They are in the studio with their sullen-looking middle-aged son. The presenter, Bill Grundy, asks them what happened and they describe the incident; they seem shocked and bewildered.

Then Bill Grundy asks their son: 'Who do you think is responsible for this?'

He has no doubt whatsoever. 'Immigrants,' he replies, angrily. 'It's because of immigrants.'

Bill Grundy looks stunned; he clearly did not see this coming. The last thing he wants to handle is a controversial racist rant on live television.

I think I understand the man's reasoning. If the government did not have to spend money on immigrants, then it could have spent that money on his parents' roof. I can see his point of view.

An organisation called the 'Gay Liberation Front' is suddenly active in the UK, bringing homosexuality out of the closet. This is the first time that I hear of such a thing (I've never seen it mentioned on television). It seems strange and unnatural; this is certainly the mainstream view. Society hates gay people and the newspapers are always

1975-76
Age: 13

exposing some famous person or other who turns out to be secretly gay. They usually have to resign from their positions if they hold jobs in the public eye, or anything that requires public trust, like teacher, police officer etc. Gay people who are 'found out' are always made to feel ashamed.

The Arabs have become filthy-oil-rich. The Saudi Oil Minister, Sheikh Yamani, gets the nickname '*Shake Yer Money*'. Oil sheikhs become a part of the British landscape, coming over to the UK and buying huge mansions, exclusive London apartments and lavish Rolls-Royces. Their many wives go to Harrods and buy expensive fur coats, to be used as bathroom mats. The UK government and society in general seems to bend over backwards to accommodate them – it's all about the money. There's a government sponsored 'Festival of Islam'. The British Museum hosts an exhibition on Islam, and there's a BBC documentary series about it as well. Apparently, Islamic science was once so advanced that they figured out a way to make ice in the desert, without electricity.

That was during the Golden Age of Islam. While Europe languished in putrid medieval darkness, Islam was synonymous with civilisation, science, art, poetry, architecture, urban planning, bathing and clean underwear. Jews fled the pogroms in Europe and found guaranteed sanctuary, and mutual respect, in the Islamic world. *Whatever happened to make all of this change?*

This oil wealth proves that Islam must be the right religion, doesn't it? As one television comedian puts it: '*Why did God give the Arabs the oil, and the Irish the potatoes? … Because the Irish had first choice.*'

But there's a puzzling anomaly. Apart from all the tales of extravagant spending, the British media is also awash with stories about Arabs drinking, gambling, womanising. It doesn't make any sense. Proper Muslims wouldn't do that. How could the rich Arabs behave like this? They are supposed to be the guardians of Islam. Aren't they afraid of what will happen in the Afterlife? *Do they not fear the judgment of God?*

The Six Million Dollar Man is one of my favourite television programmes. I read the novel on which it is based, *Cyborg* by Martin Caidin. The book raises some problems. Steve Austin is thinking about his fiancée, and how they enjoy making love. But if she is his fiancée, that means they are not married. That's not allowed! *Reverend Moore would not approve.*

There's a much more complicated issue about good and bad people. I understand that there is an Evil Russian Empire run by Communists, who don't believe in God. They are bad people; this is confirmed by all television programmes. America, Europe and the Muslim world are against the Communists, so these elements represent 'good'. Apart from a minor difference in religious belief about the nature of Jesus, we are all on the same side together, and I am comfortable with that.

The complicated issue is around Israel. I know that there is a problem between Israel and the Arab/Muslim countries. I don't understand it, but it results in a lot of bad things, like the killing of Israeli athletes by Palestinians at the Munich Olympics a few years ago. This tension between the Muslim countries and Israel messes up my understanding of who is good and who is bad. In the novel *Cyborg*, Steve Austin, who represents America and good, is sent on a secret mission to Egypt to steal a Russian MiG-27 and fly it to Israel, so that the latter country can study the MiG's technology. But Egypt is a Muslim country and therefore also good. Another *but*: what is a Muslim country doing with fighter aircraft from the godless Communists? It's very confusing and makes me very uncomfortable.

I'm not very good at sport, but it is a significant part of school life. I play football once a week. I am somewhat at a disadvantage, as I don't wear my glasses when I play, so the entire game is always something of a blur.

One afternoon, I make a particularly diligent effort. Blair Crawford is the opposing goalkeeper, and I'm approaching fast in possession of the ball. I kick that ball towards the goal with all my might. The ball rockets through the air towards Blair, who has his arms held high to stop it. At the last moment, the ball descends unexpectedly steeply and hits Blair in the sensitive parts. He collapses in agony, clutching his groin. Everyone is laughing so hard, but I feel terrible about it.

The problem of pyjamas troubles me greatly. Pyjamas always have a generous hole at the front, to make it easy for you to get the equipment out to pee. The question is: *What do you do during you-know-what?* When I see on television people who've apparently just had sex, the man always has pyjama bottoms on. (For example, in the film *Goldfinger*, James Bond is wearing pyjama bottoms. The woman he stole away from Mr Goldfinger is wearing the pyjama top.) Do you use the hole to put the equipment through, or do you take the pyjamas off completely, and then put them back on again immediately afterwards (before the long conversation)? I will need to know this before my wedding night.

We have the end-of-year exams in our form room, the Lower Tower Room, over a period of one week. Different teachers take turns to preside over us; there is no connection between the exam being taken and the subject taught by the teacher who is supervising the exam. He or she merely has to hand out the exam papers, start the clock, and collect our answer papers afterwards, ensuring no monkey business takes place during the ninety minutes or so.

1975-76
Age: 13

It's the Religious Studies exam today and I don't have to take it, of course; I can spend the time revising for another subject. Dr Luton, a Chemistry teacher, is presiding and he places a question paper on my desk. When the exam starts, I decide to read the paper out of curiosity.

They are all questions about Jesus. *Describe an incident where Jesus did this, did that, healed someone of a physical illness, healed someone of a mental illness, told a parable.* Actually, I can answer all of these. They are quite easy really.

For a laugh, I decide to answer the questions. My classmates notice that I am doing the paper; we exchange amused glances. I write about the story of the Good Samaritan. Not many people know that one of the passers-by was a priest, and he was afraid to touch the wounded man in case he was already dead; this would make the priest unclean – a great inconvenience for a priest. I write the story of Jesus exorcising a man possessed by evil spirits. 'I am Legion, for we are many.' Quite scary words; I read this account in the foreword of *The Exorcist*, that terrifying novel everyone's talking about.

I finish the last question just as the time ends. Dr Luton is collecting the papers and I don't really intend to hand mine in, but he gets to me and reaches out expectantly for it so, for a laugh, I hand my answer paper in, although I almost don't.

The following week, lessons resume as normal and our teachers are returning our exam papers to us. As usual, I am waiting outside the classroom where the Religious Studies lesson is being concluded. Reverend Moore emerges when the bell rings and, seemingly without any emotion, he hands my marked answer paper to me. On the top page is written '*62%*'.

This is not very good – 62 percent. However, inside the classroom, I discover from my classmates that it is the *second highest score*, beaten only by David Batchelor's 67 percent. (He's the class genius who comes top in

1975-76
Age: 13

everything. *Bastard!*) No wonder that Reverend Moore was somewhat cool outside; I came second in his exam about Jesus, without attending any of his lessons!

The final weeks of the summer term are unbelievably hot. Britain is having a drought, with extraordinary and unbearable temperatures. *The Sun* newspaper headline, *'Phew! What a scorcher!'*, sums it up accurately.

It's very hot, every single day. The Headmaster requires us to come to school with our ties on, but in the afternoon we may discard them; this is unprecedented. I use plenty of Lifebuoy and, as an added precaution, big handfuls of Brut 33, which I splash on all over.

My classmates and I have been together for nearly two years now. We've been through a lot and are now very close. All the earlier frictions, the insults, the abuse – it's all forgotten. My nickname has been changed to 'Super Imran', after a sports headline about a similarly named cricketer.

One lunchtime, I am on library duty, in the Lower Library. All of my classmates, except me, are outside playing a really enjoyable version of 'Tag' that we have devised. Despite the heat, they are running around frenetically and energetically, drenched in joyful sweat.

As a group, they suddenly appear at one of the windows of the library and call to me.

'Imran, come and join us!'

'Come on out, mate!'

'Come on, Imran!'

I am torn between my sense of duty and this overwhelming feeling of camaraderie, of being accepted and wanted by my classmates – my friends. It is an excruciating decision, to choose between the solemn responsibility entrusted to me – and represented by my Librarian badge – or leaping into the abyss of reckless, selfish personal pleasure. After a few moments at the edge,

1975-76
Age: 13

my sense of duty prevails, although it almost does not. I feel terrible about it, but I decline my friends' invitations to join them outside. But I have been greatly touched by this. They wanted me to be with them; *I belong.*

This is the final term that we are together as a class. Next year, there will be an intake of almost thirty boys from prep schools, and all the boys in my year group will be randomly reshuffled into new classes – to form new friendships and to help us to integrate the new boys.

I am proud of my school. It was one of the best grammar schools, it is very dignified and it has high standards.

One afternoon my father is washing his VW Fastback on the driveway. Some of the older boys from my school go past on their bikes; it is just after four o'clock and they are in uniform. One of them calls out to my father: 'Bloody immigrants!' My father looks slightly hurt – surprised rather than angry. Fortunately he did not see the badges on their blazers, so he doesn't know for sure that these boys were from Hampton School. I am deeply ashamed of this behaviour. They can insult me in school, but how dare they insult my father in public.

RAF

1976-77

Age: 14

IT'S THIRD YEAR. I'm proud and excited to join the Royal Air Force cadets and wear the blue uniform every Friday, when we have activities after school. I learn to shoot a rifle and, surprisingly, I'm very good at it.

There is one problem with being in the RAF Cadets. The uniform is made of a very rough material, and it is unbearable for me to wear the trousers against my sensitive skin all day. I revert to my childhood solution for this: I wear cotton pyjamas under my uniform trousers, tucking them into my socks.

Fortunately, we don't have PE lessons on a Friday, but I am always terrified that there will be some other event which will reveal my shameful secret. On one occasion we do have an exercise in the gymnasium, which we perform in bare feet; it involves carrying a piece of equipment across an obstacle course. When I take my shoes and socks off, I glimpse the bottom of the pyjamas and hastily pull them up. Peter Barnet stares at me with a quizzical look, but he doesn't say anything. *Did he see?*

Peldman continues to be abusive. My uniformed loyalty to Her Majesty hasn't changed his opinion of me as a Paki who doesn't belong in England. I often imagine shooting him and animate this as a real event in my mind, in precise detail, savouring the events and emotions. In one scenario I take a rifle to his classroom, walk in the door, calmly announce that I've come to kill him (amidst everyone's stunned silence), walk up to him, hold the rifle to his head and pull the trigger. There is no bullet and Peldman pees in his trousers from fear. In the other scenario, there *is* a bullet and I blow his brains out.

There's one really great thing about third year: it's Mrs Lyon, our English teacher. I find her quite beautiful, unbearably desirable. She has long, wavy dark hair and is very slim. She is quite flat-chested, but this doesn't seem to be an issue for me. I fancy her like mad.

There is a bittersweet irony about the timetable this year. We are supposed to have four English lessons per week. Because of scheduling constraints, we are assigned two English lessons on Friday and two English lessons on Monday. Friday becomes a wonderful day, because of the imminent weekend *and* because of Mrs Lyon. Monday isn't bad either; the occurrence of Mrs Lyon twice on Monday greatly softens the blow of the new week. Conversely, the three middle days of the school week become a barren wilderness, devoid of the warm, beautiful, uplifting joy of Mrs Lyon. I always sit at the front of her class.

There's something that only I know. Mrs Lyon must like me too. There's no other explanation for the marks that she gives me. I often get 20 out of 20 for technical work, and for creative work (for which she has mentioned that 100 percent is impossible), I still get implausibly high marks. It is true that I make a real effort to do well, bearing in mind that whatever I write in my English exercise book she will soon be reading, thinking about me for those few precious minutes. I want every such occasion, when she is focused on me, to be as impressive, as near perfect as is humanly possible. I write carefully, painstakingly and with absolute dedication.

For one essay, which is a science-fiction story about some descendants of nuclear holocaust survivors stumbling upon an old city for the first time (something they've only heard about in myths), she gives me 19½ out of 20. I rest my case.

Of course, the fact that I am a pupil and she is a teacher means that nothing can ever happen between us, although I often imagine it. She is absolutely professional at all times. She never does or says anything which would reveal her true feelings, apart from giving me these very high marks.

One day, I'm reading the Cadets' noticeboard in the cloisters when my head suddenly explodes in pain as a sharp and heavy blow is struck to the back of my skull. Stunned, eyes stinging, I regain my balance and look around. Peldman is nonchalantly walking away, heading inside the school.

I am furious, outraged. Without thinking, I start to follow him discreetly. I decide that I am going to kill him by smashing his skull with the corner of my metal-framed attaché case. Laden with books, the case is heavy and makes a plausible weapon. If it doesn't kill him, he will at least spend the rest of his days as a vegetable, having the drool wiped from his chin by an immigrant care worker.

As he descends a very short flight of steps at the end of a corridor, I am right behind him and the moment is perfect. I raise the case, to bring it down upon his head. I can imagine the feel and sound of metal impacting upon bone. But at the last instant, I pull back, deciding that my life is more important than his death. I just give him a half-hearted bump in the buttocks with the attaché case. He spins around furiously, a model of refinement, snarling with his usual eloquence, 'You f—ing c—!' and he gives me a kick. Mr Godfrey appears from an adjacent classroom and intervenes, closing the confrontation. It is remarkable that Peldman should be so outraged – I am the wronged party. I am deeply upset, virtually in tears and raging about what I will do to him. I see genuine compassion in my fellow pupils' eyes when I reach the classroom, which is unusual amongst teenage boys.

There's a troubling storyline in *Crossroads*. The motel has a new receptionist, a beautiful Indian girl called Meena Chaudri. Her father is an accountant and always wears a jacket and tie. Although these people are Hindus from India, their culture appears to be the same as ours (Muslims from Pakistan). Religion is the only difference between us; otherwise everything looks the same, everyone acts the same.

Meena becomes friendly with a mechanic who works in the motel garage – a blond English man named Dennis. It is clear that they are falling in love. Her parents find out and hit the roof. They don't approve of him because he's *not* Indian, he's *not* Hindu and, worst of all, he's a *mechanic*. They want to ship her off to India to get her married to some cousin she's never met. The situation seems to explode out of control; everyone is very upset. Meena ends up running away from home with Dennis. Her father is last shown sitting in his living room, weeping.

This entire scenario worries me greatly. *Am I allowed to fall in love? What are my parents' intentions? Am I supposed to marry a cousin? How would they react to me having a girlfriend?* None of this is ever discussed.

In PE, Mr Smallwood sends my class on a cross-country run: two circuits of the school grounds, which is about 2 miles in total. We are to run outside the perimeters of all the various clearly marked football and rugby fields. From the beginning, Dirk Hinrichs, the long-legged German, is in the lead, but a remarkable thing happens. Most of the class seem to slip away into the distance as I find myself running in second place to Hinrichs, with Alaric Smith the only other contender close behind me.

I know that I won't be able to pass the unbeatable German, but at least second place will be mine, if I can just keep this up. It is agonising, but stubbornly I push on. The first circuit passes painfully slowly and now we are on the second. I am utterly determined to be second in the class; what an achievement that will be! Alaric Smith is still in third place, but he hasn't found the raw power needed to accelerate past me. The certainty of the outcome is keeping me going; there is *no way* I will allow myself to drop behind, no matter *how much* it hurts.

We have only a quarter of a mile to go. I am approaching the corner of a football field, where I will make a sharp right turn, when something completely unexpected happens. Alaric Smith cuts the corner by crossing the white lines of the football field and slips in front of me into second place. I can't believe what he has just done. I have conscientiously run around the outside of every white line, without cutting any corners. I am outraged and angry. Alaric Smith is one of the class geniuses; he does well at everything – but this is cheating. *Corruption and injustice!*

I am furious over this; I won't be cheated of my rightful position. My rage helps me to find unknown inner reserves of power and I hurl myself, in agony, up to and then past Alaric Smith, also managing to find the breath to gasp 'Cheat!' as I pass him. There's only 100 yards to go. I throw myself into this; I won't be beaten.

Hinrichs has completed the course easily; he's way ahead of us. I arrive a minute later and collapse at the finish, gasping for air. I can't believe I did this. *I'm good at cross-country running!* Alaric Smith arrives a few seconds later and collapses as well. The rest of the class turn up at their leisure.

We never discuss the incident at the corner of the football field, but it just wasn't cricket.

1976-77
Age: 14

Our Easter holiday is a dream come true. We fly KLM to Toronto to visit my mother's brothers, and from there we fly Air Canada to Florida, to visit Disney World. This is unbelievable. I don't know anyone in school who has actually been to America, let alone to Disney World. (Peldman would *never* be able to guess what I did in the Easter holidays.)

We pass through US Immigration and Customs at Toronto airport, before boarding the flight. The two US Immigration officers behind the counter are very friendly to begin with, but when my father tells them that we are going to visit Disney World, they become unimaginably jovial; they exude a bright aura of genuine joyful welcome. They ask my father what he's taking with him; he answers, 'Just my pyjamas,' and they all laugh.

America is as exciting as I always imagined it would be. We fly into Tampa (we couldn't get standby tickets to Orlando), and we are supposed to be taking a taxi to the Greyhound bus station but, on the way, my father manages an uncharacteristically good deal with the taxi driver to take us all the way to Orlando for thirty dollars. We hunt around for a motel and check in to the Red Carpet Inn. The receptionist is breathtakingly beautiful, like American women on television, and I love the sound of her voice. Although it is sweltering outside, the room seems freezing cold – everywhere here is air conditioned! Disney World is incredibly good fun and everyone in America is so nice and friendly. With everything being so big, bright, colourful and efficient, with delicious food everywhere (of the kind that is always a special takeaway treat at home), and everyone exuding cheerful friendliness, all of America seems to be like Disney World.

There is only one negative incident during this entire trip to Florida.

In the motel restaurant this morning, we all order scrambled eggs on toast. Unexpectedly, the scrambled eggs

1976-77
Age: 14

are brought separately first, but there is a long delay before the toast appears – by which time the eggs are cold. My parents attempt to remonstrate with the waitress, but she doesn't appear to understand (or pretends not to). The matter is dropped from sheer exasperation, but my parents speculate as to whether this was some form of deliberately mischievous behaviour, driven by racism.

It is disturbing, but we don't dwell on it too much, or let it ruin our wonderful dream vacation.

I take many pictures and arrange these carefully in a photo album, which has Mickey Mouse on the cover. Back in school, I carry this album in my attaché case, so that my classmates will notice it – as I take textbooks in and out of my case – and will ask to see it. In this way I can show it to them without being perceived as deliberately showing off. I so much want to show it to Mrs Lyon. Her eyes do dwell on it briefly, in those relaxed, bustling moments before everyone quietens down for the lesson, but she doesn't comment on it and I can't overtly bring it to her attention.

The school has a primitive glider and, in the summer term, we RAF cadets have an opportunity to fly it. The glider is launched by means of a long elastic rope. While the one boy whose turn it is to fly sits in the glider, the other twenty or so boys heave on the giant elastic. When the rope is fully stretched, the wheels of the glider are released and the glider lurches forward. It is likely to fly about a foot off the ground and go forward maybe 50 yards. We each spend most of the day pulling on the rope, getting only a few precious moments in the pilot's seat. The key challenge is to keep the course straight. However, when my turn comes, it will be unexpectedly and dramatically different.

As the glider shoots forward, a freak gust of wind lifts it clear of the ground. I keep it straight, as it gathers momentum and surges into the air. Suddenly, I am truly airborne, the grass of the field is too far below. I see the

1976-77
Age: 14

buildings of Hampton School from above and my fellow cadets running around yelling and waving excitedly. I am excited too, but remain calm. Riding the thermals, I steer the glider in a vast circle over the school grounds, taking in the surrounding landscapes, the patchwork of fields, roads and houses. Then I bring her around and line her up for a landing in the same area from which we were launched. Keeping her steady, I bring her down in a controlled descent ...

Mr Flood's severe voice cuts in. 'Ahmad! Are you with us today? Put your back into it! *Pull!*'

When my turn does come, the glider bumps along the ground in a clumsy way and I struggle to keep it in a straight line.

One afternoon, I am walking outside towards one of the prefabricated classrooms, where our next lesson will take place. These prefabs apparently were supposed to be temporary, but they have acquired an air of permanence. Their key feature is that they seem to consist entirely of windows, which is very helpful if you want to stare outside to alleviate the boredom of a particularly dull lesson. (Actually, there are very few lessons that I find genuinely dull.)

Peldman and his class are just finishing their lesson in this particular classroom. He's in the bottom Maths set of his year group; mild-mannered Mr Smythe is probably trying to teach them basic arithmetic. Peldman spots me approaching through a window and, in just a few seconds, he is able to induce seemingly his entire class to start yelling, 'Enoch! Enoch!' at me through the open windows of the prefab. Unfortunately, this is not an Old Testament reference (too much to hope for from these Neanderthals); it is a homage to Enoch Powell, the famous Member of Parliament who advocated compulsory repatriation of all coloured immigrants.

1976-77
Age: 14

It is quite humiliating and embarrassing for me as I approach the classroom and wait outside.

'Enoch! Enoch! Enoch!'

My own classmates are arriving and gathering outside with me. Everyone is smiling with embarrassment. I smile too, as if this is just good-natured ribbing. Peldman's class stream out and some of them continue the chant as they walk past me, including Peldman himself. He is an ignorant, thuggish lout. I hate him so much. My body tenses up and my mind screams silently, 'Death to Peldman!'

Mr Smythe comes outside and, with an embarrassed smile, says, 'Sorry about that.'

I don't blame him at all. Most of Peldman's group are bigger than him and it must be a struggle to control them.

I think about what this incident means to me. I really enjoy this school; I really feel that I belong. But there is this ugly undercurrent that makes school life not quite perfect. The school is like a living organism, and Peldman is like a cancerous tumour in the body. I don't have to hate the whole body because of the cancer.

My parents decide to spend the money they made on the Putney house on building an extension to our current house. The plans are drawn up and approved by the local authority. This will involve an extension at the back of the house, incorporating a family living room, a bedroom and a bathroom. When my parents go to the building society[8] to withdraw the £5,000 in order to take it to the bank, a man in the queue witnesses this transaction and declares: 'Bloody immigrants! They've got all the money.'

We have a new neighbour, who has bought the other half of our semi-detached house. He is called Willy Johnson and he is not at all friendly, remaining quite cold whenever we meet him outside. He takes to banging on the shared wall late at night with a hammer, as if he is doing DIY. This seems implausible at 11 p.m., but we don't like to contemplate the idea that he is being deliberately provocative, so we give him the benefit of the doubt.

The end of the summer term is bittersweet. I decide to leave the RAF, because the issue of the trousers is too painful. I cannot wear the material against my skin; it is torture, like wearing sackcloth and ashes. But wearing cotton pyjamas underneath is worrying as well; it is inevitable that I will be found out at some point, and most certainly when I attend one of the training camps and have to live in a dormitory.

The other sad aspect is that Mrs Lyon is leaving the school; she is moving to some other part of the country. I will miss her; it is as if a light has gone out in school life.

The extension is completed during the school summer holiday. Willy Johnson won't co-operate with the builders, refusing to give access to his land, so it is built from our side only.

I am assigned the new downstairs bedroom and its en-suite shower room. I develop a lifelong affinity for multiple daily showers. (I never smell bad ever again.)

My optician, the well-known Mr Frith of Twickenham, recommends that I start wearing contact lenses; they will be better for my vision, giving more clarity and stability. During the summer vacation, I discard my glasses and feel quite self-conscious without them. But they did make me look like a nerd!

And now I can look cool by wearing stylish sunglasses.

I read in *TV Times* magazine an article about The Osmonds. It mentions that they are Mormons and talks a little about Mormon beliefs. Apparently, Mormons believe that black people are black *because of* what they did in some kind of earlier existence. I find this idea unacceptable (and completely un-Islamic). But on the plus side, Mormons don't eat pork or drink alcohol, so we do have something in common. The Mormon religion was also founded, apparently, by an angel appearing to their Prophet and delivering a Holy Book.

If Islam is the true religion, why is it that people in the West lead overwhelmingly comfortable lives, with much opportunity for personal freedom and happiness – whilst people in Islamic countries are mostly poor, and live in ignorance, misery and humiliation? *It must be some kind of test of faith.* God will surely reward the pious Muslims in the Afterlife, and the decadent, hedonistic and immoral unbelievers are going to get quite a shock. How else can I explain why my life is weighed down with the burden of Peldman? *What other explanation can there be?*

Wogs

1977-78

Age: 15

THE CONTACT LENSES and my own shower room facilitate a profound change in me. I develop a way of dealing with the racist lowlifes in the school, with their gutter English and unkempt appearance. I become the perfect gentleman, superior to them in every way. They may be white, but I become *whiter than white*, quintessentially English. My appearance becomes always immaculate: tie perfectly knotted, shirt pristinely ironed, hair neatly combed. My accent and enunciation become perfect BBC and I become a guardian of the English language. (Don't even think of misusing the word 'hopefully' in my presence.) My English-language skills are outstanding and I look down on people with inferior accents. (This is my way of creating some self-esteem, as a reaction to being abused as a sub-human Paki.)

Even outside school I dress smartly, or at least what I consider to be smart. I am a rebel against the scruffiness of most young people, with my deliberate strategy of being more English than the English. I do make an attempt at wearing jeans, but it doesn't work out. They don't hold their crease very well at all, no matter how much time I spend fastidiously ironing them.

There is a dreadful television programme on London Weekend Television on Saturday mornings, called *Our Show*. It is presented by a group of common, semi-literate children, of varying ages, who regularly mutilate the English language with their excruciatingly coarse accents and sloppy sentence

121

construction. The trashy 'yoof' audiences complain about having to do homework (*any* amount of homework) and other brutal violations of their human rights. The show runs for several hours, because it includes several other programmes within its time frame. This is the unspeakable scandal perpetrated by the television schedulers. I am forced to watch *Our Show*, because I want to watch the unique and exciting *Space: 1999*, but the precise timing of this quality programme is not specified clearly – it is buried somewhere within *Our Show*.

One day on *Our Show*, they announce that they are holding a science-fiction story competition. Anyone under the age of sixteen can send in a story they have written, up to a maximum length of 2,000 words. The prize is four tickets to see that amazing-looking new film that's coming soon: *Star Wars*.

It's worth a try. I have a story readily available – the one for which Mrs Lyon gave me 19½ out of 20. I copy it out from my old English exercise book (which has Mrs Lyon's sacred comments throughout), transcribing it painstakingly neatly onto a couple of sheets of A4 paper, and I mail it to the address they have given. I don't give it another thought.

My mother's youngest brother, who now lives in Vancouver, is getting married and this event will take place in Karachi, where a bride meeting the desired specifications has been sourced for him. The wedding is to be in December, so we will spend the school Christmas holiday in Pakistan. We will actually fly there on Christmas Day, when there will be no problem getting standby seats.

My parents procure suitable suits for my brothers and me, from C&A.[9] Mine is dark blue, with a fine light-blue checked pattern; it has wide lapels, generously flared trousers and a waistcoat. A spectacular (mostly orange) tie, white shirt, cuff links and shiny new shoes with big heels complete the picture. It all feels very smart and I try the suit on a few times at home, scrutinising myself in the mirror in

1977-78
Age: 15

my parents' bedroom. I so much want to be a grown up. *(If only Mrs Lyon had seen me like this.)*

The school holiday begins, and my brothers and I are getting ready for our next trip to Karachi, packing and preparing our carry-on bags. One afternoon, the phone rings and I answer it.

'Hello, can I speak to Imran Ahmad?' asks a woman, in quite a posh voice.

'That's me,' I reply, surprised. I have no clue as to who would be asking for me.

'Oh, hello Imran. My name is Victoria Poushkine and I'm the producer of *Our Show*. I'm pleased to tell you that you've won our science-fiction story competition.'

I don't believe it! I'm jumping for joy. I had completely forgotten about the competition, and now I've won it! It's amazing.

There is more good news. Victoria Poushkine tells me that they will be reading my story on *Our Show*, and they would like me to appear on the programme for this. I'm going to be famous! But ... it is not to be. We soon establish that the programme date is during the period that I will be in Pakistan, for my uncle's wedding. I regretfully inform Miss Poushkine that I won't be able to make it. She is disappointed, but understands. She will send me the *Star Wars* tickets in the post.

I think about this lost opportunity a great deal. The biggest problem I would have had, in appearing on *Our Show*, would be not having the right kind of 'street' clothes to wear. The presenters all wear exceptionally scruffy clothes, which are perceived to be fashionable and 'cool', but I have no such clothes in my wardrobe, nor any knowledge of what is 'cool'. Also, and I have no doubt about this, my accent and attitude would be so at odds with these delinquents, that they would not know what to make of me; I might even be perceived with amusement by them and their audience. (It certainly isn't cool to be intelligent,

1977-78
Age: 15   123

serious, articulate, and in any way perceived to be 'posh'.)
Perhaps it's for the best, but I still think wistfully of my lost
opportunity to appear on television.

Heathrow Airport on Christmas Day is still lively, but not
frantic. Many of the airline staff are wearing Santa hats or
reindeer horns. We have no problem getting seats and head
for Karachi.

My grandfather's house is full of people again; the
wedding celebrations are many and prolonged. There are
breakfasts, lunches and dinners to attend at various
people's houses. Being December, it is also mercifully cool,
which is a relief, because my three-piece suit would have
been unbearable otherwise.

Back in school, David 'Nobby' Styles tells me what
happened on the critical edition of *Our Show*. Kenny
Everett (the famous radio DJ) was the special guest and he
announced the winner of the science-fiction story
competition. He read the paper that was given to him and
then said to the audience, 'Here's a really English-sounding
name ... *Im-raan Aqkh-mad*.' He seemed to go to a lot of
trouble to mutilate my surname with an incorrect and
unnecessarily guttural pronunciation. He did read the story
with dignity though, and they dimmed the lights as he
reached the sombre and ominous ending.

Mr Payne, our form master and English teacher, listens
in disbelief. (He gave me just a B grade for the exact same
story, which I also wrote for him this year.)

Mrs Thatcher is doing well; she is always on the television
and she visited Pakistan (and India) recently. (The ITN
news has a laugh about a Pakistani police officer – not
really understanding who or what she was – referring to
Mrs Thatcher as 'Boss Lady'.) She visited President Jimmy
Carter in Washington, and the Americans absolutely loved

her (especially because the Russians dubbed her 'the Iron Lady' after her outspoken condemnation of Soviet military aggression). It is three years since she became leader of the Conservative Party, replacing Mr Heath after he lost the country to Labour. There has to be an election in the next year or so and, if the Conservatives win, Mrs Thatcher would become this country's first female Prime Minister. That would be amazing! I am in favour of a female Prime Minister, because women are more compassionate and peace-loving than men.

I quite like the Conservatives, because Labour wants to get rid of grammar schools – although strangely and inexplicably it was Mrs Thatcher who oversaw the decision to end the grammar status of my own school. (*I don't really understand this.*) Labour wants us all to be in big, horrible comprehensive schools, which are jungles over-run by bullies and hooligans, and where the teachers are ineffective hippies. I am so lucky to be in this school. I know that in a regular school, I would have encountered many thugs who don't like to study and don't like boys who do study.

There is still much talk of immigration; coloured people are flooding into the country, apparently, and many white people are angry and afraid about it. A lot of people on television say that they will vote for the National Front and there is much concern that this party will actually get somewhere. The spectre of being 'repatriated' still haunts me. Mrs Thatcher very cleverly harvests those frightened votes. I watch her in an interview one evening on *World in Action* saying: '… people are really rather afraid that this country might be rather swamped by people with a different culture.' Those words get played over and over again, on every news programme. *Swamped.* Some people say that she's racist, but it's very clever really – she gets the votes away from the National Front. I think it would be a lot better if the Conservative Party gets in and just stops further immigration, than if the National Front gets in and sends us all 'home'.

Strangely enough, there's a black man reading the television news these days. It seems unbelievable. His voice sounds very English and so does his name: Trevor McDonald. Well, Scottish, I suppose. *But I doubt if anyone with a funny Asian name will ever read the news. I can't imagine that.*

Willy Johnson comes out of the closet, bringing racism home to us, literally. He makes a fuss about our new extension, tears down part of the fence at the back and puts up a sign on a big piece of paper which says, '*Wogs keep off*'. Underneath this clear instruction, he has signed his name with a great sweeping flourish.

The police are called, but they say that it is a civil (not criminal) matter and won't intervene. We take down the sign and keep it as evidence. Later, Willy Johnson writes to our solicitor about the 'theft of a piece of paper from my property (value 2½ pence)'.

He has issues with the extension, saying that it has encroached on his property by one inch. He says that the brickwork of the new wall now facing his back patio has not been tidied up properly. He is suing over these items. But throughout the wall's construction he had refused to co-operate with our builder, so it had been built without access to his side of the property line.

His behaviour becomes openly abusive and causes a lot of tension for my family. We are always wondering what he will do next. Very often he will play extremely loud rock music in his house, with the speakers placed directly against the shared wall, facing towards our home. He usually goes out for a few hours while the music is playing, so that he is not disturbed by it himself.

It becomes hard for us to enjoy our garden, and we even become reluctant to go outside the front door sometimes,

1977-78
Age: 15

in case he shouts something unpleasant. One afternoon, my parents are barbecuing kebabs, but they are doing it *inside* the garden shed, so that they do not have to face Willy Johnson. Nonetheless, he sees the coming and going, smells something in the air, and stands at the gap in the fence calling out, 'What a stink!' He hasn't the faintest conception of how utterly delicious my mother's kebabs are. In fact, if he had been a nice neighbour, my parents would gladly have made some for him.

In a later development, he makes a hole in the outer brick wall of our extension that faces his back patio, and diverts his rain gutter into it, so that the rainwater from his roof is running into the cavity between the inner and outer walls. This will create dampness in our house. The police are called. I recognise the officer getting out of the police car: *it's PC Rice!* He is very kind and sympathetic as he surveys what has been done, but later tells us that his Inspector has instructed him that this is 'a civil matter'.

Willy Johnson is suing my parents and proudly declares that he has received 'Legal Aid', which gives legitimacy to his claim. (Legal Aid is apparently a system of government grants to give people money to pay for a solicitor.) My parents are taking legal action against him to put an end to his abuse, harassment and vandalism. They are denied Legal Aid. The letter says that this is because their 'annual disposable income exceeds £2,000'. *We are too well off!* Willy Johnson receives public money to sue us for something which is his fault (if it's true) – but we have to pay to prevent him abusing us and attacking our home. The system of justice in this country is sick.

This whole business weighs heavily on all of us. My mother is particularly stressed and looks it. My father is too, but does not show it; he has always been a cheerful man. I am consumed by the absolute injustice of it all. We did not ask for Willy Johnson in our lives; he has imposed himself on

1977-78
Age: 15

us. He has taken away our sense of peace and well-being at home, something he has no right to do.

I imagine how wonderful it would be to have a machine gun. To burst into his house and see the look of shock on his face. To eradicate his miserable existence with a hail of avenging bullets. Obviously, I don't have access to a machine gun, so I wonder about firebombing his house. *Could I do this without being caught? Probably not.* Fortunately, I never do any such thing, but if it could be done without any adverse consequences to myself, I would act without hesitation or regret. Willy Johnson does not deserve to live.

Where is God in all this? I wonder why God doesn't intervene and work some of His perfect justice. But I know the answer. For the administration of most acts of justice, God waits until the Afterlife, wanting to observe how we behave in this life.

School also contains racism; it must be an integral part of life. Apart from Peldman, there is another lowlife called Pyler. Like Peldman, he is also in one of the years above mine. He is a thug, a racist, a bully and a moron. He often abuses me and boasts about 'Paki-bashing'. His English is rough and low-class. The Headmaster seems to like him, calling him by his first name, which I find unfair and incomprehensible. The only reason that he is in the school is that his older brother is a pupil and is intelligent and respected.

One day, a (white) first-year boy is in the cloisters, heading for the tuck shop, and some coins slip out of his hands. One of these coins rolls away and stops in front of Pyler. Pyler is standing still, in an intimidating way, and deliberately steps on this coin. The first-year boy goes to pick it up, reaching down for it under Pyler's shoe as if Pyler will surely step back courteously.

'How dare you touch me, you little c—!' snarls Pyler and he gives the crouching boy a savage kick. The boy collapses, crying and in pain. Pyler leans back, Goliath-like, and laughs heartily, the master of all he surveys. Two of the boy's friends run up and virtually carry the sobbing boy away.

We study world religions in school. I seem to already know more about this than my classmates. There are three major religions that believe in One God. Jews believe in the One God, but they don't believe in Jesus. Christians believe in Jesus, *obviously* (they think they own him exclusively), but they have somehow fragmented the One God into a mysterious Threesome, whilst insisting that this is still One somehow. Muslims believe in One God, and in Jesus, as well as Muhammad. Hindus believe in many gods and in reincarnation (both totally un-Islamic concepts). Buddhists believe in reincarnation and seek to lose themselves ultimately in some kind of spiritual non-existence, but they don't seem to believe in an actual God.

It is easy to short-list these religions into the only ones that can possibly be true. Jesus was a real person, therefore *only* Christianity and Islam can potentially be true. All further investigation and evaluation need only be between these two possibilities. And, if one can be *proven* to be wrong, the other *must* be the true religion.

In Mathematics, I sit next to Auden and Robinson. We are always chatting while solving the problems that our bushy-bearded teacher, Doctor 'Rolf' Harris, has written on the board. These two are 'good' boys like me; they never use foul language or behave badly. One day I am speaking enthusiastically about last night's episode of *Charlie's Angels*; I find it unbearably joyful that I can watch such breathtakingly beautiful women (especially Jaclyn Smith) on television every week. Auden doesn't watch it, and there is

1977-78
Age: 15

an awkward pause from Robinson, before he says in a reluctant tone, 'We don't have a television.'

I am taken aback and embarrassed. I feel terrible that I've been enthusing about television programmes to someone who doesn't have a television. But I'm also amazed that, in this day and age, there are still people who can't afford a television, especially in a very middle-class environment like Hampton School. I feel sorry for him. We go back to the Maths problems.

I take three O-levels[10] a year early. I get an A for both English Language and Latin, and a B for Mathematics, which is disappointing, because I did very well in the practice exams. English and Latin were easy and fun, but the Mathematics did seem like hard work.

The eighth of September is a horrible day in Iran, a country I've never thought about before. Hundreds of protesters (mostly students) in Tehran are killed by tanks and helicopter gunships. What were they protesting about? We learn all about this in a television documentary. Apparently the Shah of Iran runs a brutal regime and steals the oil wealth for himself and a small wealthy elite. He has a secret police force that arrests and tortures people who oppose him. He has been in power since 1953, when the American CIA (in Operation Ajax) overthrew the democratically elected president and installed the Shah as the supreme ruler.

This is confusing and makes it hard for me to figure out who is good and who is bad. The role of America in this is very disturbing, since America is one of the forces of good in the world. They probably didn't know about the torture.

1977-78
Age: 15

Jaguar

1978-79
Age: 16

MY PARENTS, at their own expense, obtain a court injunction which instructs Willy Johnson to stay off our land and not to interfere with our house in any way. It's not a punishment for him; it's merely forbidding him to do criminal things which he should not do anyway. *Why should we have to pay for justice?*

His claim about the wall fizzles out and an uneasy peace returns.

One day, I realise that I have not been abused by Peldman recently. Come to think of it, I haven't seen him for a while. I ask around and I find out that he has been expelled from school permanently, for not doing any work in Sixth Form. Apparently, he just couldn't be bothered. *This is too good to be true!* The cancer has been surgically removed. He hasn't been expelled for racist bullying; well, no one in authority would really know about that, since I never made an issue of it or lodged a complaint. He has been expelled because he was too stupid to appreciate his grammar school place. This news is unbearably sweet. He fades into obscurity. I feel relief and great joy.

In the Sixth Form, which starts next year for me, the school has introduced joint General Studies classes with the posh girls' school next door. This means that boys from my school pay regular visits to Lady Eleanor Holles School. *I can't wait!* Also, L.E.H. girls can occasionally be seen walking in the corridors of our school. I figure out precisely when in the timetable this is and where the classrooms are. I calculate that when I walk along certain routes at these times, my path will cross those of L.E.H. girls. I always ensure that my hair, tie and shirt are immaculate, as I stride along nonchalantly with my attaché case, the absolute embodiment of masculine handsome coolness. I pass L.E.H. girls on many such occasions. They never seem to notice me.

Return of the Saint is on television, with Simon Templar driving a Jaguar XJ-S. *What a dream car!* So beautiful, so expensive – and completely unattainable. It *even has a telephone!* In one episode, the Saint is in the South of France and a beautiful woman approaches his passenger window and leans towards it. Simon Templar pushes a button on the centre console of his XJ-S and the passenger window glides down. *It's electric!*

I have a longing to have this kind of persona: that of Simon Templar or James Bond. A handsome and brave adventurer, loved by beautiful women and admired by all. Simon Templar wears smart seventies clothes, and so do I (although his are from *Francesco* of Jermyn Street, and mine are from C&A of Hounslow High Street). I scrutinise his hairstyle intently, and then carefully model my own hair in the same way; it takes a lot of combing to maintain it. It's funny, because I never see Simon Templar pay any attention to his own hair, but it always remains immaculate, no matter how much action he gets into.

Simon Templar drives his Jaguar XJ-S all over Europe, taking it as far as Italy. He finds excitement effortlessly; he couldn't even go out to pick up his dry-cleaning without something happening on the way. Occasionally I dress smartly, and casually go for a very long walk around the neighbourhood, or far into Bushey Park, looking for some adventure (and a beautiful woman) to fall into my lap, but nothing ever happens.

1978-79
Age: 16

Jaguar

The desire for his car weighs heavily. One night, I have a dream. I've won a Jaguar XJ-S, but we are keeping it in the garden shed, because I am too young to drive. One day, I cannot resist any longer. Without my parents' knowledge, I drive the enormous white Jaguar out of the shed and onto the road. The engine purrs smoothly, the interior is fabulous: leather seats, polished wood, a sumptuous steering wheel, countless instrument lights and shiny switches. I can see it all clearly; it's breathtaking. As I turn around the corner into Ormond Avenue, I see ahead of me three of my most elite classmates walking together. Alaric Smith, Jon Davidson and Michel Bowes; they are the *crème de la crème*, intellectually and socially. I so much want them to like me and to treat me as one of their clique. I am excited that I will be showing off my magnificent Jaguar XJ-S, which will give me huge credibility, but, as I approach them, it turns into a bicycle.

One morning in school, as we file towards the Assembly Hall, I notice two strange middle-aged men in dark suits, standing in the foyer with the Headmaster. One of them has what looks like a heavy Bible tucked under his arm.

The Headmaster introduces them in Assembly as two Reverends from America; they would like to address the school. The first Reverend starts off with a reading from the Bible. The second Reverend talks about faith, and ominously mentions something about singing some songs to us. When he does start to sing a song, a slow lament of some kind, without musical accompaniment, the tension in the school is unbearable.

'Oh... *Jeeeezuus* ... *my Saviour* ... *oh beloved Lamb of God* ...'

This is so *not* Hampton School, so *not* middle-class Church of England vicarage garden party lukewarm Christianity. Nine hundred boys and about fifty staff are put in a very awkward situation. The boys (and many of the staff) are trying so hard not to laugh; the first one to

1978-79
Age: 16

133

do so will set off the whole school, but he'll be a dead man. I stare into empty space and think of all the hungry people in the world. *This is unbearable.*

Even the Headmaster clearly had no idea what was coming. He is a master of self-disciplined impassiveness, but the shock and strain in his face are clearly showing, lest one of the boys bursts out laughing and Assembly erupts into a fiasco.

Possibly, the singing American Reverend notices the tension too. He decides to sing only one song. *Praise the Lord!*

We are all loitering in our classroom one lunchtime. Barry Sutton suddenly asks me a question out of the blue. 'Hey Imran! Are your parents going to arrange your marriage?' He is serious and genuinely interested.

Everyone's attention is suddenly upon me. They are all interested too. Arranged marriage is something that always happens in any television programme in which Asian characters appear. *Does it apply to Imran?*

This is the unspeakable demon which has lurked in my mind for years. It has never been discussed overtly at home, but there has always been an implicit assumption that this will be the case. Any other process will cause a huge conflagration in my family. (I imagine being asked as a grown up, *'Where did you meet your wife?'* and having to answer, *'At our wedding.'*) I can't bear to think about it. I want to be like James Bond or Simon Templar. *They don't have arranged marriages.*

'No, of course not!' I tell the class, with forced joviality.

I try to suppress this issue, to not think about it too much, but Barry Sutton has hit me in the most sensitive spot. For a very long time I've been aware that there's one fundamental difference between the two worlds in which I live.

The white people – British, American, French, *all of them* – they are all agree on one principle: you marry *only* for love. They all believe this, whether they are Protestant or Catholic or secular or agnostic or atheist. It's a universal truth to them, reflected throughout their culture, music, art, literature, drama.

But people of the Indian subcontinent – Pakistanis, Indians, Bangladeshis, or from a different perspective, Muslims, Hindus, Sikhs – they (or should that be 'we') believe the exact opposite: you marry for anything *except* love. This also seems to extend to Muslims the world over. Marrying for love is vulgar, selfish, dishonourable. It means that there has been shameful behaviour, spending time with someone of the opposite sex – enough to fall in love with them.

Instead, marriage becomes a transaction, for any other purpose except love: a business deal; community cohesion; even (most hideously) to get someone a Western passport (perhaps as a favour to a friend). The concepts of freedom, happiness, compatibility, mutual attraction and personal chemistry are alien to this mindset.

Romantic love is absolutely forbidden. And romantic love is what I want more than anything.

Simon Alloway runs into me one day and mentions something about a 'charity disco' to be held at the Methodist Church Hall in Twickenham, just before Christmas. He is supplying tickets and, apparently, quite a few people are going. Would I like to come?

This is a tantalising possibility for me: a disco means the opportunity to meet girls. I ask my mother, emphasising the charitable nature of this event and – inexplicably, implausibly and unexpectedly – she says that it is all right for me to go, as long as I return at a reasonable time (before midnight).

In the couple of weeks leading up to the disco, I have to get my act together; I have never disco-danced before. I practise in the living room, when my parents are out, setting the Sanyo music centre to a suitable radio channel. Apparently, in the music there is a rhythm, and you just have to tune your body into this rhythm, and shake your arms and legs accordingly.

Rehan and Rizwan, who attend a state school and travel there by bus, are much more streetwise than me. They observe my efforts with amusement and disdain, and dub my unique dancing style 'the Imran Shuffle'.

The longed-for Friday evening finally comes and my arrangement is to meet schoolmate Wayne Mowat, who lives nearby, and take the bus with him to Twickenham. We will meet our contemporaries at the hall.

I am dressed extremely smartly. My beige polyester trousers from C&A are tight at the waist and very generously flared at the ankles. My elegant polyester-cotton shirt is lavishly striped in shades of brown and beige, but has a plain collar and cuffs – which is the very tasteful style nowadays. The crowning glory is my special watch, the digital one. It is a bulbous and distinguished piece, shiny and gold-coloured, and it has a black LED screen. It's true that you have to push a button to tell the time, but the illuminated red LED display gives unsurpassed clarity in dark conditions, such as those to be found in a disco. On top of these chic clothes, I wear my dark-blue school-approved raincoat.

Something goes wrong with my watch on the way. I've had this problem before. The battery seems to be slightly loose, and this results in the watch resetting itself to 00:00. So, as an instrument for telling the time it becomes completely useless, but it still looks very smart.

A girl on the bus, noticing this very distinctive watch, asks me, 'Have you got the time?'

'No,' is my unexpected answer. I almost unconsciously cover the watch with my hand. She must think I'm really unfriendly, or that the watch isn't a real one.

It's a very cold, dark and frosty night. Wayne and I reach Twickenham Methodist Church Hall just as Simon Alloway and the gang are arriving. We check in our coats and head into the hot darkness. I undo my top three buttons.

During this evening, I drink a number of Cokes and dance in amongst my school friends the whole time. There are many girls in the hall, but most of us hide within the safety of our group.

We suddenly notice that Sim Jones is dancing with a girl! Later on, he is kissing her and has his arms all around her. *Lucky bastard!*

Nothing else of note occurs during this disco. When we go outside, it seems eerily quiet, as well as cold, and my head and ears feel slightly numb. My father collects Wayne and me in his car as prearranged. The much-anticipated event is over.

In school, I have an opportunity to ask Sim about the girl. He says that her name is Mary Louise and that she is 'not at all a nice person'.

I can't even begin to understand this information and the inherent contradictions. She let him kiss her; *how could he not like her?*

The Iranian Revolution takes place. The whole thing is quite worrying. The Shah is overthrown and forced to flee the country. We see on television the torture chambers of his secret police, Savak. They had racks where they toasted people alive. This revolution seems to be a just one. What disturbs me is that America supported the Shah, and continues to do so.

1978-79
Age: 16

But it's more complicated than that. Iranians are Shias, a minority Muslim sect, encompassing maybe 10 percent of Muslims. Shia Islam has a hierarchy of clergy ('*Ayatollahs*') and all sorts of unfamiliar rituals and additional beliefs; I'm not comfortable with any of it. Many Sunnis do not consider Shias to be proper Muslims at all. (In some places, this division is as intense as the Catholic–Protestant hatred in parts of Belfast and Glasgow.)

The Iranians get into a major confrontation with the United States, holding hostages from the American Embassy in Tehran. The situation seems completely chaotic – it's not even clear who is in charge and if the newly-formed and seemingly fragile Iranian government actually has any control over this situation. The hostage-takers are variously described as 'students' and 'Marxist agitators'. But they do send home most of the women and black men, keeping the remaining 52 hostages (mostly white men) while they try to negotiate an apology from America (for past interference) and the unfreezing of Iranian assets in the US. There is so much anger and rage on display, with Ayatollahs addressing crowds who scream 'Death to Amreeka!' The women are always covered in black, from head to foot, which is completely alien to me. The American hostages must be terrified, and feel so vulnerable and alone. This is all on the television, all the time. The minority faith of the furious and overtly dramatic Shias is paraded as Islam to the whole world. It's unfortunate and embarrassing. It's a mess.

Alan Wicker, the globetrotting television presenter, does an entire series of *Wicker's World* devoted to India. Apparently, they believe in thirty million gods. Can you believe this? *How absurd.* The one true God is really going to have it in for them.

There is one discussion about whether it is really thirty million *different* gods, or these are all just aspects, perspectives, dimensions, manifestations of one single God. The scholar explains to Alan Wicker that Hindus actually believe in the Oneness of God, and in the Oneness of everything *with* God. This is confusing to me; it implies that Hindus believe in a Oneness of God which is *even more* One than the Islamic Oneness of God, of which we are so proud.

Hey, this doesn't make sense. Everyone knows that Hindus believe in many gods. I put it out of my mind; it's too unsettling.

The film *Lawrence of Arabia* is shown on television one Saturday evening; I watch it with my family. Apparently Colonel Lawrence was a British officer who united the tribal desert Arabs in the First World War, enlisting their help to fight the Turks, who were on the side of the Germans.

Two aspects of this film particularly trouble me.

One issue is that all the Englishmen in the film (except Lawrence) casually refer to Arabs as 'wogs', even though they are fighting for the British. My family and I are especially sensitive to this; the word is heavily charged for us, because of him next door. Does this mean that the English always have been, and always will be, naturally racist to people like us, no matter what we do?

The other aspect is even more disturbing. In the film, an Arab from one tribe kills an Arab from a different tribe, because the latter took water from the first tribe's drinking hole, somewhere out in the desert. This is very hard for me to understand; it just doesn't make sense. It's as if the Arabs put their own tribal loyalty before the brotherhood and peace of Islam. But the Prophet Muhammad was supposed to have put an end to tribal feuding; not just for Arabs, but for all people who become Muslim. You can't kill someone for drinking from your watering hole – *that's completely un-Islamic!*

1978-79
Age: 16

And there's the further complication that both the Arabs and the Turks were Muslim, but they were fighting each other. *Perhaps the world is not as a simple a place as I would like it to be. No one is following any of the principles that they are supposed to.*

The beginning of exam season is marked by the General Election, a historic event in which Mrs Thatcher becomes Britain's first-ever female Prime Minister. In these extraordinary circumstances, it is understandable that I would take a sudden interest in watching news programmes and documentaries, and reading the more cerebral newspapers in great depth, rather than the unbearably mundane business of exam revision.

The O-level exams go okay, though. I acquire eleven O-levels in all, doing better in Arts subjects than in Sciences. (Arts subjects are also more fun.) I know that some teachers believe strongly that I should study Arts further, but the idea is ridiculous. What would I do with a degree in Classics, or English, or History? And it would make my parents the laughing stock of the Asian community. I can imagine the conversations.

> *'So, your eldest boy ... the marriageable one ... Imran, isn't it? ... What is he doing now?'*
> *'Oh, he's studying at Cambridge.'*
> *'Cambridge! Oh, ma'sh'Allah! Is he studying Meddy-sun or In-jin-eering?'*
> *'Actually, he's studying Classics.'*
> (Pause.)
> *'Clar-sic? What branch of Meddy-sun is that?'*
> *'Actually, it's the history, philosophy and languages of ancient Greece and Rome ...'*
> (Pause.)
> *'Let me get you some more samosas.'*

1978-79
Age: 16

Prefect

1979-80

Age: 17

AS I START THE SIXTH FORM, my studies narrow to A-level Biology, Chemistry and Physics, plus the mandatory General Studies, which encompasses a broad range of subjects: sociology, philosophy, history of science, psychology and so on. The only subject I really like is General Studies, and not just because some of these lessons are held jointly with the girls' school. I really don't enjoy Biology, Chemistry and Physics, but I have to study these if I am to go to medical school. I can do well if I really make an effort, but there is no pleasure in this.

My father buys a video cassette recorder, a Panasonic, from our local television shop. They know him there because he has bought two colour televisions from them over the years and they allow him to pay the £660 in three monthly instalments of £220 each. The VCR is quite heavy and I carry it out to the car very carefully.

My parents have bought this device because they like to watch Indian films, which are available on tapes from places like Southall. My brothers and I are thrilled, because this amazing invention means that we will never have to miss a television programme again (the way that I missed that critical episode of *Doctor Who*, when the Doctor regenerated from Patrick Troughton into Jon Pertwee). The VCR can be set to record one programme up to seven days in advance. The VHS tapes are quite expensive though, so we often argue over tape space; it's £11 for a one-hour tape, £14 for a two-hour, and £17 for a three-hour.

141

As for Indian films, my brothers and I find them excruciatingly long and rather repetitive. The plot line always revolves around a boy and a girl who fall in love and want to get married, but one or other of the sets of parents disapproves (because of caste, class, religion, family, village, or because they didn't choose him or her) and have other plans for their offspring. I see the inherent contradiction in this phenomenon. The societies (both Indian and Pakistani) that overwhelmingly enforce arranged marriage and family 'honour' are addicted to endless films in which the characters fall in love and resist their parents' wishes. It's as if the people who love these films can't make the connection between what they see on screen and their own attitudes.

In one such film (or is it several?), the young hero is in love with a girl, but his old dragon of a mother does not approve, and wants him to marry some other girl. She douses herself in fuel in the kitchen and threatens to set herself alight if her wayward son does not comply with her wishes. The poor young man caves in, begging her not to immolate herself and promising to marry whomsoever she wants him to. (He must be too old to be bribed by promises about Christmas presents.)

The first Indian film we watch on the new VCR does have a curious and unique twist. It is called *Amer, Akbar, Anthony*. It tells the story of three young brothers, accidentally lost by their parents and separated, who are brought up by a Hindu family, a Muslim family and Christian priests, hence their names. The film is surprising to me in that it treats all three of these religions in an equal and even-handed way, not portraying any one of them to be uniquely right, but showing positive aspects of each one. Maybe India isn't such a bad country after all.

The first General Studies option that I take is 'The History and Philosophy of Science', which is taught by the

Headmaster himself. It is held in our school, but a couple of L.E.H. girls do come over: Katharine and Judith. I am always self-conscious about not making a fool of myself in front of them.

The Headmaster (or 'The Old Man', as he is semi-affectionately known) does not make this easy for me. One day he challenges me about Islam. *Is it a scientific religion?* He is genuinely trying to extract some rational thought out of me, but I am clueless. Another question: *How do I know that the Roman gods are false and that there is only one God?* My position – '*It is obvious*' – does not carry any weight in philosophical circles. (No wonder that guardians of religion often put intellectuals to death; it's the only way that they can find to deal with them.)

In one lesson, I do shine through. The Old Man raises the question of how Christian theology would deal with life on other planets. If there *are* intelligent alien species, they presumably also would have committed an original sin at some point, in which case they too would be in need of redemption by the blood sacrifice of God's only Son. I speak up and say that there is an episode of *Star Trek* that deals with this very issue. On an alien planet, the followers of a new faith were being persecuted by a ruling race (resembling the Romans), who had earlier put to death a radical revolutionary known as 'The Son'. The Old Man is impressed by *Star Trek,* but not by my encyclopaedic knowledge of it (my intellectual capacity could have been better focused on academically useful material instead).

My birthday in September is the earliest amongst the pupils of my academic year, therefore I am the first to start learning to drive. My parents are patient and supportive. I get an appointment for a driving test in January. I practise a great deal in my mother's Mini, and the test around Teddington and Twickenham goes well. I am overjoyed when the examiner tells me that I have passed. *What could be better than having a full driving licence?*

The next morning, when I enter the dining hall at morning break, where we sixth formers gather for coffee, Paul Davey initiates a round of applause and cheering. I'm not sure what motivates him to do this, but I do appreciate the congratulations. I seem to have come a long way in Hampton School.

The Russians invade Afghanistan, in order to uphold a puppet Communist government. I am pleased to see the West, led by America, align with the Islamic world (and in particular Pakistan), in opposing the godless Communists. The freedom fighters, the *Mujahideen*, consist of both local Afghans and many Arab men who have gravitated to Afghanistan to 'fight the good fight' (*'Jihad'*). There are many television documentary programmes showing Western journalists dressed in local clothes, entering Afghanistan via Pakistan and observing the brave Mujahideen making life very difficult for the Russian military. The Americans supply advanced weaponry, explosives and training in guerrilla warfare, and the freedom fighters become very adept at using those wonderful American Stinger missiles to shoot down Russian helicopter gunships, afterwards scurrying for cover into the caves and mountain paths, which only they know well.

One day, Andrew Warmington asks me if I would like to help him to sell tickets for the Sixth Form plays. These are two pieces by Tom Stoppard: *After Magritte* and *The Real Inspector Hound.* I agree and quite enjoy the sales process, as well as being part of the administration of the plays when they are performed for three consecutive nights.

There are female roles in the plays, and these are performed by girls from the Lady Eleanor Holles School.

Katharine (from my 'History and Philosophy of Science' class) is one of them, but there is another girl called Andrea, who is breathtakingly beautiful. She has a perfect English accent, a sweet smile and delightful poise. She is everything that I long for and surely can never have.

I hang around backstage with her every evening and attempt to chat with her. She responds kindly, although I am less than inspiring.

The three nights of the performance come to an end, and we all loiter around the drama hall for a little while (it is Friday night), enjoying the exhilaration of a job well done. It is late when I leave with great reluctance, and I am gutted at the knowledge that I will not see Andrea again regularly, apart from the odd chance meeting in and outside the schools. The weekend passes with both joy and frustration; I have met someone wonderful, but I don't know how to meet her again.

Without a doubt, I have fallen in love with her, and this clouds my normally clear thinking and affects my behaviour. I cannot concentrate in class; I doodle silly things in my notebooks. I make sure that I am as smart and well turned out as can be, lest we have a chance meeting.

The following Tuesday afternoon in the Physics laboratory, Paul Davey – who is something of a loose cannon – suddenly pulls my perfectly knotted tie, just for fun. Its neatness and precise proportions are to him like a red rag to a bull.

I blurt out in a moment of reckless abandon, 'Stop it! Andrea might see me!'

Paul Davey cannot believe his luck; I have dropped a marvellous gem right in his lap. He yells out, 'Imran's in love!'

By the time of the morning break the next day, this news has spread far and wide. I walk into the dining hall to get coffee, and Blair Crawford greets me with merriment. He starred in the plays and knows Andrea well now. But,

1979-80
Age: 17

amusement aside, he asks me if am I aware that today is Andrea's birthday, she is having a party after school, and everyone from the plays is invited? *Is he pulling my leg?*

I soon determine that the story of the party is indeed true, but the question torments me: does *everyone* from the plays include *me*? I wasn't acting, I wasn't in the stage crew, I was only selling tickets and arranging chairs. *Am I also invited?*

This day is an ordeal. I am tortured by this dilemma, wracked with doubts. We have Games on Wednesday afternoon; I usually go cross-country running under the supervision of Mr Xiberras – but today I bow out under the pretext of not feeling well. I spend the afternoon moping around the school grounds and cloisters, analysing this problem without any frame of reference.

In the end, I decide to go for it. I buy a box of Black Magic chocolates from the local newsagent, and call my mother at work from the payphone in school. I tell her that I am going to 'Mike's birthday party'. Mike is a classmate who happens to live in the same cul-de-sac as Andrea, so my statement is only a very slight distortion of reality.

I enlist my trusted friend Andrew Warmington for this terrifying undertaking. He also sold tickets for the play, so surely he's entitled to come too? He is my wingman, my support; someone I can talk to, to help me appear to be at ease.

Apparently the arrangement is to meet Andrea and the other girls outside the school soon after we finish at 4 p.m. Andrew and I walk out together, with some of the other boys around us; I am practically shaking in my shoes. There is Andrea ahead; she looks so different in school uniform, but she's still beautiful. Katharine is standing with her.

Andrea sees me and calls out, 'Is Imran coming too?' *Is that surprise, joy or concern in her voice?*

I reply quickly, 'We're not invited, but we've got a present.' (The Black Magic box is in my attaché case.)

1979-80
Age: 17

Andrea seems perfectly fine with Andrew and me coming; there is no issue at all. I breathe a sigh of relief and walk along with the group. I want us to get off the main road as soon as possible. I am acutely aware that my mother (who finishes work at 4 p.m.) could come by in her Mini at any moment. We cross the road, turn off into a side road and stroll towards Andrea's cul-de-sac.

The birthday party is a civilised affair: nice food, cake, coffee, conversation. It is wonderful to be here. I am captivated by Andrea, but also acutely aware that I am just someone else in the group – no one special. I am one of the last to leave the party at nine o'clock; as I head home, I am walking on air.

In the days that follow, all of my contemporaries become aware of my turmoil very quickly, and very soon it becomes well known that 'Imran is in love with Andrea'. Everyone thinks that this is absolutely hilarious.

There are no fixed or timetabled events when I will definitely see Andrea; our meetings will be random. Her house is not far from mine, but is in the opposite direction from the schools. The post office *is* in that direction, so I take to going there after school to buy a stamp. Occasionally, I do pass Andrea – *what a coincidence!*

Cycling is a good form of exercise: it doesn't cause pollution and enables one to work the muscles, get fresh air, and get out and about. I take to cycling around the neighbourhood a lot at weekends and sometimes after school. I cycle many, many times up and down the street which harbours Andrea's cul-de-sac (although I never dare to cycle into the cul-de-sac itself). A couple of times, I see Andrea go by in her parents' car. She sees me and looks tired.

One day I'm walking down a flight of stairs at school, in my usual state of melancholy, and inadvertently (and self-indulgently) proclaim 'Oh, Andrea!' to myself. Mr Mellon, the Deputy Headmaster, appears from around the corner,

1979-80
Age: 17

ascending the stairs and trying to hide his amusement. My humiliation is absolute.

Even my parents notice my change of mood and behaviour, and suspect what the root cause is, but it is never discussed.

I have become friends with Katharine, and find her easy to talk with. I take to phoning her in the evenings sometimes, and speak freely to her, as long as my brothers and parents are in their rooms and not within earshot of me. The number-one topic of my conversation is, of course, Andrea. Katharine's message is very blunt: 'She's happy to be friends with you, but all this talk that you have generated is upsetting her.'

We conclude this conversation, with its unbearable truth, and we hang up.

A moment later, the phone rings and my mother, who is upstairs, picks it up. A couple of minutes later, she comes down the stairs, furious. Someone at British Telecom had been listening in to my call with Katharine and decided to have a bit of fun by anonymously calling our number and conveying to my mother the gist of the conversation, in a most spiteful and malicious way. My mother is not angry with me (she knows that something is up); she is contemptuous of this uncouth 'third class' woman who did such a thing. Of course, it is impossible to do anything about it; British Telecom has complete control of every aspect of the UK's telephone system. The anonymous operator can never be identified.

I am greatly disturbed by this event; how dare they do such a thing. *I hate British Telecom!*

My family and I are visiting Tesco in Teddington. My father has parked his Opel Rekord in the car park, and I have returned early to it, preferring to stand in the pleasant sunshine, in my cool sunglasses and smart clothes, and watch the people coming and going. Four white youths emerge from the back of the store, heading towards me. They are shabby, thuggish-looking, sullen faces, unkempt hair, muscular arms, T-shirts and jeans. They could be Peldman's cousins, who did not pass the grammar school exam, as he miraculously did.

They aren't here to shop; they haven't bought anything. They were probably just using the car park for convenience, and the Tesco store as a short cut to the High Street. They are wrapped up in themselves, in their own exchange of jolly mutual diatribe, when they spot me and suddenly their focus turns to me. As a team, they start hurling abuse at me, even as they walk in my direction. There is nothing original in the abuse, it comes instinctively to them: 'F—ing Paki!' and so on.

I am genuinely afraid, not for my physical wellbeing (although my body stiffens with primordial tension), but for my father's car, which they can see is associated with me. These thugs know no laws, no boundaries, they walk without fear and they are untouchable. They can do what they like, where they like. In this car park, no one will intervene, no one will witness – they can ransack and vandalise and depart at their own majestic leisure. For the police it will be but tiresome paperwork.

I lean against the car as they walk by, protecting it and turning to it for protection. Their white van is parked two spaces away. Thankfully, they limit the abuse to their rudimentary verbal skills, and seem unable to articulate anything original, although one of them does snarl 'Multi-racial society' in a mocking and derogatory way, indicating, I think, that he does not support this socio-political concept.

It is an enormous relief when they drive away, and I am glad that my parents did not have to experience it. It has been an ugly moment; it reminds me of much that I would prefer to forget. Racism takes me by surprise sometimes. Living in an affluent suburb, going to a posh school,

1979-80
Age: 17

sometimes it's easy to think that it has gone away forever, that I am now immune ... but occasionally its malice disturbs the tranquillity, the calm optimism of life.

I relax at home in the school holiday, usually listening to LBC Radio in the mornings, and trying not to wonder what Andrea is doing right now. Brian Hayes runs a daily talk show, and it's often quite amusing. One day he has a guest who believes in reincarnation. I know this is that Hindu belief that, instead of there being an eternal Heaven and Hell, you come back to this world in a state that reflects how well you lived your last life. If you've been bad, you come back as a miserable animal; if you've been good, you come back as a human. It seems primitive and preposterous. Brian seems to think so too; as he points out, if you can't remember your past life, you can't really continue to be that person. *Well said, Brian.*

It's a hot, sunny afternoon in the summer term, and a stunningly beautiful young woman drives up to Hampton School in a shiny Jaguar XJ-S convertible. She parks on the road outside and then moves over to the passenger seat. I emerge from the school, with all the boys streaming out at the end of the school day. I casually walk up to the car and open the boot. I remove my school blazer and tie, and place these, along with my attaché case, in the boot. From the back seat I take a tasteful silk tie, which I nonchalantly knot, and also an elegant fawn jacket, which I slip on. I get into the driver's seat, put my seatbelt on, slip the gear lever into Drive (keeping my foot on the brake), release the handbrake, look in the mirror, glance over my shoulder to check for anything in the blind spot (as per good driving practice), pull the XJ-S out on to the road, and drive off.

The boys outside the school watch in open-mouthed awe.

1979-80
Age: 17

'Ahmad, what's the correct equation for this chemical reaction? Can you show us on the board?'

Huh? What equation? What reaction?

There's one thing I can't understand. Willy Johnson always drives new cars and changes them often. My parents always have second-hand cars; I cannot imagine them being able to afford a new one. Willy Johnson is a racist, therefore uneducated, therefore he should not have lots of money. So how does he live in the same kind of house as we do and how does he afford new cars?

Along with a number of other boys in my year group, I am selected to be a Prefect. *Thank God.* It would have been quite humiliating for someone like me, who has acquired a reputation for being a square (too smart, too tidy, too conservative) to be passed over for this 'promotion'.

Since the first year, I have looked up to Prefects. Being a Prefect is a privilege for the final year at Hampton School. There is a 'Prefect's Room', complete with armchairs and a pool table. Prefects perform a range of supervisory, crowd-control and rule-enforcement functions. Prefects are empowered to hand out punishments, such as detentions and writing assignments. As soon as I am given the good news by Paul Pemberton – the new 'Captain of the School' – I head for the school office to buy a Prefect's tie. It is black, with gold rampant lions. The Headmaster summons us to his study (I haven't been here since my interview) and briefs us on the great responsibility we now bear, and his high expectations of us. In some ways, I feel that I have made it, become part of the establishment, integrated into the fabric of English society.

To demonstrate that I am truly 'one of the boys', my classmates – those who have not been chosen to be Prefects – drag me outside and throw about 20 gallons of water over me. I am delighted to be so accepted (although

Spock would certainly disapprove of such illogical behaviour). Fortunately, it is an extremely hot and sunny day, and I dry off in no time. My new Prefect's tie remains perfectly knotted throughout.

The end of term is near. The Upper Sixth Formers are doing their A-levels and will soon be gone, making my contemporaries the true elders of the school. I walk the corridors with the authority that my many years here and my Prefect's tie have earned. It's as if I've lived an entire lifetime in this school; how long it's been since the fear and misery of the first year.

I walk into the Sixth Form common room, carrying a cup of coffee. I am shocked to see Peldman in here, talking to some of his friends. He is wearing a black-leather jacket. He really shouldn't be here, but he has slipped into the school to catch up with some of his old classmates. I try not to acknowledge him, but my body tenses inadvertently, from years of conditioning. I am supposed to be a Prefect now, but for a moment I feel like a little boy, wondering what the big bully will do.

He walks close by me on his way out. Peldman looks at my Prefect's tie and scowls.

The James Bond film *On Her Majesty's Secret Service* is screened on television. I tape it on the VCR (I'm the only person I know in the school whose family has one) and watch it several times. Not only does it have great music and action, but it has a special connection to *me*. James Bond rescues a beautiful woman; her name is Contessa Teresa di Vincenzo ('Tracy' for short). Later, he bursts into the office of Tracy's father (the head of a powerful criminal organisation) carrying a dagger. Tracy's father says, 'Do not kill me, Mr Bond, at least not until we've had a drink.' Bond considers for a moment, then throws the dagger at the wall calendar; it embeds itself in '14 September'. Tracy's father scrutinises the calendar, then declares, 'But today is the *thirteenth*, Commander.'

The thirteenth of September – *that's my birthday!* This is a magic film, and this scene has a special message for me. Tracy's father explains why Bond should marry Tracy, and indeed she is the perfect woman. She is beautiful, intelligent, independent, vivacious, a lover of adventure, and not afraid to drive a car with passion. Contessa Teresa di Vincenzo is the kind of girl for Bond, and the kind of girl that I should marry. I know this with all my heart.

My father buys a Mercedes! A posh car, second only to the Rolls-Royce. It is four years old and a basic model, but it is a Mercedes nonetheless. I think this is some kind of milestone achievement for him. Inside it is refined and quiet. The doors close with a finely engineered 'clunk'. The distinctive Mercedes three-pointed star at the front of the bonnet is magnificent. My father is really happy and we are all excited. This is another step on our road to elevated social status. *Hardly anyone has a Mercedes!*

Willy Johnson stares at the Mercedes on our driveway and scowls.

Satan

I HAVE MADE a complete fool of myself as far as Andrea is concerned, by talking about how I feel to many of my contemporaries. I am clearly inexperienced in these matters and this was not the right thing to do. My preoccupation with Andrea is causing her much discomfort and embarrassment; she does not want to have anything to do with me. I learn this from Katharine. My misery is complete.

The Iraqis invade the land across the border with Iran and start a long, bloody and agonising war, which claims a huge number of (mostly young) lives. Saddam Hussein is the secular despot who rules Iraq. He receives the full backing of America (weapons, training, intelligence) in this unprovoked aggression; they are using him to punish the Iranians for overthrowing the Shah and the subsequent American Embassy fiasco. Iran is completely Shia, but Iraq is also overwhelmingly Shia, although it is ruled by Saddam Hussein's minority Sunni government and presents itself as a progressive secular country. So, essentially, this war is Shia killing Shia over some swampland.

The West is worried about the war, because of its effect on the oil supply. The Saudis increase production to compensate.

Sixth-formers take turns to run a regular Assembly for our year group. This is always a general discussion about some topic of interest, not a religious service. One morning,

Auden and Robinson lead such an Assembly, and what they present is quite a shock. Unexpectedly, they reveal themselves to be Christian fundamentalists. They talk about something called the 'Rapture', a miraculous event in the near-future, when all Christian Believers will be literally lifted up to Heaven by God, with the rest of us *left behind* to suffer from horrible events here on Earth. This is a call to *believe now* and be saved, or endure the most horrible suffering that will befall all the non-Believers. A wave of amusement runs through the audience – but I am taken aback by the deeply serious demeanour of Auden and Robinson.

They talk about the fulfilment of end-time prophecies, which includes a belief that all the world's Jews *must* return to the Holy Land which God gave to them thousands of years ago (and which does not belong to the Palestinians, who are living on it now). The mosque in Jerusalem known as the Dome of the Rock (the third most sacred place in the Islamic world) will be demolished (by God or man), so that the Temple of Solomon can be rebuilt on that site.

They then go on to make an attack on Islam, quoting Qur'anic verses supposedly urging Muslims to attack Christians and Jews. I am outraged, but say nothing. I know that those verses are not referring to Christians and Jews, but to the savage and idol-worshipping pre-Islamic Arabs who were trying to eradicate the early Muslims, and they are *survival* verses, telling the early Muslims it was okay to fight for self-preservation. At this time, I don't have enough specific knowledge to be able to quote similar (but even worse) biblical verses giving orders to '*slay every man, woman and child*'.

Everyone else in the audience finds all of this hilarious, but I am the only Muslim present and I am totally stunned. My cosy perception of the warm and friendly coexistence of the three great religions, which all believe in one common God, is being shattered.

1980-81
Age: 18   156

Later in the day, Auden and Robinson deliberately corner me in a small, quiet music room in the Garrick Building and, working together, they scare the hell out of me with their story, including this imminent Rapture, and many accounts of miracles that they have heard of, at second and third hand. Blair Crawford witnesses this meeting through the glass door, but does not come in.

This is a strange, sinister, frightening Christianity they tell me of – not the Christianity I know and am fond of. They talk about biblical prophecies that have been fulfilled already, proving that others will also come to pass, and that the Rapture is a real event, which will surely happen soon. They talk about the Antichrist. This will be a powerful and charismatic man (possibly the Head of the United Nations, the Pope, or Prince Charles) who succeeds in bringing about global peace but, in so doing, he is really uniting all the non-Believers in order to oppress the true Christians.

They say that there is an airline in America which has a secret policy of not assigning Believers as both pilot and co-pilot on any flight, out of concern for those who would be *left behind* on all the aircraft that would crash after their Christian pilots had been Raptured away. Apparently, it will be possible for those left behind to be saved, by embracing Jesus (when they realise that the Believers were right after all), but they will have to suffer hideously in the Tribulation that will follow the Rapture; non-Believers will torment them to force them to deny their faith in Jesus. Only if they keep to their new faith, even if tortured to death, will they be saved. Eventually, Jesus will arrive in a cloud of glory, there will be a huge battle of Good versus Evil in the Middle East, and the united forces of Evil (mostly Muslims, but also Catholics, Hindus, secular humanists, Communists and so on) will be utterly vanquished, falling into the depths of Hell for all Eternity, as their punishment for opposing the will of Almighty God.

1980-81
Age: 18

I am completely taken aback by all of this. They are saying that peaceful coexistence is not an option; that we are destined to fight a horrible global war between Believers and non-Christians and that this is promised in the Bible. I feebly argue that the Qur'an has incredible scientific facts in it, describing the 'Big Bang' and the condensation of stars from gas. Muhammad could not possibly have known about these scientific phenomena, therefore the Qur'an *must* come from God.

Robinson has a different argument: the Qur'an comes from Satan and its purpose is to mislead people away from being saved by Christianity. I never thought of this possibility. He's talking about a *conspiracy by Satan.* I am taken completely by surprise. Their *absolute certainty* scares me. (I've never had such certainty.)

Satan is a very clever and powerful entity, Robinson tells me. He creates and supervises many deceptive schemes. Satan controls the media and uses television as a particularly effective means to drive lies, immorality and un-Christian ideas directly into people's homes and into their very hearts and minds. This is why, like many believing Christians, Robinson's family does not keep a television set in their house.

Auden tells me that he has only recently become a Believer, thanks to his friendship with Robinson; Auden's own family are atheists. He tells me that his life has been completely transformed since he surrendered himself to Jesus. He can feel the power of the Holy Spirit working in his life, and it will redefine my life too, if I will only let myself *believe.* They tell me that there is a greater awareness of this miraculous truth in America than in England, but this country is slowly waking up as well.

I go home this evening, deeply disturbed. *Could Christianity really be true?* Does God really require redemption by belief in blood sacrifice? Was Islam really created by Satan to keep people away from the truth of Christianity?

1980-81
Age: 18   158

Will my family and I burn in Hell for all eternity if we don't convert? It weighs on me very heavily. I feel as if I'm not an honest member of my family anymore, because a part of me now believes Christianity to be true.

The next day, Blair Crawford (one of only two A-level Religious Studies students) seeks me out and deprogrammes me. He explains the history of the Bible, the timeline of the Gospels (they were written many decades after the events related), the biased selection of the approved Books of the Bible at the Council of Nicaea in AD 325, the issue of versions and translations, the implausibility that this collection of books could be the absolute, 100 percent infallible, literal 'Word of God'. As for the 'Rapture', it's an outlandish belief that was unheard of before the nineteenth century, when it was cobbled together by some marginal Christian leader. The Americans have become excited about it recently, due to some book that says it's okay to trash this planet (and no need to worry about global pollution, the ozone layer and the 'greenhouse effect'), because God will give true Christians 'a New Heaven and a New Earth'. But the Rapture has no foundation in the words of Jesus.

I am so relieved. What Auden and Robinson were alleging about the Divine integrity and absolute infallibility of the Bible cannot possibly be true. I don't have to become a Christian to save my soul after all. I am happy with all the scientific facts in the Qur'an, which prove its authenticity.

I try to put all this behind me and return to my normal view of the world.

I read an article in *New Scientist* magazine that proposes a link between stress during pregnancy and the occurrence of homosexual traits in the child. This implies that homosexuality is something over which the individual has

1980-81
Age: 18

no choice or control – it's not their 'fault'. But this raises a religious dilemma. I am quite sure, from what I've heard from all sides, that the God of the Jews, Christians and Muslims does not like gay people. But God couldn't be angry with someone for a characteristic that was His doing, not of their own free choice. That wouldn't be fair.

The time to organise our futures has come. I apply to St Thomas' Hospital Medical School, which is in the heart of London, across the Thames from Big Ben and the Houses of Parliament. I am invited to attend an interview one morning and deliberately walk the long way to the train station, so that I pass Andrea walking to school on the other side of the road. I am perfectly attired in a blue suit, white shirt and grey tie, and I want her to see me looking so smart, but we ignore each other.

The interview goes well; my accent is, of course, flawless. To the selection board of white, conservative, distinguished upper-middle-class men, I present myself as the perfect English gentleman-physician candidate. Two days later I receive a formal offer in the post, and the required A-level grades are easily attainable for me. Everything is clearly laid out: I'm all set to go to medical school.

In WHSmith I pick up a heavy volume of four collected James Bond novels, by Ian Fleming. I start reading and I'm absolutely hooked. They are brilliantly written, compelling, exciting, erotic. Fleming is a storytelling genius and these novels are absolutely intoxicating. The character of Commander James Bond is a compelling role model. He's actually Scottish by birth, but he represents all that is quintessentially British (like me), and he's an ex-military man (like me).

I even look like him! I match his description almost perfectly.

1980-81
Age: 18

James Bond	Me
'dark, clean-cut face'	Yes, and I shave every day
'eyes … wide and level'	Sure
'straight, rather long black brows'	Yes
'hair … black'	Absolutely!
'parted on the left'	Yes, since childhood
'longish straight nose'	Yes (I used to deny that I have a long nose)
'short upper lip'	Could be
'wide and finely drawn but cruel mouth'	My mouth can be cruel
'jaw … straight and firm'	I think so
'a three-inch scar … right cheek'	No, but dimple on chin (right side)
'dark suit'	Black blazer and trousers
'white shirt'	Always
'black knitted tie'	Prefect's tie is black. *(What's a 'knitted' tie?)*

James Bond always has a bracing cold shower, after his hot shower. I start to do the same – cold showers make me feel great! He smokes a lot and drinks vodka – things which obviously I cannot do – but for breakfast he has scrambled eggs, washed down with an entire pot of coffee and a whole jug of freshly squeezed orange juice. This becomes my favourite breakfast too, on non-school days – although I have to make do with just a carton of not-quite-so-fresh orange juice. I also have to stay in for a while after consuming all of this.

Instead of working for my exams, I am reading James Bond novels. This is not good and I know it.

It's the Christmas vacation a few months before the big exams, and I'm at home all day, every day. This time is supposed to be dedicated to exam preparation. I'm reading *Goldfinger*. There is that scene near the end in which a character is sucked out of the jet aircraft window at high altitude and falls to his death. (In the film it is Mr Goldfinger, who goes feetfirst – but in the book it is his Korean henchman Oddjob, who goes headfirst, giving James Bond a moment to disparagingly contemplate his broad backside.)

I think about this manner of death. How awful it would be, to be falling for so long, seeing the ground gradually approach, and knowing what is going to happen, not being able to do anything about it, and all the while screaming with terror. I think: '*God would never make someone die in such a terrifying way.*'

The next morning I'm listening to the Brian Hayes programme on LBC Radio, as usual. I should be focused on studying, but I convince myself that the audio stream doesn't really distract me. Brian reads the news and one item is about a Saudi Arabian airliner. A tyre had exploded inside a wheel well, at high altitude, rupturing the hull. Two Pakistani children sitting in that location had been sucked out over the Arabian Gulf.

I am speechless, stunned, afraid. *What's going on? This is a coincidence, right? What else could it possibly be?* I know that God, who is omniscient and omnipotent, knows everyone's thoughts. But He wouldn't have read my mind about what a horrible way that would be to die, and how He would *never* make it happen, and then just tossed those Pakistani children out of the airliner, just to prove a point? That would be unspeakably cruel. *So, it must be just a coincidence.*

I think about the two children. How terrified they must have been. How alone they were as they plummeted to their deaths. Only children. Now I'm afraid to think anything and I just want my stream of thoughts to stop. I wonder who's listening.

1980-81
Age: 18

After 444 days of captivity, the 52 American Embassy hostages in Iran are finally released through negotiation, a few minutes into the presidency of Ronald Reagan. The Iranians have delayed this deliberately. It was so obvious that President Carter was absolutely desperate to get the hostages released during his term (even authorising that military helicopter rescue attempt which went tragically wrong in the desert), the Iranians decided to deny him this satisfaction. It is President Reagan who gets to announce the wonderful news, just moments after delivering his inauguration speech. He heralds in a new era in which a strong America will have the world's respect, by being militarily powerful and absolutely resolute, and not taking crap like this from any barbarians ever again.

As the crucial exams approach, I see the University of Stirling on a television programme about the severe spending cuts in higher education. I have never heard of this place; it is a beautiful campus with a lake, surrounded by mountains and forests. It is utterly captivating. Strangely, I instantly *yearn* to go there. Well, that can't happen. I am definitely going to St Thomas' Hospital Medical School.

I will need God's approval and co-operation to become a doctor, so I finally get into the habit of performing Islamic prayers. But I only do the night-time prayer (four *rakahs*), every night before going to bed. That should be enough to secure success; I'm quite a good person, on the whole. Also, my desire to be a doctor is a noble one; I want to be a doctor because I want to help people. (*Oh, I've passed the interview stage; I don't have to say this anymore.*) I also want to make lots of money and enjoy the elevated social status which comes with being a doctor.

As a Prefect, my turn comes to read in Assembly, in front of the entire school. I discuss this with Reverend

1980-81
Age: 18   163

Swarbrigg. The passage we select is the one about God asking Abraham to sacrifice his only son. I have a practice session with the Reverend one lunchtime, in the main hall. I never realised how difficult it is to project one's voice in a vast room.

The day of the Assembly, I am nervous, but this is an inevitable part of my social progress. Reverend Swarbrigg introduces the passage, saying that it is a very important story in the Jewish, Christian *and* Islamic traditions.

I launch into the reading, but with my nervousness my voice has lost its energy. However, when I get to the part where the Angel of the Lord appears suddenly just as Abraham is about to kill his son, William Irvine (a Prefect) has the audacity to hit a couple of dramatic notes on the organ. The hall erupts in laughter. I'm oblivious to the funny side of this, but nonetheless the incident re-energises me and my reading concludes in a much more spirited fashion.

I'm still drawn to the Christians in school. It's their absolute faith that impresses and disturbs me. I attend some of their discussion groups. They believe the Bible, including Genesis, to be the absolute and literally true Word of God. They have a scientific discussion about this. Apparently the Earth is only about six thousand years old and, before the Flood, it was not tilted on its axis. It had a very temperate climate all over its surface and so people really did live to be many hundreds of years old, as described in Genesis. The vast deluge of water, as it hit the Earth, caused it to tilt on its axis. This created seasons and a variable, more hostile climate, so people do not live as long anymore.

'What about evolution and dinosaur bones?' I ask.

'These are deceptions of Satan,' they tell me.

In Islam, Satan is known as the '*sneaking whisperer*'; he's that little voice telling you to make the wrong decision, to do the bad thing. He tries to drown out the voice of your conscience. He can't do anything more than tempt you and, if you keep to the Right Path, with good intentions and deeds, he is impotent and won't succeed. But the Christians are telling me of a more powerful and sinister Satan, a brilliant, deceiving evil genius, who has a massive and highly professional team of agents working for him. He has masterminded many schemes (such as Islam, Buddhism and secular humanism) to mislead people away from their only hope of salvation – belief in the blood-redemption sacrifice of Jesus. The Qur'an, with its amazing scientific facts, is just another clever scam in Satan's master plan.

America will lead the world in the war against Satan and in the fulfilment of biblical prophecy, which will bring the Rapture ever closer. All of these things they are telling me are already well known in America, they assert with absolute conviction.

Both Auden and Robinson are straight-A students in Science and Mathematics. They can both solve the Rubik cube in under a minute, which is like witnessing a miracle. They are 'good' boys, cultured and well spoken; they never use bad language. I am intimidated by their intellects and unsettled by their faith.

Andrea is having a birthday party on Saturday night and it seems that everyone is invited – everyone except me, that is. I wouldn't want to go anyway; I have been embarrassed, humiliated and made miserable by this whole 'affair', and it's really my own fault.

I am watching television late on Saturday night; my parents and brothers have gone to bed. The telephone rings and my father, awakened by it, picks it up upstairs. I have a bad feeling about this, so I rush over to the extension in the living room and pick up the phone. It is indeed for me; there is loud party music in the background. I can tell that my father is still listening, as a slightly inebriated classmate

1980-81
Age: 18   165

of mine (I don't know who) tells me that Andrea's party is really great and that she would like me to come. I'm sure the first detail is true, but the second is unlikely to be so; he is winding me up. Acutely aware that my father can hear everything, I just want to get this call terminated. I thank the caller kindly and tell him that I won't be coming. I just want him to hang up. I don't want to hang up myself and leave open the possibility that the drunken prankster might speak indiscreetly to my father. Fortunately, the joker does give up when he realises I'm not convinced and hangs up. I return to the film I was watching, but my mind is elsewhere.

On Monday my investigations reveal that it was my friend 'Gus' Fraser who made the call. What the hell was he doing there? *He doesn't even know Andrea!*

The Mercedes is often parked in the road outside our house, its tail end projecting in front of Willy Johnson's house. One day we discover a long, malicious scratch in the paintwork of the boot lid. It has been made with a flourish, sweeping up and down. The number-one suspect would be Willy Johnson, but we have no proof and, in any case, what can we do? The police aren't going to take him away and give him a hundred lashes, which is what he deserves. I am so angry; I am sad to see my father's hard work being abused in this way. But there's nothing to be done.

I am complacent, lazy and I hate exam preparation. I expect to get the required grades for medical school, because God will make it so. There's nothing else that I can be, except a doctor, and so God will make it happen. The right questions will come up in the A-level exams, I will saunter through answering them and I will get the necessary grades. God will make it happen. All I have to do is show up.

In the last formal days of school, I have a feeling that I have neglected many things, across all three of my science subjects. I'm not sure that *any* Physics knowledge at all has passed through my brain. I have only a memory of 'guilty ease' – relaxing when I know I should be studying. In one of the last Physics lessons, we are given some free time to devote to individual studies. I don't think anyone is actually studying, judging by all the chatter.

For the first time *ever* in Hampton School, I happen to be seated next to Richard Bleakey. Finally, all the bitterness and anger of the Panda competition defeat cannot be suppressed any longer. I confront him and accuse him of deliberately sabotaging the contest for us, because he was sulking about not getting into the grammar school. He doesn't acknowledge this to be true, but he doesn't deny it. He's guilty as Hell; I can see it in his face. He cost us the Panda competition. We would have reached the Grand Final, and Leslie Crowther (the famous television comedian) was the quizmaster for that final contest! We missed it because of him. *Bastard Bleakey!*

The time finally comes and I sit the A-level exams in a half-hearted, lacklustre way. I really am expecting God to take care of this for me. The exams don't go particularly well; I have a feeling my performance is mediocre, but the grades I need are not that high, so it's a done deal.

After the last of the exams is over, we have afternoon tea with our teachers to say goodbye. It is in the same dining hall where we first assembled; wet, dishevelled and afraid. After seven years at Hampton School, it is a very poignant feeling not to belong anymore.

I make a visit to the National Gallery in London one afternoon. (I'm actually killing time before going to see the latest James Bond film, *For Your Eyes Only*, in the adjacent

1980-81
Age: 18   167

Odeon cinema in Leicester Square.) This gallery is an endless maze of interconnected rooms, with a magnificent collection of old paintings. The artificial light and still air cut one off completely from the outside world, be it summer or winter.

Many of the paintings are from the Renaissance and Reformation eras of Christian history. It is interesting how they depict God, as an old man with a beard who unmistakably resembles the Roman god Zeus. He lives in the clouds with an army of angels and looks down on humanity. This blatantly anthropomorphic Christian perception of God is very different from the Islamic (and Jewish) view. In Islam (and Judaism), God is without physical form; He is everywhere and is definitely never characterised as a man in any way.

In the summer, we make a family trip to Pakistan. In the lazy days here, I read *The Odessa File* by Frederick Forsyth, which includes an account of a Nazi concentration camp. The rounding-up and extermination of Jewish people is described in heartrending detail. I feel a deep outrage about the Holocaust. How could human beings behave in this way? And apparently some of those Nazis are still holding down respectable government jobs and the money which they stole from their Jewish victims is still being looked after for them by self-righteous Swiss bankers. It makes me very angry.

My grandfather's house is directly opposite the entrance to the neighbourhood mosque. My brothers and I sleep on rope beds arranged under a covered area on the roof of the house, in front of the big room which is up there. From here the call to prayer, the *Azaan*, is impossible to miss. Some mornings I perform the impossible; instead of rolling over and diving back into sleep when I am awoken by the *Azaan*, I manage to drag myself off the bed, perform the ablution in the rooftop bathroom, and walk across the road

1980-81
Age: 18

to the mosque in the cool, still silence of the pre-dawn, joined by many men and boys who surge quietly through the streets from all directions. The early-morning prayer is the most difficult and spiritually it seems the most rewarding. But I have an ulterior motive, which is not entirely spiritual. I am painfully aware that I need certain grades to go to medical school, I have some uncertainty about whether I have achieved those grades, and this matter is entirely in the hands of God.

Throughout our stay in Pakistan, my grandfather is not at all well. His heart has been giving him trouble for years. I can't quite face the implications. One evening, while he is lying on the bed suffering from chest pains and troubled breathing, he insists on talking to my father about the management of his affairs. What this means is too painful to contemplate. We return to London in August with a deep sense of foreboding.

The day that the A-level exam results come out, they will be sent to the school and the school will send them to us in the mail. That day is a Saturday and it is rumoured that if you go to the school, you can get the results directly.

I drive my mother's Renault 5 to school (this is completely unnecessary, as it is walking distance). I enter the school and run into Mr Creber, who is uncharacteristically wearing jeans and a T-shirt. He says that the results are on the noticeboard in the staff room and it is okay to go in and take a look. I enter the staff room for the first time ever and approach the noticeboard with trepidation. The list is arranged alphabetically, so my name is right at the top.

I see the Biology grade. It's too low! There's a pain in my gut. The Chemistry grade … it's okay, but it doesn't make up for the Biology one. General Studies is good, but it doesn't count. The Physics grade is too low. I am stunned and my legs feel weak.

I haven't made the grades. I can't go to medical school. I can't be a doctor. I am shocked, devastated. I can barely walk as I stumble back out to the car. *God, how could you allow this?* It doesn't make any sense. *I thought God would take care of this for me.*

Sitting in the car, I pray to God to help me out. I don't exactly know what I'm going to do in my life now. I've wanted to be a doctor for years – I never thought about anything else.

But then suddenly I think, *'Now I can go to Stirling!'* For some inexplicable reason, I feel excitement and anticipation about this.

Back at home, I have to break the awful news to my parents; they are more disappointed than I am. Being a doctor is the most respectable, most sought-after profession for children of the subcontinent. Their spoiled and inept son has foolishly thrown this opportunity away by not studying hard enough. Curiously, I seem to accept this loss quite readily. A part of me is secretly relieved. *Did I really want to be a doctor?*

Now that I am not qualified to get into medical school, I am actually *free* to go to Stirling to study a less competitive subject. It appears that in disaster there is opportunity. I decide that I want to study Biochemistry and Physiology, but I look it up in the universities guidebook and find that Stirling doesn't offer Physiology, so I decide to do just Biochemistry. The need to go to Stirling appears to be overriding; more important than the subject I study.

I look up Stirling in the atlas and discover that it is in Scotland. *I never knew that!* I had assumed it was somewhere in England. I have never been to Scotland.

My application goes smoothly and, on the telephone two weeks later, they confirm that they are giving me a place.[11] My mother is just coming home from work; I run outside

1980-81
Age: 18   170

to tell her. I am excited, but she seems quite sullen about it. My parents are finding it harder than me to accept that I will not be a doctor.

I am sent an application form for campus accommodation. Apparently, there are four halls of residence on campus that will accommodate first-year students. One of these is segregated; the males are in one wing and the females are in the other. Most of the rooms in all the halls are for single occupancy, but apparently a few are shared. The idea of sharing a room is not at all appealing to me. On the application form, under 'Any Other Information', I write: *'A single room please, for religious privacy.'* Seeing my name, they will know that I am a Muslim and they know that Muslims pray a lot, so they will definitely give me a single room.

I do pray to God *not* to put me in the segregated hall; it will be harder to meet girls there.

Scotland

1981-82
Age: 19

IN SEPTEMBER, my parents drive me up to Scotland. We set off in the Mercedes at 6 a.m. on a Saturday morning; my bicycle is on a rack on the roof. Stirling is over 400 miles away, in the vicinity of Bannockburn, near the places where William Wallace and Robert the Bruce fought the English.

All the way up, I am praying and hoping not to be in the segregated hall. We arrive on campus and I head for the Accommodation Office. The good news is that I have been given a single room, for my 'religious privacy'. And, since I'm clearly a very religious person, they have put me in AK Davidson Hall, the segregated one. *Why, God, why?*

I am walking through campus with my parents and there are posters everywhere for the 'Freshers' Disco'. My father says to me earnestly, *'Disco meh nay jannah!'* ('Don't go to the disco!'). I think happily that my father will be safely hundreds of miles away and he does not need to worry about matters like this.

Clutching my papers from the Accommodation Office, I enter the foyer of AK Davidson Hall, while my parents wait outside in the car. At the front desk, there is a girl chatting with the hall porter. She is obviously not a first-year, as she is very familiar with the porter and they are completely at ease with one other.

She is absolutely beautiful; she has curly dark-brown hair, is of medium height and has a fabulous figure. Her manner is energetic and she is utterly vivacious. I've only been on campus for thirty minutes and I've already met the girl of my dreams. *I have arrived in Paradise.*

But as I listen, I realise that something is not quite right. It's her accent: it's very Northern. It grates on me slightly and offends my insistence that there is only one way to speak English, the way followed by the BBC, Prince Charles and myself. The girl isn't perfect, alas.

The porter's deep Scottish accent is almost unintelligible; I have to rapidly retune my ears until my brain can interpret the signal. He gives me the keys to my room on the third floor up.

The room is basic, with whitewashed breezeblock walls, but promises a life of independence and opportunity. There's a wardrobe, a large washbasin, a narrow wooden bed, a bookcase, a long desk on the far side that runs across the width of the room, a chest of drawers, overhead storage cupboards, a desk lamp and a plastic chair. I feel as if I'm moving into my own bachelor pad.

After we've moved my stuff, my parents drive away slowly in the Mercedes; I wave them goodbye. (I hope some girls are watching, because of the car.) I am alone and free for the first time in my life. I immediately fall in love with Scotland. It is beautiful.

I am glued to the window of my room. Opposite me is the girls' wing, and behind every one of those windows is a girl.

The next day I meet an irritating Northerner called Milton, in the corridor where my room is situated. He insists on being nice to me. When we first meet, in the kitchen, I am reheating some delicious kebabs and tandoori chicken which my mother has packed for me. Out of politeness, I offer to share the food with Milton, who (to my greedy and selfish relief) declines. We are able to converse, although I look down on him because of his Northern accent. He is from Newcastle and he is a third-year (of a four-year

1981-82
Age: 19

course). He had been supposed to go to Cambridge University, but did not get the grades and ended up at Stirling.

Milton mentions that he spent some time in London during the summer and visited the National Gallery. We exchange details and realise that we were both in the National Gallery on the same day at the exact same time. How funny. A meaningless coincidence.

The Wallace Monument overlooks the campus from the top of a nearby hill. It is an ancient-looking tower and is visible from the window of the kitchen. I go up there later in the afternoon and I am filled with joy at being in this wonderful place: the beauty, the tranquillity – it's spectacular. It no longer matters that I did not get into St Thomas' Hospital Medical School in London; for some reason, this is where I am glad to be.

The first week is quite wonderful. Just the processes of Registration, administration and total freedom. I register for classes, attend the first couple of lectures, discover that money is necessary for necessities I took for granted at home, and singularly fail to impress any girls. I eat, sleep, relax as I please. It's exhilarating.

One day, I'm in a queue for another part of the Registration process. It's to obtain our photo ID cards. There are certain documents required and I have them all, carefully arranged, in my folder. The girl in front of me reaches the desk and only then starts looking for the necessary documents in her bag. She says aloud to herself, 'Oh, would you believe it, I can't find them,' in a Northern accent. Impatient at being kept waiting, I am filled with a sense of contempt and superiority. Some people are *so* stupid.

Every time I pass Milton, he insists on saying 'Hello, *Imran.*' It is his way of memorising my name.

Milton is quite scruffy; he always wears jeans and a baggy white sweater. He doesn't shave every single day and is quite scraggly-looking. His room, which is just opposite mine, is a disgrace. Books, papers and miscellaneous items are strewn all over the floor. However, there is something welcoming about his room and we sit here often, chatting and drinking coffee, while he strums his guitar. He introduces me to the music of Paul Simon and Joni Mitchell; we often listen to their albums. Milton also went to a boys' school. We share all the insight that we have about women, which is none whatsoever.

Curiously, Milton has never flown and has never been abroad, apart from a school bus trip to Germany. He tells me that he is terrified at the thought of flying. I can't imagine that; airports and flying are part of my life.

Stirling is what they call a 'new university', although it is now about fifteen years old. It is completely unique in the UK, having an American system of two long 'semesters' per year, instead of three terms like most British universities. There are other American aspects too, in the way that courses and options are selected. Instead of studying only a single subject from day one, you begin by choosing three subjects, gradually whittling these down to develop a Major and a Minor over the years.

I am quite overwhelmed by the beauty of the surroundings. The campus is built around a small loch, Loch Airthrey, the halls of residence being on one side of this and a footbridge spanning it to the other buildings. There is a nine-hole golf course and Airthrey Castle, which is really a big house in the shape of a castle. The campus is bordered by a hill forest and in the distance is a mountain peak. I have no idea how far away or how high the mountain is, being a city dweller my entire life. I know it is

1981-82
Age: 19

called Dumyat and has one of those beacons on top that are lit all across the country during major royal events (like Charles and Diana's wedding recently), or so I am told by that fellow Milton.

AK Davidson Hall (known affectionately as 'AKD') is a warm and comfortable residence. The girls' wing opposite is a tantalising place. Men are not prohibited, so occasionally I walk over there, striding through the corridors purposefully, as if I'm going to visit someone I know (and hoping to have a chance encounter that will somehow change my life). The girls' wing has an amazing smell; a thousand different fragrances all blended into one, which hangs in the air and which I remember forever.

I awake on Saturday morning, having been here a week, with a world of possibilities open to me. I reflect that I have viewed the magnificent surroundings in the distance, but have not really immersed myself in them. I decide that *today*, I am going to do that; I am going to explore Scotland. I do not get around to starting this until early afternoon, having spent a lazy morning getting up and finding something to eat.

Finally, I set off on this expedition. I am wearing a brown checked shirt, a beige woollen sweater, a brown polyester safari jacket, a pair of light brown corduroy trousers, and my best pair of formal brown-leather lace-up shoes. I am definitely in autumn colours – a sort of camouflage, I suppose. I need only the flimsiest amount of daylight to justify wearing my aviator sunglasses. Over my shoulder I sling my binoculars in their case. This is certainly an adventure, because I have never explored the countryside before.

I walk out of AKD and into the car park. It is a changeable day: not quite sunny, not quite cloudy; breezy and fresh. This is the characteristic, living climate of Scotland whose embrace I will grow to love.

1981-82
Age: 19

I head in the direction of Airthrey Castle, past the golf course, because this seems to be one place where the hill forest comes down to meet the campus. Behind Airthrey Castle, as I walk towards it, I gaze at that tantalising mountain peak.

I follow a path at the edge of the forest that leads upwards and into the hill forest. It is amazing: so peaceful, so alive, so unspoiled. It is teeming with invisible life. To a lifelong city dweller like me, this is another world. The path winds around inside the hill forest, going ever higher. I come upon an ancient stone wall which runs in both directions as far as I can see, but it has a big hole in it – clearly a well-used doorway. I pass through and onto another path which runs alongside this wall.

I walk along with an explorer's curiosity, wanting to get lost, flirting with danger (as long as I can get home before dark). The path emerges onto a country road, very narrow, not really room for two cars to pass, and no pavement of course. This road goes upwards and, with inexhaustible energy, I eagerly follow it.

The road takes me uphill and brings me out of the forested area into very open countryside – Scottish countryside. The air is clean and fresh, the silence is magnificent, the views of the hills spectacular. Sheep punctuate the scenery, near and far, and the very air seems to muffle sound, creating a peaceful tranquillity.

I follow the road ever higher and come to a point where a well-trodden walking track heads off from the road at 90 degrees and up into the infinite distance of the hills. I cannot resist it. I come off the road, climb over the fence where the steps are, and head along this path, up into the sky.

Soon the road is gone as I walk along the path over a succession of hills, going ever higher. The ground is thick

1981-82
Age: 19   178

with unfamiliar vegetation, interspersed with sheep droppings, and everywhere is that amazing uncanny silence, just the wind providing an eerie but peaceful backdrop. The sky is blue and grey and bright and alive.

The views become ever better as I climb. Soon the Wallace Monument is far below me, amidst its beautiful surroundings.

At this point, I witness an amazing phenomenon, one that I have never seen before. The bright sun is partially hidden in an isolated cluster of clouds, and its rays are lighting up those clouds into magnificent, brilliant whiteness, and bright, vertical, visible columns of light are coming down, illuminating the countryside below, where they hit the ground, leaving the surrounding areas comparatively grey and dull.

This immediately reminds me of paintings I have seen in the National Gallery, in which Heaven is portrayed as an illuminated place in the clouds, with an elderly sky-dwelling God sitting on a throne and sending shafts of brilliant light earthwards, angels *et al* in attendance.

As I witness this amazing sight, I think to myself, '*No wonder they used to think that Heaven is in the clouds.*' Then I immediately dismiss this as a blasphemous thought, because my omnipotent, omniscient and omnipresent Islamic God does not live in the clouds; that is primitive, anthropomorphic Christian imagery, which demeans Him.

I continue along the path.

As I come over another rise, I reach a sort of plateau between hills that is grassy, silent and stretches as far as I can see. There is something extraordinary, almost magical and mystical, about this path.

In the distance, I see a Scotsman approaching from the other direction. It is obvious to me that he is a Scotsman,

because he is wearing a kilt and other traditional clothes.*
He is of medium height and build, has brown hair and a
neat moustache. As we pass, his clear, wise eyes look at me
with a slight, wry smile and he says, 'Hello.' I say, 'Hi' back.

I continue along the path, across streams, over gates and
rocky steppingstones, ever upwards. It is windy and chilly,
but I am hot and perspiring from the exertion. There is a
final hill to climb and I seem to reach a big, rocky and
grassy peak. There is a large unlit beacon on top of a pile of
rocks. I have reached the top of Dumyat, without even
meaning to! The wind howls around my ears as I admire
the view, now able to see miles in every direction.

From somewhere, a quintessentially English voice calls
out, 'Hot?'

I turn around to see a tall, dark-haired man in his late
thirties. 'Yes, rather,' I answer.

We start to chat. His name is Dr Ted Porter and he is a
Chemistry lecturer at the University. As we walk back down
together, he gives me two pieces of advice.

The first is never to climb a mountain dressed the way I
am. I am now sweaty from the climb, but the wind is
making me cold; I have no effective protection from it.
One should climb the mountain lightly dressed for the
exertion, but carrying an anorak that one can put on at the
top, to shelter from the wind. Remember: *hot sweat + cold
wind = pneumonia*. Also, my shoes are totally inappropriate. I

---

* Being new to Scotland, I had no idea how implausible this was. I
spent the best part of the next six years in Scotland, and never saw
anyone wearing a kilt high upon a mountain, especially on a cold,
breezy day. Twenty-one years later, on an overnight flight from
Atlanta to London, it was explained to me who this person was.

1981-82
Age: 19

should be wearing mountain boots, otherwise I could easily break an ankle in a moment's carelessness.

The other piece of advice is more troublesome. Dr Porter basically tells me – at great length and with considerable emphasis – that success in exams is in direct proportion to the amount of effort expended in preparing for them, and that I am at university primarily for the purpose of academic achievement (not girls), and should therefore ensure that my number-one focus is on academic study and exam preparation.

His car is parked at the bottom of the mountain path and he gives me a ride back to campus. We shake hands and he says he'll doubtless see me around.

Dr Porter is definitely right on the first matter. I don't get pneumonia, but I do get 'flu', within a couple of days of this expedition.

On the second matter, I completely ignore his advice, but it takes longer for me to understand that he is right.

Later in the week, when I call home, my brother Rehan (who is doing his A-levels now) tells me that our grandfather has died. My mother has flown to Pakistan to be with her family. I feel sad. I'm not sure how I'm supposed to behave. I pass Milton the next day and he asks me how I am. I tell him about my grandfather and he is immediately sympathetic. He seems to be a decent fellow.

The days pass and I fall into the routine of university life.

I'm approaching a lecture-room door one day when suddenly it flies open violently and the metal handle hits my left hand, grazing a finger quite badly. An idiotic young man is on the other side of the door. He is holding a heavy cardboard box with both hands and it is clear from the position of his foot that he has just kicked the door open. He has brown hair, glasses, a 'pretty boy' face, and he's

1981-82
Age: 19

wearing jeans and a black-leather jacket. He realises that he's done something stupid, but the idiot mumbles something that isn't quite an apology and walks off.

I am left nursing my finger, which is bleeding slightly. Because my skin is so sensitive, the wound is slow to heal and remains a sore spot literally for months.

A couple of weeks into the new semester, the lab classes start. I am walking towards my first Chemistry lab one morning, carrying my white coat over my arm, when I notice a girl from AK Davidson Hall in front of me, walking in the same direction, also carrying a white coat. I can only see the back of her, but what I see is very nice; she is about five feet and four inches tall, with stunning red hair, and tight jeans accentuating her superb figure. I cannot help but notice in particular her perfectly formed backside.*

In the lab our places are already marked out by name, along the benches, and the dazzling redhead is placed next to me!

The first task we are required to do is perform an inventory of the lab equipment (such as test tubes and beakers) in our individual lockers under the worktop, but it soon turns out that we have to work in pairs throughout the semester in this lab class, and it's obvious that, because we are next to each other, this girl and I should be lab partners.

Her name is Janice and she has a regional accent (to me, it seems Northern), but I am able to disregard this because she is very attractive, and our conversation flows freely. Janice is from Leicestershire, from a town improbably called Melton Mowbray (which is famous for pork pies, she

---

* Note from grown-up Imran: I'm sorry – I'm just being honest. After all those years at the boys' school, I remember vividly that this sight mesmerised me.

1981-82
Age: 19

tells me) and she was supposed to study Medicine in a London medical school, but she did not get the grades and ended up at Stirling. *Perfect! We have so much in common.*

It gets better. She clearly considers herself to be posh (this is a revelation for me, that a regional person can be posh) and admires Margaret Thatcher. (My politics have been somewhat undecided until now, but suddenly I realise that I am a Conservative.) She approves of my father's Mercedes, but her father (who is a company director) has a very nice car as well – a Jaguar XJ6, Series III, in metallic bronze with tan leather interior. This is a company car, but they also have another car, a cream Honda Accord hatchback. Since her mother does not drive, this Honda Accord is effectively considered by Janice to be *her* car. Both cars were acquired brand-new, of course. She lives in a detached house in an exclusive cul-de-sac on top of a hill; this place is understood by all the locals to be the nicest place to live in her little town.

I think about my family's Renault 5. It's really *my* car, isn't it? I just happen to let my mother use it when I'm not there. This is what I convey to Janice: I also have a car back home.

Janice is perfect. She is beautiful, intelligent; she has class, dignity and independence. She's a competent woman who loves driving in the fast lane and has no time for losers. *She is Contessa Teresa di Vincenzo!*

I look up the Honda Accord in *What Car?* magazine. It says that it is a very good car, and comes with power steering and a five-speed gearbox as standard. That *is* good.

Janice and I become lab partners, lecture partners and friends. As the weeks pass, I spend every moment that I can with her, but this is usually in the context of classes; I don't generally go over to the girls' wing to see her in a spontaneous act of socialising, as I lack the confidence to do so, but I do go over 'on business'.

One Saturday afternoon, I collect our lab write-ups (my mark is 85 percent, Janice's is 67 percent) from the Biology department, and I kindly take Janice's document across to the girls' wing. Janice is in the kitchen with her two best friends, Joan and Suzanne; they are clearing up, having just had lunch together. Janice looks stunning in an olive-green sweater and matching corduroy trousers; this outfit goes spectacularly well with her red hair. I yearn to be part of this group, and imagine having lunch with them all the time, being involved in the cooking, the eating and the washing-up. Janice is quite welcoming but cool, as she concentrates on putting some sauce away in a Tupperware container.

'I made apple sauce, as we had roast pork for lunch,' she says.

'Oh, that sounds nice,' I say, mentally meaning the sauce and not the pork. I cringe to think what I would have done, if I had indeed been invited to this lunch.

I am receiving As for my lab write-ups, whilst Janice generally gets a lower grade. What soon develops is that we establish a Friday-evening study 'date' in my room, in which we jointly review the lab-class material and do the write-up collaboratively. I have nothing to gain from this except the pleasure of her company; it's a chance to chat with her and develop our relationship in private.

I never discuss religion with Janice and rarely mention Pakistan. I don't want to say anything that will make her think of me as 'different' and derail our imminent romance.

But we never seem to cross the line to boyfriend–girlfriend. *How can I achieve this?* As I am now totally in love with her, I am desperate that this should happen as soon as possible.

A Paul Simon song I've heard several times in Milton's room has begun to resonate so much:

> *First thing I remember*
> *When you came into my life*
> *I said, "I'm gonna get that girl*
> *No matter what I do"*
> *Well, I guess I'd been in love before*
> *And once or twice I'd been on the floor*
> *But I never loved no one*
> *The way that I loved you*
> *And it was late in the evening*
> *And all the music's seeping through*

I discuss the problem with Milton a lot. He tells me what he did. He was obsessed with this girl called Annabel last year. They were both in a large group of friends who all hung out together. One day, he and Annabel ended up walking to the shops together. This was the moment that he had been frantically waiting for. In the midst of a perfectly relaxed conversation, he suddenly blurted out, 'Will you go out with me, Annabel?' He felt a wave of relief at having finally done it.

It didn't go quite as he expected. Annabel was thrown completely off guard, and could barely articulate her response, which was along the lines of: 'I think we should just be friends.'

'Oh, okay, that's fine …' stammered Milton.

The two of them continued their walk in awkward silence. Milton couldn't wait to get away from her so that he could relax again. The awkwardness between them persisted for quite some time, but it did fade eventually, within the framework of their interaction with all their mutual friends.

I am quite certain from Milton's account that this is not the way to proceed. My approach will be more dignified

1981-82
Age: 19

and thus much more likely to be successful. I know that I'm in love and every day brings a joyful promise of something wonderful happening; now I really understand the expression 'walking on air'. Janice and I were made for each other and will surely get married one day. As James Bond said about Tracy: 'I know I'll never find another girl like you.'

An acquaintance of Milton is Magnus. I meet him one evening in Milton's room and we chat. He is a tall, bearded Christian evangelist who takes an immediate interest in me. (I find out much later that he has been on an American course in converting Muslims and has selected me as his field project.)

He is able to use as leverage my confusion about what Islam really is (all mixed up with un-Islamic Arab culture). He says that the Qur'an is false, it's not from God, it's copied from the Bible, or there's stuff in it about Jesus which is complete rubbish, because it's not in the Bible at all, such as that the Qur'an says that Jesus sometimes spoke like an adult, when he was just a baby: 'What garbage! That's *not* in the Bible!'

Magnus points out that the Qur'an says that God asked Abraham to sacrifice his son *Ishmael*, whereas the Bible, which came first, says that it was *Isaac* he was asked to sacrifice. Hence the Qur'an is *so obviously* wrong on this.

But his greatest contempt is for the fact that the Qur'an denies that Jesus was killed by his enemies (and therefore was not resurrected). Muslims deny that Jesus actually died on the cross, but don't articulate a clear explanation of what really *did* happen. Without belief in the Crucifixion and Resurrection, there is no Christian salvation; this is the foundation of Magnus's belief, and the critical difference with Islam (in which entry to Heaven is by good deeds and God's Beneficience). By making us deny the Resurrection, Satan is leading Muslims to Hell, Magnus tells me.

1981-82
Age: 19   186

Magnus and his fellow true Believers are looking forward to the Rapture, which will surely be coming imminently. Jesus is suddenly going to lift them all away to Heaven and the miserable non-Believers (like me) who are *left behind* are going to suffer horrible events on Earth and will be wishing that we had listened to people like Magnus. Then we will fight a global war against Jesus' forces and we are going to be completely and utterly defeated and hurled down into the flames of Hell.

I've heard this before, and it comes as no surprise when Magnus asserts his view that the Qur'an is a deception of Satan, who deliberately created Islam to misguide as many people as possible away from the salvation of Christianity. But, unlike Auden and Robinson, Magnus has an ace card which supports this view.

He shows me a passage in the New Testament, in Galatians (written by Paul), warning against an alleged Angel of Light bringing another gospel. 'But though we, or *an angel from heaven*, preach *any other gospel* unto you ...'

I am stunned. My heart stops and I feel a deep, foreboding pain in my guts. Is Paul warning against 'Gabriel' bringing the Qur'an to Muhammad? Is this proof that the Qur'an *really is* from Satan, designed to mislead people from Christianity? Again, here is that concept of *satanic conspiracy*, first introduced to me at Hampton School, but this time with *proof*.

Magnus observes my anxiety and looks smug and certain. His evidence has had the desired effect. As he points out, this passage in the Bible was written hundreds of years before an alleged angel came to Muhammad with the Qur'an, which is definitely 'another gospel'. The same warning applies to the Mormon Church, which was also founded on 'another gospel', delivered by an apparent angel.

This is turning my world upside down. I am confused and deeply frightened. When I return to my room at the end of the evening, I am terrified that Satan is going to jump out at me from somewhere. I am too scared to perform my night-time Islamic prayer, the only one of the five daily prayers that I actually do. I am afraid that someone or something scary will be behind my back when I prostrate myself in the direction of Mecca. Not only that, I am coming to grips with the possibility that Islam isn't just misguided, it is in fact deliberately engineered by Satan, to lead people away from salvation by Jesus, and to Hell. *But how could God allow this?*

I can barely sleep during the night. *Is my grandfather burning in Hell?*

What about that crippled man in Mecca, who had to shuffle along on all fours like an injured animal and could not raise his head up from the pavement; his faith and humility put me to shame. *Will he burn in Hell for all eternity?*

I lie awake, anxious and sweating. Perhaps I do drift off, but then I am brought wide-awake by the sound of muffled laughter. It seemed to have come from within my room. I am too scared to look. I face the wall with my eyes shut. Sunday morning comes eventually; it's a nice day, but this sense of doom hangs over me.

I have been placed in a state of extreme anxiety and I cannot shake it off; the worry persists. What really bothers me is Magnus's *absolute certainty* that he is right. He makes me both angry and afraid. (The truth is that he is more sure that he is right, than I am of being right, because I have *always* wondered, 'How do we *know* that we follow the right religion?')

These conversations with Magnus go on for two years.

My university career is off to a great start. I am consistently top of my classes, with very little effort or focus on

1981-82
Age: 19

studying. I'm drifting along doing fine. The question of how I achieve boyfriend status with Janice is my main preoccupation.

At mid-semester we will have a few days of vacation, and both Janice and I will be going home. Her father will be coming to get her in the fabled Honda Accord. I am walking back to AKD on the last afternoon of classes when I see the vehicle in the car park. I know instinctively that it is the one. It is a sporty two-door hatchback, metallic cream in colour, absolutely immaculate and shining in all the right places. It has been reversed into the parking space, allowing it to show off the distinctive fog lamps at the front.

I walk deliberately slowly. I know that Janice will be leaving at any moment, and I want to meet her father. (*'Marry my daughter, Mr Bond.'*)

I loiter inside the lobby; there's no sign of them. I check the 'A' mailbox fastidiously for any letter for me, although there won't have been a delivery since I looked this morning. There is nothing. I walk very slowly towards the door of the boys' wing. I reach the door and I am just going through it, when I look over my shoulder and see two figures emerging from the girls' wing across the other side of the lobby; one of them has stunning red hair.

I turn around, wave, and walk back to meet them in the middle of the lobby. Janice's father is a pleasant man. We exchange greetings and shake hands. I don't know how much she's told him about me, but he does seem to have heard of me. This is very promising. I wish them a good drive down.

I go home the next morning by taking a bus to Stirling station, a train to Glasgow, a taxi to Glasgow Airport, a plane to Heathrow and a bus to our home. As I'm walking up to the house, I see something wonderful. There is a 'For Sale' sign outside Willy Johnson's house. (A few months

1981-82
Age: 19   189

later he is gone.) My mother is pleased to see me, but I can tell that she is still saddened by her father's death.

Back at Stirling, Janice and I spend all our 'work' time together, we sit together in the MacRobert coffee bar, and we walk around together between classes. We have so much in common. We look down on most students as lazy, scruffy, uncultured 'Lefties' (especially the ones who study Sociology). We even share the same favourite car, to which we both aspire: the Jaguar XJ-S.

One dark, wintry evening after the day's lectures are over, we wander into the campus supermarket together, to buy a few groceries before walking back to AK Davidson Hall. Janice wants to buy a loaf of crusty bread, but it's more than she needs, so I agree to buy it jointly with her and split it. *Could we be any more like a couple?*

I know that many people see us together all the time and perceive us as boyfriend–girlfriend, and I'm proud to be associated in this way with such a beautiful and desirable girl, but I also know deep down and most painfully that this is not really the case, that in reality I am kidding myself.

But it's only a matter of time before it will become true.

Janice comes to see me in my room later this evening. She is very upset. She has a special ring, from a very posh jeweller, and she has lost it. Have I seen it anywhere? I haven't, but I am very sympathetic and I feel sorry for her.

The next day, I approach this problem logically. If someone has found her ring, then they may have handed it into the Lost Property Office, if such a place exists. I make enquiries and learn that it *does* exist, in the Cottrell Building. I go there and discover that *they have the ring!* It was found in the supermarket and handed in by a lady who works there. I am not able to persuade them to give me the ring, as I'm not the owner and I can't describe it in detail, but that doesn't matter. I am excited about how grateful Janice will be.

I find Janice working in the library. I instruct her to come with me and, when she hesitates, I repeat firmly, 'Come with me, *now*.' I am so enjoying this. She has no choice – my manner is so insistent. I lead her to the Cottrell Building, up to the mysterious top floor, and to the Lost Property Office. At the last moment, I tell her that I have found her ring. She is overjoyed. She describes the ring to the custodian of lost property, practically jumping up and down with excitement, and she is given the ring as her reward for getting the description right.

I am so pleased with myself, but the feeling soon fades – nothing changes between Janice and me.

The science-fiction society is screening the film *Alien*. I ask Janice if she would like to see it and she agrees. This is very exciting for me, but the irony is that it is *not* a date. It is just two university friends going to see a film together. Nothing happens.

One afternoon, we walk back to AKD together. In the lobby, a scruffy young man emerges from the girls' wing, proclaims, 'Hi Janice!', grabs her by the arms and kisses her on the forehead, before proceeding out of the hall.

'Who's that?' I ask, trying not to sound too concerned.

'Oh, that's Anna's boyfriend,' replies Janice.

I am relieved, but outraged. *Who the hell is Anna's boyfriend and how dare he kiss Janice on the forehead?* (Why can't I do that?)

I conspire to do this very thing. At the end of one of our Friday night study sessions in my room, I walk her to the door and then, in a rather awkward and contrived way, I say, 'Goodnight partner' and kiss her on the forehead. Her skin feels wonderful, warm and soft. She seems slightly taken aback, but recovers smoothly, says goodnight and retreats gracefully down the corridor.

I feel ecstatic. *I did it!*

I become obsessed with giving Janice a nice Christmas present. One Saturday morning, I go into town on this special mission. I wander into Liberty and settle on a beautiful shimmering blue silk scarf. It costs me eight pounds. The woman in the store wraps it for me in delightful Liberty paper. I find a nice Christmas card and write in it, *'Here is a rag for you to dry the test tubes with.'*

I want the delivery of this present to be special. As the final lab session of the semester approaches, I go to the laboratory and persuade the custodian to let me place the package inside Janice's equipment locker, as a surprise. He is bemused, but co-operative.

The day of the final lab class, I have a sense of nervous excitement. I try to act completely normal, as Janice and I review the details of the experiment together, before we will assemble the equipment for it. The time comes when she opens her locker with the key and looks inside it. There is the flat package with the card attached, standing upright amongst the 250ml glass beakers.

It does take her by surprise *('Oh, what's this then?')* and she does seem genuinely touched for a moment, but then she regains her composure and we proceed to have a perfectly normal lab session – *or do we?* I think there is a slight change in the air, an almost intangible sense of a joyful, unspoken connection.

However, things return to normal almost immediately afterwards. The lab sessions are over, soon the lectures will end, the exams are approaching … and still I have not crossed over the line.

It's the AKD Christmas party and we are all dressed in our finest clothes, enjoying the roast turkey and Christmas pudding. The smell of perfume and aftershave hangs in the air, along with a lot of sexual tension. There are many beautiful girls, including Janice, heavily made up and in provocative dresses. I still haven't figured out how to impress her; Milton's been no help at all.

Another record starts to play and many of the girls react emotionally, almost tearfully, as they recognise it and listen intently. I am not familiar with it, but it seems to be called '*Imagine*' and from what they are saying, it is by John Lennon, the ex-Beatle who was shot dead last year. I listen and pick up a few of the words. The gist of what he is saying is, 'Imagine there's no Heaven, Hell or Religion.' *How foolish!* What he really means is, 'Imagine there's no God.' Of course there's a Heaven and a Hell. The purpose of life is to earn one or the other from God. True religion shows you the Right Path. He must have had quite a shock when he met God.

A couple of weeks before the exams, I have a brilliant idea; something unique that Janice will remember forever. I need Milton for this. He is an excellent songwriter, guitar player and singer (I cannot sing to save my life). I put the proposition to Milton. In exchange for six Yorkie chocolate bars, he will write and record an album of songs for Janice, sung on my behalf. I will give this tape to her, and she will know how I feel about her and be overwhelmed. Our relationship will be a *fait accompli*.

Milton is delighted to do this, for two reasons: Yorkie chocolate bars are expensive and anything's better than preparing for exams.

I meet him in his room many times over the weekend of this project. We review the lyrics and he composes the tunes. The first song is really joyful, with a deliriously ecstatic chorus – a bit like a typical song from *The Carpenters*:

1981-82
Age: 19   193

THE PERFECT GENTLEMAN

You make the sun shine in my heart as bright as day,
I don't know how, it's only you that knows the way,
I'm like a king and you play good Queen Janice's part,
You crown my reign, by making sunshine in my heart.

The next two songs are serious and intense, with verses like this:

Janice with your wide warm eyes,
Come drink my dry white wine,
Fill the space between us,
Like some warm lovely dreamer,
You make my time here fine …

The fourth one is funny and lively, for some light relief:

Let's be smooth together Janice,
Let's make campus smart,
Let's both work to James Bond music,
Tear my life apart.

Let me kiss you on the forehead,
Will you let me please?
When you say I can, you know,
I go weak at the knees.

Let me buy you costly pressies,
I'm generous and refined,
To gift you with such stylish ease,
Oi, 'scuse me, where's mine?

Let's hear classic symphonies,
Let me find your ring,
Compared to cuddly Aliens, oh,
You're a wild, wild thing …

1981-82
Age: 19

The last song is absolutely magnificent, musically brilliant, poignant and deep:

Janice [pause], *don't get me wrong* [intense], *if I say I feel for you*
   [emotive],
Though oceans of people swirl through your changing gaze,
To fall on another side, of the shifting borders of your mind.

I have many deep questions to channel your energies into me
   [mysterious],
And the power that flows through the earth and through the
   atmosphere [surreal],
To eagles who focus into the spectrums of your hair [inspiring] …

Finally, all five superb songs are ready. The recording session is in my room; the tape is prepared on the little TV/radio/cassette recorder which my parents gave me for my eighteenth birthday. We record one song at a time; the tension is palpable as we need to get through each track without error or interruption, but the session proceeds with very few retakes. Finally, it's done. *The tape is fantastic!*

Everyone watches *Dallas* in the television room on Sunday evenings. I sit next to Janice, which is perfectly normal (she looks gorgeous in a cream jumper and matching trousers), but my attention is not really on the episode (although I do notice that Cliff Barnes is now driving a Jaguar XJ-S; *lucky bastard!*). Finally, when *Dallas* is over, I ask her, 'Will you just come up to my room for a few minutes?'

She is perfectly amenable to the idea, but asks 'Why?' out of curiosity. I tell her that I have something for her and she is intrigued (or bemused).

She makes herself comfortable on the bed and I sit on the plastic chair by the desk and operate the tape player. I am almost apologetic and self-deprecating as I tell her that this is just a little something which I have commissioned for her. The songs begin and she gives a little embarrassed (*but flattered?*) laugh when she hears her name for the first time.

I sit through the five songs in a timid, defensive but smug way, knowing that the songs will do all the talking. Janice listens intently to all of the lyrics, but she tries to remain impassive, not wanting to let her face reveal the emotional whirlwind which she must be feeling.

We are both relieved when the tape ends. I bring matters to a close; I want her to enjoy the tape and to think about it, not to put her on the spot right now. I give her the tape and show her to the door.

The exams begin on a Monday morning. The Friday before, Janice comes to my room for a little talk …

It doesn't go quite as I hoped. She tells me that I'm a really nice person, we share many of the same ideals and ambitions, and she values having me as a friend, but she does not wish to be in a 'relationship' with me. She does not see me that way. I should not be upset about this and the fact that I appear to have fallen in love with her – this has happened to many boys and men before me. It is almost inevitable, because of her 'magnetic personality'. Also, there is someone else whom she's interested in, a guy called Rick. (I know of Rick; he is a friend of Suzanne's boyfriend and he has a car – a Triumph Dolomite.)

I think I've had a crusader's sword plunged deep into my chest; that's exactly how it feels.

I manage to get Janice to qualify her position about how she feels about me with an 'at this time', thus keeping the door open for a future change of heart. Janice and I agree that we will remain friends and that our friendship will not be affected in any way by this little talk. I see her to the door.

It is snowing heavily this evening. Campus is buried deep in snow and everyone is out having snowball fights, as

1981-82
Age: 19

a relief from exam preparation. I can hear and see them through my open window; it sounds like fun. There is no more joyful, privileged and rare form of recreational conflict than a snowball fight – *if* you don't have a heavy pain in your chest, that is.

Paul Simon knows exactly how this feels:

> *A winter's day*
> *In a deep and dark December*
> *I am alone*
> *Gazing from my window*
> *To the streets below*
> *On a freshly fallen, silent shroud of snow*
>
> *I am a rock*
> *I am an island*

The exams pass miserably, and the end of the semester comes upon us. Janice gives me a Christmas present too, on our last evening before we head home. I unwrap it reverently. It is a book called *The Splendour of Scotland*, filled with beautiful photographs of this wonderful country. On the inside she has written, in her elaborate script: *'Imran, Best Wishes for a Merry Christmas and a Happy New Year! Janice.'*

I carry the book with me on my long trek home (much of which is spent sitting in a fog-bound Glasgow airport), admiring the photographs, but I am drawn again and again to her inscription – scrutinising it to decipher the hidden message. *What does she really mean?*

At home on Christmas Day, which is not a formal event for us, I am sitting by the telephone in the living room all day long. I have an expectation, a dream, a wholly irrational belief, that the phone will ring and it will be Janice saying, 'Hey, why don't you come up to my house for Christmas dinner?' I will explain to my mother that 'a friend' has invited me to her ... to *their* house for Christmas dinner and ask, 'Is it okay if I go?' I will rush out to the Renault 5, which happens to be washed, fuelled and ready (oil, water, tyres – all A-OK), and drive off to Melton Mowbray in Leicestershire. On Christmas Day, with no traffic, I estimate that it will take less than two hours. I sit in the living room all day picturing this – but the phone doesn't ring. I stare out of the window.

My mother sits opposite me for a while, perhaps noticing that I am anxious about something. She decides to make a very generous offer, which shows how tolerant and understanding she is. She says that I can marry anyone I want to, as long as she is a Muslim Pakistani girl. 'You *will* marry a Muslim Pakistani girl, won't you?' She explains at great length all the problems I would have if I married outside my religion and ethnicity, and all I can think is: '*The biggest problem is you, Mum.*'

I wonder if I really want to succeed with Janice, if I will ever allow myself the privilege of such joy? Because if I do, I will have my parents to deal with, and that may be a greater struggle than convincing Janice to be with me.

During the holiday, I watch the movie *Gandhi*. At one point, dealing with inter-religious rioting, Gandhi declares: 'I am a Muslim. I am a Hindu. I am a Christian.'

A nice sentiment, but not rational. Only one religion can be true, and when you choose your religion on the basis of evidence, reason and logic then, by default, other religions, no matter how appealing, cannot also be true.

I am resisting the possibility of caving in to Christianity. The idea that the One, omnipotent God had a Son (making another god), who then had to be sacrificed in order for God to forgive Mankind their sins, is unpalatable. *It doesn't make sense.* What limited Islamic studies I have undertaken have indoctrinated me with at least this much.

1981-82
Age: 19

During this vacation, I study the Qur'an more. It very helpfully says specifically that it is *not* written by a deceiving devil. It's very scientifically sound and gives more credible versions of biblical stories. For example, the Great Flood was not a universal flood; it was just a local flood where Noah lived, and he saved his family and *farm animals* with himself, not *every* kind of animal in the whole world. *Hey, that's exactly what Reverend Moore said.*

The Qur'an also says that everything in the Universe originated from one piece of matter, which exploded violently. The stars and planets condensed from the resulting gas. All life came from water and evolved in many stages. This is all good stuff and *proves* that the Qur'an is the Word of God ... but the *absolute certainty* of the fundamentalist Christians still bothers me. They say that this information comes from Satan, who wants to keep people from believing in the blood sacrifice of Jesus, which is the only true path to eternal salvation.

I don't know what to think. I just *don't know.*

We all return to campus in early February, for our second semester. Janice and I visit each other's rooms on the first evening, while we are both unpacking. She tells me pointedly about the hi-fi she received for Christmas, and then is confused when I don't reciprocate in the expected way, by telling her what I received. There is an awkward moment, but I fill the silence by talking of something else. But she won't let it go – she *must* find out. Later, she asks the dreaded question, in an almost coy and awkward way.

'What did *you* get for Christmas?'

I try to sound as casual and unconcerned about it as I can. 'Oh, nothing. We don't really *do* Christmas much.'

Her 'Oh' is both disappointed and confused. She wanted to know, so that we could compare (to determine whose was better). But my opting out in this way is not playing the game. How can anyone *not do* Christmas? She

1981-82
Age: 19

realises suddenly that there is something strange and sinister about me, below the outer mask of suntanned middle-class English Conservatism.

The routine of second semester begins quickly in the next few days. Janice and I are back to normal, lab partners again and so on. There is no sign of this guy Rick around AK Davidson Hall. It seems that he wasn't really that interested in her. *Ha!*

The first Saturday is Valentine's Day. It is quite beyond me *not* to do something. I buy Janice a Valentine's card and a rose. While she is watching *Dallas* in the television room, I persuade the reluctant hall porter to let me place them in her room, on the pillow.

The outcome is not quite as I expected. Janice is furious about this invasion of privacy and lets me know it at our next lecture. She reprimands me and I feel sheepish and like an idiot.

But there is a more sinister undercurrent of events taking place. Janice begins to be seen around campus with a man, who clearly is developing into the role of 'boyfriend'. I see him with her on a few occasions, but we never speak of him. He has brown hair, glasses, a 'pretty boy' face, and he's always wearing jeans and a black-leather jacket. I can't believe that she would go for such a person! It's a betrayal of our common ideals.

He drives a dark-blue Mini Clubman with a heavily dented front and rear. *Bastard!* I can't compete with a guy who has a car.

I learn later that his name is Ben and she met him at the Valentine's Day disco, at the Sports Pavilion, which she went to with her friends that night, after watching *Dallas* and finding my card and rose on her pillow. She was pretty angry with me, apparently.

One day I break the ice by going up to Janice and Ben when they are together, saying that 'It's time we met' and

1981-82
Age: 19

shaking his hand. He seems surprised and unable to articulate a sentence (which pleases me and is what one would expect from a leather-and-denim-clad Neanderthal). Janice is certainly happy that I am able to accept Ben as her boyfriend, and still be her friend and lab partner. (I'm just biding my time.)

Apart from the existence of Ben, there is another uncomfortable development this semester – the Falklands crisis. Argentina has invaded some obscure British-owned islands in the South Atlantic (islands which no one I know has ever heard of before), and now Mrs Thatcher has sent the British fleet there. We seem to be at war.

I find this deeply disturbing. The media love this – it's the biggest news story for years – but I don't find war entertaining or simple. I don't think that the 'Argies' (as the tabloids so easily fall into calling them; sounds too much like 'Pakis') are any less human than us. This is a political dispute and human beings – sons, fathers, brothers – are dying because of it; an orphan in Argentina is no less a tragedy than an orphan in Britain. I am acutely aware of these realities, all the time, and cannot really enjoy the war like everyone else seems to be doing.

Things turn especially ugly when the Argentine ship *General Belgrano* is sunk by the Royal Navy, and hundreds of Argentine sailors are drowned. *The Sun* newspaper seems to sum up the national mood, with its '*GOTCHA*' headline; everyone seems to gloss over this tragic loss of human life and the dead Argies are completely dehumanised. And apparently the *General Belgrano* was not even inside the 200-nautical-mile exclusion zone that Britain has declared around the islands. Later reports indicate that it was actually sailing away in the other direction.

But any doubts and any residual humanity are abandoned when, two days later, the Argies manage to sink the HMS *Sheffield* with a French-built Exocet missile. Now I even hear friends of mine talk about 'nuking Argentina'. This is a horrible affair; it brings out the very worst in us.

Internally, my Britishness is under severe strain. Do I just cave in and jeer at the deaths of Argies to show how British I am, or do I express disquiet at the loss of 'enemy' human life and thus show myself to be a foreigner after all, not really committed to Britain? Mostly I say nothing, except to Milton, who shares the same concerns.

Janice doesn't make any of this easy for me. She has no doubts about the absolute righteousness of our conduct in this matter, proudly declaring that, 'Mrs T. has it all under control.'

I prefer not to discuss the Falklands war with Janice.

One Friday evening on campus, I see a little handwritten card on one of the noticeboards. It says:

VW Beetle for sale. Blue. 1969. £200.

Irrational excitement grips me. I have £400 in the bank to last the rest of semester (about ten weeks). My rent is already paid in advance and I have a book of meal coupons worth about £80. I reckon the insurance will cost me about £100, leaving me about £100 to live on. And I can have a car! There is no better status symbol than a car. *Girls 'dig' guys who have cars!*

The Beetle is in a village called Bridge of Allan, close to campus. I call the number and the middle-class woman who owns the car is practically able to sell it to me on the phone. I agree to come over the next morning.

I excitedly tell Milton about it and he agrees to come with me.

The car, when we see it, could barely look more pathetic. Three of its four wings are dented, as well as the back end. It seems to run okay though.

Milton and I converse in low tones. 'I think you should buy it,' he advises. My hand is shaking as I write the cheque. This is not, by any means, a rational decision. I have allowed my heart to overrule my head, and it is exhilarating and frightening.

The woman drives the Beetle to campus for me and parks it at AKD. I cannot drive it until I buy the insurance on Monday morning. This weekend passes painfully slowly; a few times I go out and sit in the car, playing in it like a child.

The insurance is duly arranged and costs me £114 – it is very close to my estimate. I call the car 'Tracy'. She gives me access to Scotland in a way that wasn't possible before. Milton and I go on many trips that take us to lochs, forests and mountains. When I know my way around, I will be able to persuade some girl or other to come on a drive with me, including Janice and her friends.

I don't tell my parents about the Beetle (I phone home a couple of times a week), but I am rumbled when the insurance company sends my policy documents to my home address. When I next call, my mother is disapproving about this reckless purchase, but my father sounds quite excited (the document tells him that it is a blue VW Beetle) and he wants to hear all about the car.

Ben always parks his Mini illegally by the entrance of AKD when he comes to visit Janice. Although I cannot see Janice's window from mine, I can see the hall entrance, so I always know when Ben is visiting. On the one hand, I don't want to know. On the other hand, I can't *not* see his car. He often spends the evening here, leaving around midnight.

One Friday at mid-morning, Janice and I come out of a Biology tutorial and start walking back towards AKD. It is a beautiful spring day, with brilliant sunshine and a lovely blue sky; the air is fresh and cool. Casually, I say that I'm going to go for a drive in the country. Would she like to come?

'What, *now*?' she exclaims, and then, '*Yes!*'

We dump our stuff in our rooms and meet in the lobby, then walk out to the car. Exhilarated, I drive out of campus and through Bridge of Allan, towards Callander and Loch Lubnaig, which takes about forty minutes. There is a car park, where we pull in, with a beautiful view of the loch and the mountains. I have brought my camera and take pictures; my favourite is one of Janice leaning against my car, the loch in the background. Her face and her hair look radiant. It's the most beautiful girl in the world, with the most beautiful car (you cannot argue with this, it's all in the eye of the beholder).

We have lunch at a hotel in Callander: smoked salmon, with a little caviar sprinkled on the side. She pays.

'Let's just hope our children grow up to enjoy things like this,' Janice says casually.

'Yes … I hope so …,' I stammer, my mind reeling with delirious joy.

I drive the Beetle fast and we make it back to campus in time for a double lecture session in the afternoon; Chemistry and Biology. The lectures pass delightfully. There is a renewed energy between us, a sense of joyful anticipation about the future. I can feel it.

When we emerge from the final lecture, we see Ben waiting nearby. She looks at me apologetically, says, 'There's Ben,' and goes to him. This is the right thing to do; at this point, she has no choice. He is still officially her boyfriend – she hasn't broken up with him yet. But change is in the air; it's imminent.

In the night, I am going to bed and I see that the Mini is parked under my window, which is not unusual. So, she hasn't quite broken up with him yet; she must be waiting for the right moment. It won't be long, and then she and I can have more wonderful days like the one we had today.

1981-82
Age: 19

The next morning it is sunny and promising. I look out of my window at the new day. *Oh God! No! No, no, no! Dear God, this can't be true!*

The Mini is still there.

This semester becomes a wilderness for me. A deep unhappiness is with me at all times, a sense of incompleteness, a longing for what I cannot have. I wander around campus in a semi-daze, waiting for something or someone to happen to me. I wear a tie and jacket and go for drives to lochs and forests, looking for some adventure to befall me, the way it always does to Simon Templar: a beautiful woman, a conspiracy, villains, action, danger, justice done. It's true I have a beaten-up old Beetle and not a Jaguar XJ-S, but it's still a car. However, nothing happens.

Relief comes, from an unexpected quarter. My classmate and friend Martin (who is scruffy, scraggly and extremely bright) teaches me to play golf, on the University's course. I am hooked. I seem to have Beginner's Luck (which does diminish eventually). On the golf course, I focus on the ball and forget Janice, although I'm always conscious of the fact that Janice's room overlooks the course and she may witness me enjoying myself without her, having a life that doesn't need her to be complete. That will show her.

We have to apply for accommodation for our second year. The results come out and on the noticeboard I see that I have been granted my room in AK Davidson Hall again. Janice and her two closest girlfriends have not been given a campus place; they will have to find private accommodation off-campus. On Saturday morning, I take the three of them flat-hunting in my Beetle. They are able to secure a lovely flat in town, which actually is owned by one of our Chemistry lecturers.

They are grateful to me for the help, with my car. Where is Ben when you need help? *Ha!*

1981-82
Age: 19   205

There's a catastrophe. My Beetle was at least as good as Ben's wrecked old Mini, but his parents buy him another car. It's a Ford Cortina 1.6 Ghia, and it's only four years old. It has fog lamps and flashy wheels. It's a real car, not a student jalopy. Now, this is the car which I am forced to observe frequently parked under my window (and increasingly overnight).

I hang out with Janice's girlfriends, because they are my friends too. I am determined to be part of the fabric of her life. One evening I am in Joan's room, doing her ironing for her, which is easy for me. (In Hampton School *no one*, pupil or master, had clothes more sharply pressed than mine.) Of course, my ulterior motive is to find out what is going on between Janice and Ben, and how serious it is. The subject of conversation gets onto Ben and casually I mention how surprised I am that he now stays the night a lot, in the girls' wing (obviously in Janice's room). Joan agrees, then realising what I am thinking, blurts out, 'Oh, she's not had sex with him!'

My heart leaps with unexpected, unimagined joy, which I struggle not to display too obviously. It was worth doing the ironing to learn this. *She's not had sex with him. Thank God!*

My financial planning was not so good. I'm running out of money and decide to sell my bicycle. It's just a regular bike, a Raleigh Wayfarer – not a racing bike or anything special. I ask Milton for advice and he says, 'It's crap, not worth more than twenty-five quid.' I duly advertise it for £25 on a campus noticeboard and, by the time that I return to my room an hour later, two people are waiting to see it. The first one buys it immediately. I hurry back to remove the notice. Milton's an idiot – *it was worth a lot more than twenty-five quid!*

1981-82
Age: 19

I eventually borrow £100 from my father to see me through to the end of semester, and then another £30 in the last couple of weeks – otherwise I will not be able to pay for the petrol to drive home to London.

One day Diane mentions to me that she saw Janice and Joan last night, sitting together in the *Westerton Arms* pub in Bridge of Allan, having a drink. They were both smoking.

This can't be right. I know that Joan smokes, but Janice definitely does not. Diane must have got it wrong. It must have been some other redhead she saw.

At the end of the semester, I am able to meet Janice's mother as well, when her parents come to collect her in their magnificent metallic bronze Series III Jaguar XJ6. From my window, I can see my Beetle in the car park across the road, and suddenly I see the mighty car arrive and pull into a space near my old banger. I check in the mirror, tidy my hair and quickly rush down … so that I am casually walking out to my car when, coincidentally, I encounter her parents coming the other way.

(The reason I have time to achieve this is that Janice's father took a minute to apply a cleaning cloth to the front of the bonnet and the radiator grill of the magnificent car, meticulously wiping away the flattened insects which were unfortunate enough to get in the way. I remember Janice telling me about this: 'You have to wipe off the insects as soon as possible, otherwise they're a bugger to remove when they've dried in.')

Of course, I recognise her father from over six months ago, so I say, 'Hello!' with pleasant surprise in my authentic polished middle-class voice. He says, 'Oh, hello Imran.' ('*Marry my daughter, Mr Bond!*') He introduces me to his wife and I shake both their hands. I enquire as to whether they have had a pleasant drive. I act like the perfect English gentleman (which I am) and leave it to them to make the comparison between me and the denim-and-leather-clad caveman they will surely meet later.

On the last day of term, I say goodbye to all my new friends and set off with Martin on a slow and steady drive down to London, in my thirteen-year-old Beetle called Tracy. I never exceed 55 miles per hour; I don't think that she can take any more. I could not afford to buy membership of the Automobile Association, so I have to be very careful. Many lorries pass us and sound their horns in irritation.

At home in London: I get a vacation job in a government building, which requires me proudly to sign the Official Secrets Act (organising the relocation of heavy boxes of official forms from the old storeroom to the big new storeroom – I'm sorry, I can't tell you any more than that); work all through the summer; sell the Beetle; buy my mother's white Renault 5, making a deal with my father. (We bought this used 3-door French hatchback last year; it has quite low mileage, but no service history.) My father buys my mother another Renault 5, a sporty blue one.

One afternoon, I pass Auden on Teddington High Street. I look away, hoping that he hasn't seen me. I really don't want to speak with him. He really makes me feel uncomfortable with his beliefs and his certainty: Rapture, Armageddon, global war between Believers and non-Believers (meaning Christians and Muslims), the end of the world. *What if he's right?*

1981-82
Age: 19

Renault

1982-83

Age: 20

I RETURN TO STIRLING UNIVERSITY in my washed and polished Renault 5 (and with newly purchased Automobile Association cover). It is wonderful to be back on campus, and back in the same room in AKD. Milton has the same room again as well. We continue our joyful journey of self-discovery and learning how not to impress women.

Because she is now living in the town, Janice brings her Honda Accord to the university. Despite being three years old, this car has done only 7,000 miles, and it is absolutely immaculate. It seems very advanced; there is an electronic display that shows which of the doors are open. It is one of the smartest cars to be seen on campus.

Janice is my lab partner again, and classes are going well. Ben is still around, but I try not to worry about this. She will realise what she's missing out on eventually. I try to find another candidate to be my girlfriend but, despite having a car, I am not successful. It doesn't matter. Janice is the one for me; it's only a matter of time.

I have a private conversation with Joan and Suzanne about this. I tell them what Janice said when we were having lunch in Callander last Spring: 'Let's just hope our children grow up to enjoy things like this.' Whether it was intentional or a subconscious slip of the tongue, it definitely means something.

Joan and Suzanne look taken aback and exchange a concerned glance. Then Joan explains it to me.

'Oh, she didn't mean your and her children, from the two of you *together*. She meant your children with your wife, and her children with her husband, *separately*.'

I don't know. It didn't sound like that to me.

It's Milton's birthday in October and I take him on a long country drive, ending up on the shores of Loch Lomond. He's been drinking tea all day and he has another pint before we go, so he won't get thirsty. I have to stop three times so that he can run behind a bush. It's a cool, breezy, slightly damp day, cloudy with intermittent sunshine. This is typical of the Scottish climate, and there is something wonderful about it. *Scotland is alive.* It resonates with something deep within me. It's hard to explain, but I love Scotland and the gentle caress of the wind and the rain.

At mid-semester Janice is going to drive home, down to Leicestershire. Although I can easily get a cheap ticket to fly home to London, it seems unbearably exciting to me to drive down to England in my car, accompanying Janice. This will be such fun.

We set off immediately after the last lecture, on Tuesday morning. I am acutely aware that her car has a maximum speed of 95 mph, whereas for mine it is 82 mph, but I do not believe that this will be a problem. I am wrong. Once we are on the motorway, Janice begins to drift ahead, 70 … 80 … 90 and I struggle to keep up. (*She is Teresa di Vincenzo.*) I lose sight of her, but proceed as fast as I can. Fortunately we have a rendezvous at Southwaite service station, just south of the border; she gets there a minute before me. I park alongside her and we eat our sandwiches in the Honda (I am very careful not to drop any crumbs in her car), before setting off again.

Once again, she begins to drift ahead. If only she would keep to 80 mph, I would have no problem, but she insists on doing 90. The other problem for me is that it takes the Renault 5 (with its one litre engine) an eternity to accelerate from 70 to 80. Janice begins to disappear into the distance. I keep my foot to the floor and clench my teeth, speeding in the fast lane. The Renault 5 accelerates excruciatingly slowly: 70 ... 72 ... 74 ... 76 ... 78 ... 80. A car pulls out in front of me and I have to brake hard. *Stupid bastard!*

I sound the horn, flash my lights, and slowly pull past him. Again, I accelerate as fast as I can; there is nothing more that I can do. I can still see the tail of the Honda on the distant horizon as the Renault drifts to 80, then 82 mph. The Honda disappears and I just happen to glance in my rear-view mirror to see dark smoke pouring out of the Renault's exhaust. Shocked, my heart pounding, I come off the pedal and let her slow down to 70 mph. The smoke disappears. I am deeply anxious about what has just happened and consider myself lucky that something didn't 'blow'. I continue the journey home at no more than 70 mph. I don't see Janice again today.

On the drive back to Stirling on Sunday afternoon, I pull into a service station in Yorkshire for a break. As I walk back towards my Renault, I see something unbelievable. Janice is just reversing her Honda into a parking space; her parents are with her. I have an unexpected opportunity to meet them again and I surprise them when I walk over. They are quite welcoming; we have a delightful chat and share amusing anecdotes.

There's an interesting story about Dr Singh, who lives in their exclusive cul-de-sac. (I think that Dr Singh and his family are the only other Asians they know. I must remind them of him, although he has a beard and a turban of course, being a Sikh.) Apparently Dr Singh recently bought a brand new £28,000 Mercedes 500 SEC, and this exclusive

1982-83
Age: 20

car just suffered an engine fire while he was driving it, in the middle of Leicester. *How unbelievable!* But to the company's credit, Mercedes-Benz sent a new engine from Germany without delay. I smile and nod with great interest.

Thank you, God! What an amazing 'coincidence' it is, to be meeting Janice and her parents in the middle of Yorkshire. I know I'm going to marry Janice one day.

The reason that Janice's parents are with her is that her father will drive the car back home; she will not be keeping the Honda at Stirling during the winter months. This car has spent most of its life safely in the garage and is too valuable to be left outside during the cold, wet, dirty winter. Janice will be taking the bus instead.

Magnus and I discuss Islam and Christianity a lot. I am mesmerised by the fire in his eyes and his absolute conviction. He is a compelling character, with a certain charisma; he carries himself with absolute self-confidence (he would call it 'faith'). Sometimes he attends lectures wearing a three-piece suit. He is academically gifted and highly ambitious; I am thoroughly intimidated by him. In his room there is a large photographic poster showing a bolt of lightning and the caption: *'You don't have to fear the power'*. His bookshelves are lined with Biochemistry texts, as well as books by American preachers explaining that the world is a battleground between God and Satan (and Muslims work for Satan), describing in precise detail the horrible events which are soon to come, and how to be saved from them. They also helpfully illuminate how so-called scientists have confused and misled people.

Magnus says that God and Allah are not the same. His is a God of Love and forgiveness. Allah is a false god, a god of Fear, a mean and judgmental entity. If I don't embrace Magnus's beliefs, I will go to Hell.

Magnus tells a joke to emphasise that Allah is not God. 'A man falls out of an airplane over Arabia. He remembers how his Arab friends always talk. "*Oh Allah, help me!*" he cries. A big black hand emerges from a cloud and, taking him in its palm, lowers the man gently to the desert sand. "*Thank God!*" gasps the man. A big black foot comes out of a cloud and stamps on him.'

The joke seems funny and arrogant at the same time.

'What about little children, who die before they've had a chance to accept Jesus?'

'They have not had a chance to sin, so they go to Heaven.'

'What about people who've never heard of Jesus?'

'That's God's problem, not yours. You *have* heard the good news from me, so you have *no excuse*. If you don't accept Jesus as your saviour, you will be left behind from the Rapture and spend eternity in Hell.'

During the winter vacation, which runs all through January, I am back at home as usual. The Renault 5 suffers a major breakdown; the timing chain breaks and it is a huge job to repair this. I don't have any money to do this, as I struggle to live from one grant cheque to the next.

My father arranges the repair and pays for it; the cost is several hundred pounds.

The drive back to Scotland in early February is tenuous, the car having just been repaired, but it goes okay.

One Saturday, Surinder and I are going into town in my car. The Renault 5 is parked in a campus car park, as usual. I unlock my door, get in, and I'm just reaching over to unlock the passenger door when Surinder opens it by himself.

'How did you manage that?' I ask, surprised.

'It wasn't locked,' he replies.

This doesn't make sense to me. I am scrupulously careful with my car. I would never have left it unlocked.

The next time that I am performing the under-the-bonnet checks for oil and water, I discover that the oil cap has disappeared. I can't believe it. I would *never* have left the oil cap loose enough that it could fall off. It does not make sense. I have to drive to the Renault garage in town to buy a new one. It does not cost much, but they have to order it, and they tell me not to drive the car much without one; the loss of oil could destroy the engine totally. I am sombre, grateful that I had decided to look under the bonnet when I did.

Campus is a relatively small community. The car-owning crowd is even smaller still. I am aware of another Renault 5 on campus, a battered piece of junk, and I know its owner by sight – a scruffy, long-haired excuse for a student. Doubtless he knows me by sight. We are opposites.

One afternoon, I am walking through campus, heading for the chalets where some friends live. The other Renault 5 is standing in the middle of a car park, its bonnet is open and the owner and his friends are gathered around it, looking at something. This is of no concern to me whatsoever, other than that I must walk around this obstacle on the way to my destination. However, most interestingly, as soon as they see me coming, their chattering stops, replaced by an awkward silence. I don't understand this. I don't know any of them personally. The only commonality is the Renault 5; its owner probably knows me by sight, having noticed me driving mine, just as I have noticed him driving his. But that is all.

I walk past them and the tension is palpable. It's as if they are expecting some reaction, some comment from me. I continue on.

Later, it hits me, in a flash of inspiration. That little shit had needed an oil cap, and successfully used his key to open my passenger door (the bonnet release is on the passenger side). He had stolen my oil cap, and left me at risk of totally wrecking my engine if I did not discover this loss soon enough. For the sake of two pounds, he had put my entire car in jeopardy, a car that I had worked hard for and look after with extreme care. Doubtless, he had told his friends, and they had all been aware of it and guiltily became nervous when they saw me approaching, irrationally concerned that I had somehow figured it out. Ironically, it was this tension on their part that gave the game away.

I am at a loss how to deal with such selfish, criminal behaviour. *My entire car put at risk, to save himself two pounds!* I am angry, mad as hell. It will be relatively easy for me to exact revenge. I can go out late at night, puncture his tyres, maybe put sugar in his fuel tank. There are many possibilities.

But there is a problem. Even though I know intuitively what has happened, I cannot be sure, beyond reasonable doubt. I cannot do this, if I might be wrong. And I remember that both the Bible and the Qur'an tell us to forgive our enemies (except in those passages where they both instruct us to slay them). '*Vengeance is mine, sayeth the Lord.*' I think that means we should leave it to God. There is nothing I can do, except be grateful that I noticed in time. I haven't really forgiven him; I've just acknowledged that it is not appropriate for me to take any action.

In Islam, entry to Heaven is gained by the doing of good deeds, not by religious belief. Correct belief merely encourages you to do good deeds. In Christianity, according to Magnus, entry to Heaven is solely by belief in the sacrifice of Jesus. I can resist becoming a Christian, because the theology doesn't seem fair.

What really does bother me is their Holy Spirit phenomenon. They are always saying that *the Holy Spirit did this, said that, prophesied whatever.* Magnus often talks about what the Holy Spirit has just told the assembled Christian

Union in one of their closed-door campus meetings, but says, 'I can't share it with you. It's confidential, for Christians only.' His absolute certainty causes me great disquiet.

The Holy Spirit protects Magnus; no harm can come to him. The Holy Spirit listens to and speaks to Magnus and ensures that all his needs are met. Magnus says that he has a hotline to God. I'm sure that there is a real phenomenon here; that he's not making it up. But how do I explain it?

Magnus is very sure. 'When *I* pray, the Holy Spirit always answers my prayer. When *you* pray, there's no one listening.'

The Israelis invade Southern Lebanon. In the ensuing anarchy, nearly two thousand Palestinian refugees in the Sabra and Chatila camps, mainly women and children, are slaughtered by factional Lebanese militiamen – with the Israeli invasion appearing to provide them with this opportunity. The manner of the slaughter is particularly hideous: it takes a couple of days, is mostly by knife and often preceded by rape.

I am horrified by this event; I can't believe that it happened *now*, in my lifetime. Even Magnus – an apologist for Israel and a deep believer in the need for fulfilment of biblical prophecy prior to his longed-for Rapture – is somewhat concerned.

Magnus and I agree on one thing; God does not like gay people. Magnus has absolute conviction that this is the true Christian viewpoint and, not to be outdone by him, I assure him that the Islamic position is no less severe. (I don't know where this is in the Qur'an, but it obviously must be written somewhere – although I never do find it.*)

---

* Because it's not there.

1982-83

Age: 20

Why do I spend so much time with Magnus? He treats me with virtual contempt, yet I am drawn to him. It is because I am afraid that he might be right. I am affected by his conviction.

I have always assumed that choosing a religion is a rational process of evaluating evidence, and that there remains an element of uncertainty as to whether we have made the correct choice. The fact that Magnus has *absolute certainty* leads me to assume that he has access to some fact or knowledge of which I am unaware, and that this additional information brings him the absolute certainty. This makes me very uncomfortable.

Magnus is unable to convince me to take the leap of faith required to surrender to Christian belief, but his attitude towards me has a side effect. I become very wary of evangelical (or 'American-style') Christians; I am always deeply suspicious and mistrusting of them. I prefer my friends to be lukewarm (or 'British-style') Christians: the kind who have never thought these matters through to this extent, the kind who don't believe that I will burn in Hell for all eternity.

A friend convinces me to try Karate. I start attending twice-weekly sessions on campus. The exercises that we have to do to increase our stamina are excruciatingly painful, but leave me with a sense of exhilaration afterwards.

In one session, we are all lying on our backs in a long line, and the instructor makes us lift our legs high and low, open and close them, do the scissors motion and the riding-a-bike action, but we must *never* let our legs touch the ground again. It is particularly arduous holding our feet just six inches off the floor. This goes on for a number of minutes, although it seems like an eternity. Everyone is groaning in agony, but we are all determined not to give up. His voice and attitude alone are enough to motivate us. I cannot believe how long this activity lasts, or that I am indeed able to succeed – but miraculously I do manage it.

1982-83
Age: 20

When he lets us rest, it's like entering Paradise. I lie on the ground exhausted, gasping and moaning with relief.

There is one aspect of this martial art with which I am uncomfortable. In Karate, you have to do a lot of bowing. I know that in Islam, bowing is reserved only for God; no human, object or place is worthy of receiving a person's bow. Despite this discomfort, I follow the rituals along with everyone else, hoping that God does not perceive me as being disrespectful of Him.

There is an Exchange Programme to America which takes place in the third year. About twenty students from Stirling University swap places with students at American universities for one year. Selection for the programme is by an application form and interview process.

Janice and I attend a seminar about this Exchange Programme and we both become quite excited about the possibility of going. I think that it will be great fun; it is also an exclusive, prestigious experience. For sure, Janice and I will end up at the same place, Ben will be left behind (he is in the year above us and doesn't qualify for the programme) and Janice will finally fall into a relationship with me, in sunny California! *It can't get any better. ('Let's just hope our children grow up to enjoy things like this.')*

I spend all night working on the application form, the day before it's due in. I am smugly satisfied to be called to an interview, which is scheduled for 8 p.m. one evening.

I present myself as the ideal ambassador for Stirling University; I choose to wear a suit and tie. This may be a mistake; the Selection Board is dressed quite casually. They ask me questions about why I want to go: I say that it will be a 'good experience'. The scruffy student representative on the board, who went on the programme the previous year, asks me if I believe in Evolution or Creationism? I launch into a long discourse on how I believe that God created Man by means of Evolution (which is what I believe is hinted at in the Qur'an).

The results are out at the end of the week. I approach the noticeboard with absolute confidence. There are twenty selected candidates and a reserve list of five. I scan the list anxiously. Janice's name is there: she's going to San Diego. My name isn't on the list. Then I see it at the bottom. *I am last on the reserve list!*

I feel a pain in my gut, a weakness in my legs. This is just like when I didn't get the grades for medical school. I feel disappointment, rejection, humiliation. The chances of the fifth reserve going are negligible. Five of the successful candidates would have to drop out.

This ache of disappointment stays with me a long time. I am demotivated and lethargic. I can't even jog all the way up the hill to the Wallace Monument anymore; I've lost the willpower. I feel as if I've been rejected unfairly. *How does this fit in with my faith that I will marry Janice one day?*

I do wonder if God is testing me and whether it will all work out after all. Perhaps five people *will* drop out, for whatever reasons. I yearn to be able to stand on the beach at San Diego and pray to Him from there. The University of California at San Diego has a magnificent campus, adjacent to the Pacific Ocean. I picture it intently and imagine being able to thank God from that beach. The ocean is deep blue, the sand stretches in both directions as far as the eye can see, there are palm trees dotted about. I am standing there at dawn and the place is deserted. It is tranquil and breathtakingly beautiful.

A very strange thing happens. I'm lying in bed early one morning, when I hear a high-pitched buzzing noise around my head. It seems as if something is trying to communicate with me, but I can't tune into that frequency. In frustration, so it appears, whatever it is seems to lift my head and slam it into the pillow a few times. I don't have any control over this action. The buzzing stops and I am left wondering what happened and what this was. What troubles me is that – thanks to Magnus, Auden and company – I have been introduced to a whole dimension of existence which I don't understand – Satan, angels, demons, the Holy Spirit – and I fear that this event has something to do with all of that.

My university career is going okay, although I'm not shining as much as I used to. I'm sulking about not being selected for the Exchange Programme and I've lost focus on my work. What I haven't realised is that the studies are getting harder; more work is required, not less.

I will miss Janice while she is in America. I have to give her a farewell gift, so that she will think of me often. I buy another silk scarf from Liberty, this time a yellow one; just like before, it is wrapped beautifully. Once again, I win over the custodian of the Chemistry laboratory and the package is placed in Janice's equipment locker. Yet again, she is taken aback when she finds it. This time the card wishes her luck in America and expounds on what a pleasure it has been to work with her.

Dr Porter, who is running this lab class, looks on in bemusement.

Janice and I have three exams to face. Biochemistry is on Tuesday morning, then Chemistry 'A' is on Tuesday afternoon, and finally Chemistry 'B' is on Wednesday morning. A few days before the exams, I realise that I have run out of time for revision; I have been negligent this entire semester. I decide that I will leave the revision for Chemistry 'B' until Tuesday evening; I can cram all through Tuesday night. It will mean only one night without sleep. Then I can sit that exam on Wednesday morning (it's only two hours) and afterwards collapse into blissful slumber.

This allows me to focus the remaining time before the exams only on Biochemistry and Chemistry 'A'.

This does not go quite as I planned. For some inexplicable reason, I am completely unable to sleep during the night before Biochemistry and Chemistry 'A'. I lie in bed the whole night, fully conscious, feeling like a prisoner due to be executed at dawn. The morning comes and I proceed sombrely to the exams, feeling a dullness in my head from lack of sleep.

After Chemistry 'A' in the afternoon, I have no choice but to remain awake all night revising for Chemistry 'B' – spending a second consecutive night without sleep. 'Revision' isn't really the right word; it implies that you are reminding yourself of things that you have already studied. In fact, much of this material I seem to be considering for the very first time now. Having not slept at all the previous night, this night is a horrendous ordeal. I force myself to stay awake, guzzling huge amounts of coffee. A Paul Simon tape I borrowed from Milton is playing all night long, on auto-reverse. A certain verse sticks in my mind, and remains on indefinite repeat inside my head.

> *Couple in the next room,*
> *Bound to win a prize,*
> *They've been goin' at it all night long.*
> *Well I'm tryin' to get some sleep,*
> *But these motel walls are cheap,*
> *Lincoln Duncan is my name,*
> *And here's my song, here's my song.*

The middle of the night is the loneliest time, but the middle of the night before an exam you are woefully unprepared for is the *very worst* time.

It's a beautiful May morning when I proceed to the exam with a throbbing head, feeling slightly dizzy. I struggle to remain conscious and to focus. Everything

1982-83
Age: 20

seems to be happening in slow motion and Dr Walker, who is supervising the exam, seems to be talking from a great distance, from behind some kind of veil or wall.

Strangely, after the exam is over, I feel such exhilaration that my energy and clarity of mind seem to come back. Implausibly, I take Fiona and Jo (contemporaries of Milton that I'm friendly with) on a long drive in my Renault 5, past Loch Lubnaig and to the swirling waters of the Devil's Cauldron. We walk along the forest paths and enjoy the heady fresh air and glorious sunshine. I am so glad that the exams are over; I seem to be drunk with relief. Arriving back on campus late in the evening, I collapse on my bed at last, in another dimension. *To sleep, perchance to dream …*

… there's a persistent knocking on my door, forcing me to uncomfortable, head-pounding wakefulness. It's nine in the morning, much too early to get up when I'm so exhausted. Martin is at my door, reminding me that I promised to drive him to the village of Kinbuck on Thursday morning, to collect his car from the cheap garage that we know. It's true; I did promise. Miserably I tell him that I'll meet him downstairs in a while.

The exam results are out just a few days later; I read them on the noticeboard. Fortunately, I am alone at this time. My performance has been appalling (whereas Janice has done very well). I have not secured a place on the Honours programme in Biochemistry. I will have to re-sit exams in the summer if I want to study Biochemistry. Or, the alternative is that I can switch to Chemistry as my Major. This isn't any easier, and I'm not any better at it, but the process of selection for Honours in Chemistry is deferred until the daunting Honours Qualifying exam – which isn't until early next year. I select this route, because it buys me another six months to prepare.

1982-83
Age: 20

This is Milton's final year, as he is two years above me. On the last day of the semester, with Fiona and Jo, we go on a pre-dawn climb up Dumyat, that wonderful mountain which can be seen from campus. It is cool, damp and silent. We reach the top and wait for the sun to rise.

There is a poem that comes to mind; I saw it taped on someone's wall.

> *And all that fills the hearts of friends,*
> *When first they feel, with secret pain,*
> *Their lives thenceforth have separate ends,*
> *And never can be one again ...*

The walk down is very subdued.

I have to drive back down to London this morning. Despite not having slept all night, I am confident that I will be fine, as I have spent many nights awake writing essays that were due in the next morning, or frantically studying for an exam that had finally come upon me. I know that I always get through the next day without a problem. I appreciate having the opportunity to make an early start on the 420-mile drive.

Within 50 miles, the Renault 5 breaks down. The engine runs, but has no power. The patrolman from the Automobile Association arrives and he determines that the vehicle cannot be repaired by the roadside. Under the terms of my membership, they must transport my vehicle and me to my destination, which is London. The AA operates a series of 'relay stations' up and down the country, and each tow truck only takes me to the next relay station, where I wait for typically two or three hours each time for the next tow truck. The journey takes all night and is particularly arduous, as I have not slept the night before either.

I am deposited at home in Hampton about twenty hours after leaving campus, in a state of psychotic exhaustion from lack of sleep.

I cannot afford the repair of the car. My father takes care of it. It was a blown head gasket.

I get a summer job in the same government building as last year (still bound by the Official Secrets Act) and spend the months shifting boxes of official forms and dispensing ballpoint pens and staples (I'm sorry, I can't tell you any more), and trying to save money. Robin, one of Milton's contemporaries, is moving down to London from Scotland and asks me if I would consider helping him move his stuff, in my car, in August. This sounds like fun to me, so I take time off work and we drive up to Scotland together.

We stay one night at his parents' house and then head back down; the Renault 5 is laden with all of Robin's worldly goods. The drive down is problematic; the engine is not running smoothly. In the afternoon, in the Manchester area, the engine totally self-destructs. There is no doubt about it. The clunking noise it makes when you turn the key speaks of broken metal.

The Automobile Association relays us to London overnight. It takes about sixteen hours. We arrive at my parents' house at about 6:30 a.m. and my father is just leaving for work. Irrationally and ungratefully, I attribute blame to him for buying this car in the first place and selling it to me. He is hurt and upset. I am exhausted and my attitude is shameful – self-centred and totally egocentric. He leaves for work to provide for us as usual, and I take Robin to his destination in my mother's car.

A week later, I borrow my mother's car to go to a car breaker's yard, where I have located a working Renault 5 engine that I can buy. I bring this engine home and attempt to find a garage that can replace the old engine in my car.

The truth is that I don't really have enough money to pay for this.

My father takes care of it, arranging both the engine transplant and paying the bill. People at a bus stop one weekend morning are treated to the sight of a blue Renault 5, with a spare engine in the back, towing a white Renault 5 to the garage.

Yellow

1983-84

Age: 21

I RETURN TO STIRLING after the summer vacation. As fifth reserve, I did not get to go to America on the Exchange Programme. Janice has left for San Diego, as expected. At least Ben is left behind.

The drive up to Scotland begins on a Saturday morning and is undertaken with much trepidation, the Renault 5 having just returned from its engine transplant. About 80 miles north of London, the red *engine temperature* light comes on. I pull over on the motorway and open the bonnet. The glass expansion bottle for the radiator cooling fluid has slipped loose of its flimsy mounting and smashed. It is not a major engine problem, *thank God*.

However, the AA is unable to perform a roadside repair. A new bottle is required from Renault and this cannot be procured on a Saturday afternoon, when the service departments are all closed. I know the drill now. I am relayed to Scotland. The first tow truck driver tells me something very interesting. He says that he is an independent contractor, who does work for both the Automobile Association and its competitor, the Royal Automobile Club. Because I am with the AA, he will only take me to the nearest AA relay station. If I had been with the RAC, he would have been asked by them to take me *all the way* to my destination, as the RAC does not operate any relay stations.

I arrive at AK Davidson Hall at about 6 a.m. on Sunday morning, after a twenty-two-hour relay.

I've started to wonder: '*Dear God, what have I done wrong? Why can't I just drive between London and Scotland without breaking down?*'

The repair itself is quick and simple. I am able to buy a new bottle from Renault in Stirling for three pounds and I fit it myself.

I take stock of my life this semester.

I'm in love with Janice, who is the perfect woman for me; I want to marry her one day. I ache for her, but she's in California and she's not in love with me. If she does eventually fall in love with me one day, and agrees to marry me, my parents are going to go ballistic, because she's not Pakistani and she's not Muslim. So that's another challenge altogether.

My friend Milton is not here anymore. I miss him a lot. It's quite inexplicable that a scruffy Northerner and I could have become such good friends.

My professional life is about the study of Chemistry, which I really don't enjoy. It is hard work and not at all interesting. It's even worse now that Janice is not beside me in the lab classes and lectures. I miss the smell of her hair. The Honours Qualifying exam is coming soon and if I don't focus and do the work necessary to pass it, I will not be able to stay for the fourth year and an Honours degree. I will be booted out at the end of this year with only a General degree. The consequences of this for my future career (whatever that is) are too horrible to contemplate.

I have a troubled relationship with a car that has cost me – but mostly my father – a lot of money. I shouldn't really have a car, because I can't afford the maintenance, but I can't imagine living without one. So I keep this car and drive it with much anxiety, always worried about whether it will break down again and cost a lot of money to repair (money I don't have).

1983-84
Age: 21

On top of all this, I am afraid that maybe I am not following the right religion. I have been deeply disturbed and humbled by the faith of the evangelical Christians who keep appearing in my life (a depth of faith that I don't have), and they sincerely believe that I am destined to spend eternity in Hell if I don't convert. Their absolute certainty really affects me. They tell me with a disquieting conviction that Jesus will be returning soon to lead a global war between Good and Evil, and I will be on the wrong side, which will result in me being cast into the pit of burning sulphur forever. This is rather worrying. (I hate the smell of sulphur.)

I consider the plus factors in my life. At least at university I can eat fish and chips whenever I want to.

There's a stranger in Milton's room. (Well, it's not Milton's room anymore, I suppose.) His name is Bill Wellman and he's from Chicago; he's come from the University of Illinois on the Exchange Programme. I begrudgingly acknowledge that he would be considered good-looking: slim, fit, blond hair, bright-blue eyes. We become acquaintances and then friends. So the accursed Exchange Programme took away Janice, but brought me Bill as token recompense.

His father is a General Motors car dealer. What did Bill get for his seventeenth birthday? A brand new Chevrolet, of course. I imagine with futile longing what it would be like to have a brand new car. Bill does not seem to be short of money. He mentions that his father wires him all the money that he could ever need. 'Wires money' – I don't even know what that means.

Bill has a wardrobe full of smart clothes. He shows me how to iron a shirt without using an iron. You hang the shirt up and hold a boiling kettle in front of it. I'm not sure I like this technique; it does seem to remove the creases, but it makes your room steamy, and what if you were to spill the water on your foot?

Magnus and Robin both left Stirling last year, but Robin still shows up on campus sometimes. He shocks me with some news: Magnus succeeded in converting him into a true Believer. Robin tells me what happened.

'I was in Magnus's room, and he was Bible-thumping as usual, and I was just ignoring it. Then suddenly he started praying out loud, asking that I be made to see the Light, and I felt this incredible cloud of Love descend over me and completely wrap itself around me. It was the most wonderful, warm, amazing feeling. It was real, it was absolute Love, it cocooned and protected me, and it was God.' Robin speaks in an earnest, intense, uplifted manner. I believe that he is telling the truth about what happened.

I am deeply disturbed and scared by this account. This sort of thing does not happen in Islam, which is rational belief based on evidence, common sense and absolute trust in a remote and aloof God. We don't do *feelings*. I am afraid that if such a thing happened to me, I would be torn apart by the conflict between the cold (sometimes brutal) logic of Islam, and the exhilarating emotional pull of Christianity. It's my angel-or-demon dilemma.

Robin troubles me now, and I avoid him as much as possible.

I continue to do Tenshinkan Karate two evenings a week, which I started last semester.

On this occasion, for some reason, I have reverted to the Beginners' group. I think this is because I have not yet purchased a white Karate suit, and am wearing a tracksuit, like all the other Beginners. Or is it because I have spotted a beautiful girl in the Beginners' group?

She is absolutely gorgeous; quite possibly the most beautiful woman that has ever walked the grounds of this

1983-84
Age: 21

University. She is of medium height, and very slim, with medium-length wavy brown hair. Her eyes are sparkling and she exudes vivaciousness. The word 'vivacious' was specifically invented for this girl, I believe. There is something more in her eyes and face, and the way that she conducts herself; she has intellect and class and *je ne sais quoi*.

I am not the only male in the group who notices her. It is obvious that she is new, a first-year, because we have never seen her before. Of course, as males do, we assume that somehow looking cool, aloof and macho will bring about the desired result. As for actually trying to talk to her, that is out of the question. *Communication?* We don't do that!

Anyway, Beginners' Karate is mostly about strenuous and painful exercise routines, and any conversation is forbidden once the big guy has initiated the session. He is a tall, fit, young Scotsman, exuding all the authority and confidence that a black belt in Karate gives you. We do the usual warm-up exercises, all trying not to be the wimpy one who fails in some way.

And then the unbelievable happens. The instructor orders, 'Get into pairs and line up by the wall.'

My first thought is, '*How can I pair up with that beautiful girl?*' I envy the lucky man that will have that privilege.

I casually eye the girl, who is a few feet away, whilst nonchalantly attempting to team up with someone. For some reason, I am unable to catch anyone's eye, mainly because I am trying not to. The number of single individuals rapidly diminishes, as the pairs slip away towards the wall. I cannot believe what is happening. Suddenly, there is just the girl and me left – so we have to pair up. I make a sort of '*Oh well!*' shrug of the shoulders. One thing needs to be clearly understood by the girl: I have not *deliberately* sought to partner with her; it has just happened. It was completely random. The idea that I might deliberately want to meet her is too embarrassing; who am I to reckon my chances with such a supermodel?

Not a smile cracks my face, nor does a quiet and cheerful 'Hello' slip past my lips. I could look her in the eyes with my own eyes sparkling and friendly, perhaps flirtatious, but I do not. I am a complete idiot. I have no idea how to relate to her or establish communication. *Men are so stupid!*

The exercise that he wants us to do involves stretching our legs outwards and upwards, taking turns to support each other's outstretched foot in our hands. My first encounter with the most beautiful girl on campus is thus extremely intimate. Frankly, whilst there's nothing wrong with my feet, they are not the first part of me that I want a potential girlfriend to examine in detail. Fortunately, I believe that mine are reasonably fresh and the toenails are trimmed and clean, as usual.

However, during this completely surreal exercise, when I am taking turns to stretch and grunt and support feet, with this astonishingly beautiful girl, I cannot bear to maintain eye contact with her, and not one word comes out of my mouth. I know that we are not supposed to talk during Karate, but I could whisper something, anything, to establish communication; maybe, '*This is harder than it looks* ...' At this point, she does not even know for sure that I speak English.

Men are stupid and I am particularly stupid.

The Karate lesson ends and I have said not one word to the most beautiful girl on campus. The girl chooses not to continue with Karate; I never see her at a session again.

I am in the kitchen of our corridor one evening, making beans on toast, when Bill Wellman comes in and comments on how odd this is.

'What do you mean?'

'I mean pouring beans *on top of* toast.'

'But this is standard British gastronomy – we put everything on toast: beans on toast, eggs on toast, sardines on toast, spaghetti on toast …'

Bill comments that this sophisticated cuisine is completely alien to him, and suddenly something dawns on me. The apparently obstructive waitress in Florida wasn't racist at all – she simply had no concept of 'scrambled eggs *on* toast'. That was a cultural chasm between us. I relate the incident to Bill, and he immediately leaps to the waitress's defence.

How bizarre! The Americans can put men on the moon, but they have no idea about the delights of putting all kinds of food *on* toast.

Janice and I exchange letters every couple of weeks. In one epistle, she breaks some surprising news; she is going out with someone – a guy called Bill. He is also a student at San Diego and he has a Toyota Corolla, which he lets her borrow.

Well, at least she's broken up with Ben. *No, wait.* Wouldn't I prefer it if she was still going out with Ben, but thousands of miles apart from him, than being with someone she can see every day? That's much worse, from my perspective, especially as I'm not there, enjoying the sun and blue sky and ocean of California. I remember Florida so well and I'm sure California must be similar – the joyful, heady exhilaration of America. This yearning – combined with my unbearable longing for Janice – reminds me how miserable and unfulfilled my life is.

Okay, here's another problem. In university, I'm not doing as well as I used to, because I haven't been making the required effort. I was lulled into a sense of complacency by my earlier, easy success. Everyone else has been working harder, as the work gets more difficult, but I have not ramped up my effort, so I am plunging into mediocrity.

1983-84
Age: 21

Dr Porter never fails to remind me of his most important advice: studying for exams is the only priority.

Also, I'm spending too much time in the wrong part of the library, reading about Theology and especially the Sufis, who are a mysterious branch of Islam ('sect' is not the right word, as they seem to transcend being Sunni or Shia). They view and describe God in ways that are not consistent with mainstream Islam, such as the '*Beloved*' and so on. This is strange, but fascinating, thought-provoking and enjoyable.

One Sufi text states that there are many paths to God, and all are valid, but most of the adherents of these paths are too busy bickering with each other about who is right, and this is a complete waste of energy and focus. I'm not sure what this actually means. Surely there is only one *true* path, but God doesn't mind if people follow other paths, as long as their intentions and deeds are good?

I'm jealous of people who are allowed to study this for their degrees (it never occurs to me that I could have done the same), but surely this won't build a secure future and career for them. I have to study Chemistry, a sensible subject, but I hate it. It really is *work* for me.

I'm in a campus phone booth one day, calling home. That little shit who stole my oil cap is in the next booth. Now that I think about it, I haven't noticed his Renault 5 on campus this year. The reason becomes apparent from his phone conversation, which I partly overhear. He had to scrap his Renault 5 in the summer; he could no longer afford to keep it running. He had replaced it with a motorbike … and this has just been stolen.

Thank you God! Not only for exacting vengeance on my behalf, but also for the additional favour of letting me find out about it.

I tell an Indian friend about this incident, during a discussion we are having – it surely proves that there is one God who is in charge of everything.

1983-84
Age: 21   234

He says, calmly and with a quiet assurance, 'This is an example of Karma at work.'

I don't know what that means.

An acquaintance of mine has joined Amnesty International. He wants me to join, but this presents a dilemma for me. Amnesty International does a lot of good work, especially in God-forsaken, corrupt countries where there is no concern for justice. But it also opposes the death penalty, and this is the issue I have with it. I can understand that Amnesty International believes in compassion and humanity for all human beings. But what about those horrible IRA terrorists who have been bombing trains and public places in England for as long as I can remember? I don't see how we are going to make the world a better place without being able to execute bad people.

At my parents' home in the mid-semester vacation, I read an interesting letter from Auden's mother in the local newspaper. She is berating the Cambridge Christian Fellowship and how they brainwash young students and alienate them from their families. I remember Auden (who is now at Cambridge University) telling me in school that his parents were atheists. She is expressing a mother's pain at losing her son; I feel for her. I hate Auden, though; he and I must be theological enemies forever. He will never see his precious Rapture, but what a shock he will get on the Day of Judgment, when he finds that he is wrong and I am right. *(I hope.)*

Back at Stirling, Bill Wellman has a favour to ask. A friend of his is coming to visit the UK, and Bill is going to hire a car for the two of them to use for a trip this weekend. But Bill has never driven in Britain before (on the wrong side of the road) and he has never driven a manual transmission car, a 'stick shift' as he calls it. Bill would like me to come with him to collect the car and show him how to drive.

We take the train to Glasgow and make our way to Hertz Car Rental, where a brand new Mini Metro is waiting for us. It has 17 miles on the clock and the interior smells like Paradise. Bill would like me to drive the car out of the city, and then let him take over. This is fantastic; I have never driven a brand new car before and I relish the experience.

Once we are out of town, on the A-road to Stirling, Bill and I switch places. He struggles with the gear box, torturing the brand new car, which protests with metallic shrieks of agony. As we approach a roundabout, Bill is looking down at the gear lever, fighting with it awkwardly. Bill has never driven on a roundabout in his life (he calls it a 'traffic circle'). I am looking with horror at the shocked driver who slams on his brakes as the (to all intents and purposes) driverless Mini Metro drifts onto the roundabout into his path. Today I nearly experienced Paradise in more ways than one.

It is a Saturday morning and we have an all-day Karate training session, prior to our yellow belt exam at the end of the afternoon. It is an extremely arduous day. We have a rest break and I go next door to the Sports Union bar to eat something. I am wearing my Karate outfit (with only a Beginner's white belt).

The most beautiful girl on campus is serving behind the bar. Apparently, she has taken a part-time job at the Sports Union. *She is beautiful.* I ask her for a Mars bar and a Coke. She gives me a Mars bar and a Coke. She tells me the price. I give her some money. She gives me the change and I thank her.

Well, at last I have spoken with her, but that is the full extent of the communication. I could have said something, anything, some pleasantry to start a dialogue, but I was too embarrassed and afraid. *Idiot, idiot, idiot.*

I pass the Karate exam today, although I was very afraid that I would not, so I *have* achieved something.

Bill Wellman is pretty damn mad about something. He's been getting B-grades for coursework and mid-semester tests, and it looks like he'll get B as the final grade for some of his course units at the end of semester. The trouble is that, before he came to the UK, his Grade Point Average was a perfect 4.0; he had never failed to get an A for every course. Now his flawless score has been reduced to a '3 something'.

I explain that at Stirling, and in British universities in general, a B is considered a very good grade; it is extremely difficult to get an A. In fact, I can hardly think of anyone who has had an A in any subject, in any semester.

This is not enough to ease his pain; his perfect GPA[12] has been ruined. Who knows what this will do to his career?

My last-minute attitude to exams and lack of real effort finally have an impact. I am very worried about the Honours Qualifying exam, which will take place in the January vacation, just before the start of the Spring semester. I realise that this is going to be a hugely challenging exam, covering all the work that we have done so far, and I am not prepared at all. I feel as if much of the material has passed by me in the last five semesters without me even thinking about it.

It's November now and the Honours Qualifying exam is only seven weeks away. I recognise how I feel: it's the same way I felt as the A-levels approached. There's that sense of guilt and inadequacy and paralysis and impending doom.

A very special episode of *Doctor Who* is aired one Friday evening, called 'The Five Doctors'. The television rooms in all the halls of residence are packed for this. Here again I see Sarah Jane Smith (I love her; her accent doesn't matter), the Brigadier, daleks, cybermen, adventures unimagined. We all watch, riveted; it's a poignant journey through our childhoods. When it's over, I walk out into the darkness and I feel miserable. Whatever happened to the joys and dreams of childhood? My life is now about Chemistry, which I don't enjoy, and there's a constant emptiness, a longing for something I don't have. But I know that I really have to get my act together; if I fail the Honours Qualifying, it will be a disaster for me. I go into a panic and I decide to spend the entire Christmas vacation on campus, cramming; making up for my earlier guilty ease.

During this vacation period, most of the halls of residence close down and those few students who are staying are consolidated into Andrew Stewart Hall. I seem to be the only UK student here; the others are all overseas students who can't afford to fly home to their distant countries for the holiday season. They think that I must be one of them, but I'm not; *I'm British*.

This is a particularly brutal Scottish winter. About two feet of snow lies on the ground and the loch is frozen solid. In the dark, the illuminated windows of campus make it look like a futuristic base on some hostile alien moon. My white Renault 5 is lost in the snow. I have to fight my way to get inside it. I run the engine just to keep the battery charged, but there is no question of driving it anywhere.

Despite making this sacrifice of staying on campus over Christmas to focus on exam preparation, it seems to be the last thing on my mind. The amount of time that I spend genuinely studying each day is pitiful. I busy myself with other priorities: buying groceries, preparing meals, doing laundry, going for walks to get fresh air. The last thing that I want to do is study Chemistry.

In theory, there is enough time to cover all the material, but the days and weeks slip by and I do only a fraction of what is required.

My classmates return to campus for the Honours Qualifying and it is almost a relief to sit the exams, so that I don't have to study for them anymore. Some of the exam questions are impossible for me, but some are fine. In my mind I conduct endless analysis of my performance and I realise that it will be very, very close.

The day of the exam results, I can see the class standing around the noticeboard, as I approach down the long corridor of the Chemistry Department. The results are there and they've already read them. I don't look at anyone as I go straight to the board to scrutinise the white piece of paper pinned to it.

I have failed the exam, just barely. The required pass mark for the Honours Qualifying is a B- grade, and I have achieved a B/C.

This means that I must leave the university at the end of next semester, with a three-year General degree, instead of a four-year Honours degree.

I am quite shocked. *How could God let this happen?* What is a person of my inherent talent and intellect supposed to do without a proper degree? I have no clue. My life is in ruins (again).

The worst thing is that when Janice returns from America and starts the fourth year, I won't be here. I was counting on having the fourth year for her to fall in love with me.

This weighs on me heavily, like not getting into medical school, and not getting selected for the American Exchange Programme. I am getting used to reading bad news on noticeboards.

1983-84
Age: 21

This evening, the Chemistry class is meeting at the Settle Inn, the oldest pub in Stirling. I decide to go along; I have nothing else to do. My Renault starts up, but in the sub-zero temperature its clutch plates are frozen and it won't get into gear. I abandon the car and trudge into town.

At the inn, the class is gathered around Dr Porter. He says to me, 'I told you so,' only briefly, before revealing my last-chance strategy. I can *still* do an Honours degree, but it will be called a GRSC, which is administered by the Royal Society of Chemistry, and it will mean spending the fourth year at another college (as Stirling University does not offer a GRSC). The Royal Society of Chemistry will have to approve my General degree from Stirling University in order to give me exemption from Part One of the GRSC, and allow me to proceed with Part Two, at one of the colleges that offers this. *Get it?*

I get it. I am overjoyed that there is another chance, but I also know that this is my academic *last chance*. I promise myself that I am finally going to follow Dr Porter's advice and work hard for exams, *well before* the exams.

This semester is poignant, because it is my last. All of my friends will be here next year, Janice will be back from America, and I will be gone, exiled. It's a personal disaster, quite apart from the academic and career implications.

I'm sitting in my room one afternoon, cross-legged on the bed, reading '*How To Make Love To A Woman*' by Michael Morgenstern – a book which caught my eye in the campus bookshop. (When I bought it, I also purchased a birthday card so that the young woman behind the counter would assume it was a present for someone else.) Beethoven's *Pastoral* symphony is playing on the Sanyo stereo and the afternoon sun is generously illuminating the leaves of my now massive Swiss Cheese plant. (Since I bought it last semester, it has grown enormously, due to the healthy stimulation provided by my tasteful music.) A beautiful handmade Pakistani carpet is spread over my floor; visitors are always impressed by it. I have created such a refined and elegant environment for myself, and now I have only a few weeks left to enjoy it – thanks to my laziness and foolish ineptitude.

There's a knock on the door and I call 'Come in!', simultaneously putting the book face down on the bed.

A young man in jeans and a black-leather jacket steps into my room. *Bloody hell! It's Ben!*

Probably sensing my speechless shock, he says politely that he just needs a moment of my time. I stutter 'Sure' and motion him to sit down on the bean bag.

I have to concentrate very hard, because of his strong Scottish accent and manner of speech. He asks me if Janice has any mid-term exams coming up, or anything of similar academic importance. 'I'm wanting to break it off with her and I don't want to upset her at the wrong time.'

Break it off with her? Haven't they broken up already? But … 'She's going out with someone.' *Oops. Did I just say that out loud?*

'She's going out with someone?' Ben repeats back. He seems surprised and inexplicably pleased. 'Oh, that's okay, then! She won't mind and it won't upset her. Thanks. See ya.'

In a moment he is gone, leaving me stunned and bewildered. How could he want to break up with Janice? How could he not appreciate her stunning beauty, her intellect, her vivaciousness, her elegance? Even though she's thousands of miles away, I would give anything to be 'going out' with her. It doesn't make any sense.

I understand later, when I see him around AKD a lot, visiting another girl. I reflect wistfully that both Ben and Janice are of 'the beautiful people'. They get a choice of candidates to go out with. As for me, I don't get any.

I wonder what Martin is doing. Perhaps he'd like a game of golf?

Bill Wellman and I reflect on the academic year which is now drawing to a close, his time on exchange from the University of Illinois. He tells me that, during the year, he went to bed with three different girls on campus. I am stunned; *how did this happen?* Well, each time the girl met him somewhere, he chatted with her, she seemed to like him, invited him back to her room for coffee and then, instead of putting the kettle on, she proceeded to rip his clothes off.

'What about … you know … protection?'

'Oh, that was never a problem. I always carry a rubber in my wallet. Don't you?'

I am taken aback by all of this. It seems that, just as I find American girls to be exotic, British girls find American men to be exotic. Bill has seen more action in two semesters than I could ever dream of; *bastard!* It's true what they say about the trouble with Americans on campus; they are overpaid, oversexed and over here.

I leave Stirling University at the end of this semester, packing all of my possessions into the Renault 5 and hoping that I will one day return for a PhD (because Janice mentioned once that she is interested in doing a PhD at Stirling). To make this possible, I have to excel in this last-chance opportunity.

It's the summer vacation and I sell my Renault 5. Putting together all the money I have and with the help of a cash advance from my Barclaycard, I buy an Alfa Romeo Alfasud, an Italian two-door sports car which is pale orange in colour and has a unique driving style. To help pay for it, I get a job selling advertising.

I watch a documentary on that new Channel Four, *The First Christian*, written and presented by Karen Armstrong. It is about the life of Paul, author of much of the New

Testament. Paul is not a popular figure in Islam, as it is considered that he is responsible for much of the deification of Jesus, taking the events of Jesus' life and interpreting them in the framework of the old redemption-by-blood-sacrifice myth. The remarkable thing is, this appears to be close to what Karen Armstrong is saying: Jesus didn't create Christianity, Paul did. Jesus' message was simple; Paul created a complex and mysterious theology out of it, weaving it into his existing beliefs.

I am amazed. It seems that Western scholars think exactly as we Muslims are supposed to believe. If I had known this stuff before, the Christians could never have disturbed me so. How could they try to convert me with a clear conscience; didn't they know any of this about Paul and the history of Christianity? Perhaps they needed to convert me, to reinforce their own shaky faith.

When I start this job, although it is a 'permanent' position, to me it is just something that I will do temporarily until the Royal Society of Chemistry has approved my first degree from Stirling as being adequate to admit me to their GRSC programme.

What happens subsequently is that I am seduced by the working life. I enjoy putting on a jacket and tie, driving my Alfa Romeo and earning £90 per week, which, after my student grant, is a very liberating flow of money. I begin to lose interest in going back to college. When the first letter comes from the Royal Society of Chemistry, stating that they do not recognise a General degree from Stirling as conferring exemption from Part I of their GRSC course, a part of me is secretly excited. *Perhaps I don't need to worry about studying and exams ever again.*

But still, I go through the agreed motions of forwarding this letter to the Chemistry Department at Stirling, who have promised to negotiate with the RSC on my behalf.

1983-84
Age: 21   243

Several weeks have passed since that first letter and I am now thoroughly disillusioned by this job of phoning businesses and trying to sell them an advertisement (display or small print) in the *London and Local Advertiser*. Not only is it very difficult to cold-call someone, get their attention and convince them that placing an advert with this publication will greatly increase their business turnover, but I have also received feedback from some of my customers, those who *have* placed adverts, that these resulted in *no response whatsoever*.

This leaves me feeling somewhat disillusioned and guilty. I just can't sell an advertisement to someone – possibly someone struggling to make ends meet in a small business in a difficult economic climate – if I believe (as I do) that the advert will be of no benefit to them whatsoever. The *London and Local Advertiser* is a ridiculous publication; a jumbled assortment of advertising without any particular market niche. But we have been trained in techniques of persuasion and equipped with a virtual library of counter-arguments.

Now, getting that approval from the Royal Society of Chemistry and returning to college is my only hope.

Not only that; I am determined – quite irrationally and without any prior success on which to base this plan – that I am going to get no less than a First Class degree and return to Stirling for a PhD. I envision this in my mind, even though I have never succeeded like this in the past. It's a fantasy. (But it's the only way to be with Janice, if she returns to Stirling for a PhD.) My academic career is a sorry tale of underachievement due to laziness, not to mention the fact that I have been doggedly following a Science path, when all of my natural talent, success and enjoyment have been in the Arts subjects.

It is sad how we constrain ourselves in chains and boundaries of our own making. I could have studied 'Politics, Philosophy and Economics', really enjoyed these

1983-84
Age: 21

subjects and been very successful. (I've never had an interesting conversation with anyone about Chemistry.)

Today, it is a horrendously hot July day, one of those for which London is not equipped. The tie around my neck is choking me and I am a prisoner of this desk and telephone. I am doing nothing that I believe in and I am waiting for that approval from the Royal Society of Chemistry.

Please God, give me another chance.

I have a Yellow Pages on my desk. I use it to select businesses to cold-call, to convince them that my publication can somehow be more effective than this legendary medium. The window is wide open and a welcome gust of light breeze comes through and blows across the pages of the yellow holy book.

The Yellow Pages falls open on a certain page and my eyes instantly lock on an entry: *Royal Society of Chemistry.*

Without a moment's hesitation, I grab the phone and dial the number. On being greeted, I ask for the Membership department. A woman answers.

As I introduce myself, she says, 'Oh yes?' with immediate recognition in her voice. I pose my question and she answers it.

'It's funny you should ring right now. I'm right *this moment* in the middle of typing a letter to you. Yes, the answer is "yes". We've had a letter from Stirling and we accept your qualification for the GRSC.'

I thank her profusely and, when I hang up, I am a transformed, uplifted individual. I am going to quit this job and return to college to do that degree, I *am* going to get a First and I *am* going to return to Stirling to do a PhD. I feel a burden lifted from me and a sense of enormous excitement.

1983-84
Age: 21

And yes, the significance of the gust of wind and the Yellow Pages at that moment in time is not lost on me. It is a synchronicity for which I will be eternally grateful.

Janice returns from America. I call her at home and my heart leaps when I hear her voice. We talk on the phone for an hour. I've arranged to do four weeks of paid Chemistry research work at Stirling before I start at my new college, and Janice suggests that I stop at her house on the way to Scotland. *I have dreamed of this.*

It's a glorious, hot, sunny August day when I drive the Alfa Romeo up the M1 motorway towards Leicestershire and the ancient town of Melton Mowbray, around the old marketplace and past the sign for *Ye Olde Pork Pie Shoppe*, to Janice's house on top of the hill, as I have often imagined doing. It's a dream house, detached with a *double* garage. She is looking radiant, but I notice that a year in America has broadened her noticeably (not just her mind). We talk for a couple of hours in her house, and then I say goodbye to her again and head off to Stirling. My faith is restored. It will all work out one day.

Stoke

1984-85
Age: 22

I START THE GRSC at North Staffordshire Polytechnic, in Stoke-on-Trent – an industrial town which is a far cry from the beauty of Stirling.

On the drive there, I stop my Alfa Romeo at a motorway service station. There is a uniformed representative of the Royal Automobile Club, selling membership. I remember that the RAC does not operate any relay stations; the tow truck that first picks you up is the one that takes you *all the way* to your destination, regardless of how far away that is. I buy the membership immediately. I must be his easiest sale ever.

In Stoke, I am placed in an elegant old house – in a cul-de-sac called The Villas – which has been converted into a hall of residence, with about sixteen rooms in it, and five bathrooms. Each of the rooms is unique. Mine is L-shaped, with ornate and aged furniture. Villa Hall is nothing like AKD, but it has a certain charm and I enjoy it. The important thing is that I must sit regularly at my desk for many hours studying, not making excuses. I have to walk about a mile to college every day, and I quite enjoy this morning exercise, watching the town wake up and feeling the seasons change.

This time at college, I am really determined. I constantly *visualise* getting a First and returning to my beloved Stirling to do a PhD. Dr Porter himself had done a GRSC and had got a First. He is my role model, my mentor. It's a very good thing that we met on top of the mountain; he took an interest in encouraging me after that. We exchange letters and he reiterates that advice which he first gave me on top of Dumyat; he really motivates me and I follow his advice at last. (If only I had done so at Stirling, this would not have happened.) I am going to prove to the world that I *am* capable (more than my dismal prior record indicates). I know that this is my last chance and I am a little afraid.

This year in Stoke is an interesting experience, but for once in my life, I actually execute the plan. I study hard and prepare for the final exams from the very beginning. I study and practise and study and practise. I also jog at night around Stoke-on-Trent and I play squash occasionally at the college, with a couple of classmates. It is a very holistic year.

I am afraid in case God decides that I don't deserve a First and will sabotage the exams for me in some way, but I press on.

In October, Indira Gandhi, the Prime Minister of India, is assassinated by her own trusted Sikh bodyguards. They were angry about the attack that she had authorised on their Golden Temple in Amritsar, to flush out some militant Sikh separatists who had been holed up in there.

India explodes into Hindu riots against Sikhs. Thousands of Sikhs are killed, often being burned alive. I feel sorry for the Sikhs; I'm relieved that it wasn't Muslims who killed her.

I am particularly annoyed by one of the residents in my hall, an older student named Brian. He is in his late twenties and has returned to education after a long spell working in some dead-end job. Brian is of the opinion that the thirty pounds deposit we all had to pay as residents of Villa Hall should be considered as 'money spent'. In other words, we should *not* bother to maintain the hall in good condition or to refrain from reckless and destructive activities. We should just have a good time and let Villa Hall suffer whatever damage occurs in the process.

I am thinking about this one Friday afternoon as I'm doing my laundry. I am furious at Brian's attitude. Thirty pounds is a lot of money. How dare he decide that we should consider it 'spent', just so that he can behave as irresponsibly as he wants to? *How dare he be so selfish?* I am completely alone and, thinking about this, get quite angry. My pent-up emotion is vented as I cry out: 'Death to Brian!'

On Monday morning, I meet my friend Alan at classes as usual, and ask him about his weekend. He says that it was terrible. His best friend back home in Sheffield, whom he's often mentioned to me, was killed in a car accident at the weekend. His friend … *Brian.*

This is just a coincidence. There is no other explanation. A dark, unspeakable guilt overcomes me and I never discuss this 'coincidence' with anyone. Never!

In December, after my first term ends at Stoke, I arrange to pay a visit to Stirling University for a couple of weeks (the Stirling semester ends much closer to Christmas). There is a bedroom in one of the halls which someone allows me to use; the official occupant actually lives with his girlfriend in another room.

I drive up with great excitement; it is a joy to cross the border into Scotland, especially in an Alfa Romeo. I arrive on campus; it is dark, cold and beautiful as always. Snow is on the ground and Christmas is in the air. I love this place.

I surprise Janice in the car park; she is walking back from a lab session, towards the chalet where she now lives. She is beautiful; she has a new hairstyle, but her red hair is as dazzling as ever. We share a hug.

This is an interesting time. Janice and I talk a lot over the next few days; more than we have ever done. I tell her honestly about my problems with the Renault 5. I had kept all this from her previously, because it would reveal signs of failure – the *inferiority* of having a car old enough to suffer breakdowns. I tell her about my ungrateful argument with my father about the car, and how bad I feel about it. I am no longer trying to be 'Mr Cool'; instead I talk openly and honestly about my concerns, experiences and emotions. She listens intently and is sympathetic.

We go for a walk in the hill forest; both the forest and Janice are beautiful to me, each in their own way. She even agrees to have dinner with me.

The next evening, we go to Stirling's best Indian restaurant, *Qismat*. We talk and talk, until there's hardly any other customers left. I hear the waiter saying of us, in Urdu, 'They've just ordered *another* cup of coffee.' When the only other remaining couple get up to go, at around 11 p.m., we decide that we must go too.

We drive back to campus in my Alfa Romeo and end up in her room. She seems to be laughing at all my jokes. I seem to be making jokes effortlessly. I am sitting next to her on the bed, we are physically close, my hand makes it up her arm to her cheek.

I say, 'May I kiss you?'

She responds, 'You don't need to ask' and slips into my arms easily, naturally.

We spend a few minutes embracing and kissing. (It's pleasurable, but it's not quite as I imagined; it seems to lack the electricity I thought there'd be.) Finally, she tells me that I must go and manhandles me gently towards the door.

I am utterly elated as I walk away from my first sexual experience (involving someone else). It has finally happened. I always knew it would. Janice is my girlfriend. My girlfriend is Janice. She will marry me one day. *Thank you, God.* I walk around campus in the dark, in a daze.

1984-85
Age: 22

Will we be making love soon? I expect so. That's not really allowed, but I don't think that God will mind, as we will be getting married. I stand on the bridge over the loch, staring vaguely into the pure, cold darkness of the water mingled with the night, and I pray to God to forgive us if Janice and I make love, because we will get married and it won't be just casual sex. *'Qismat': it means 'destiny'.* Eventually, I return to my borrowed room and sleep a busy sleep, dreaming of a smiling Janice and delightful anticipation and niggling doubts and upset parents.

The next morning, I go to see Janice, with the intention of planning our day together. It doesn't go quite as I expected.

She is utterly cold, a veritable ice princess. It was just a bit of fun. Nothing has changed. She is *not* my girlfriend, we do *not* have a 'relationship'. (Ever since she's come back from California, she's been sounding like *Cosmo* magazine.) 'Why must you always be so serious?' she berates me.

I try to hide my shock and disappointment, to salvage some self-esteem, but it's a lost cause. I stumble back outside the chalet and walk across the car park; there is a pain in my chest and it is snowing heavily. I am without purpose; I don't know where to go or what to do.

In one of the campus shops, a pop song is playing on the radio ... something about 'Last Christmas' ... Apparently, the singer gave his heart to his beloved, only for her to dump him the following day. I know exactly how he feels.

In a state of utter misery, I end up driving to Edinburgh and visiting Milton, who lives there now. We stay up half the night, talking. His old rented flat – with its very high ceilings – is freezing, because it doesn't have proper central heating. I have a severe throat infection, which is killing me, and I sip neat Scotch whisky for medicinal purposes. I bring Milton up to date with the latest in my Janice saga. It's strange how things turn out.

1984-85
Age: 22

It's a very grey Christmas holiday, but I can't afford the luxury of moping around in self-pity, not this time. It's my academic last chance.

Back at Stoke, I'm sitting with Alan in the student cafeteria one freezing January morning. It's actually still vacation time, but we are both at college to study and work on our degree dissertations. There are hardly any students about. A couple of girls walk in, dressed warmly in jackets, gloves, scarves and boots. They walk around the cafeteria as if they are not familiar with it. One is blonde, but it is the brunette who catches my eye. She is absolutely beautiful; she has curly dark-brown hair, is of medium height and has a fabulous figure. Her manner is energetic and she is utterly vivacious.

I'm talking to Alan, but I'm also discreetly eyeing the two girls as they walk past us. Suddenly, the beautiful brunette breaks through my outer shell and surprises me by asking, 'Excuse me. Weren't you at Stirling University?' Her accent seems Northern.

I look at her in shock and stammer that I was. There *is* something familiar about her. She tells me that she was at Stirling as well, and she finds me familiar. Her name is Susan Tebbitt. We exchange notes and determine that we both lived in AK Davidson Hall, although she was a couple of years above me. She is doing a business course at a nearby college, and she and her friend have just stumbled into our cafeteria while on a long walk.

She asks me what I'm doing in this college, and I mumble something about further studies. I am too ashamed to let her know that I did only a General degree at Stirling, not an Honours degree. There is so much joy and friendliness in her but, inadvertently, I come across as dismissive and aloof, because of this reluctance to talk about my degree.

1984-85
Age: 22

252

The two of them walk away towards the door. For a moment I think about going out on a limb, asking Susan if maybe she'd like to meet for coffee one day, to talk about old times at Stirling University. But I'm reluctant and afraid: she *is* beautiful, but she is not right for me; I have to study for my First; I have to return to Stirling; I'm in love with Janice, and she will surely return to Stirling for a PhD too; she will marry me one day. I think of all the reasons why I shouldn't ask to meet Susan again, and through the door she disappears ...

I experience a strange phenomenon that occurs from time to time. I seem to wake up in the middle of the night to find myself paralysed. I know that I'm lying here, but I can't move. This paralysis is accompanied by an intense high-pitched noise and a perception of a brilliant white light. I'm not sure where the light is; it's not illuminating the room. The strange noise reaches a peak and then stops. The light disappears and I return to normal. I don't feel threatened by this, but I have no explanation. This happens perhaps once a month. I know it must be something to do with that other dimension which I don't understand, and which hasn't gone away, although I'm trying to avoid thinking about it.

I purchase a stack of cheap A4 paper about six inches thick and use it constantly to practise exam questions and to write down what I have memorised, again and again. This is exactly how Dr Porter told me to study, on the mountain, years ago. It is a departure from my previous technique of merely reading my notes once or twice (or not at all). The old exam papers scare me into studying even harder.

The exams approach. I have not wavered from my intent. I have studied and practised hard. Previously in life, I have not focused, even when sitting in the exam room. I would sometimes take it too easy and fail to complete an exam paper, thinking that the examiner would see that I ran out of time and would give me a break. *How idiotic!*

This time I practise so much that I can practically take the exams in my sleep.

Each day of the actual exams, I remain focused, upbeat and joyful. I walk to college in my aviator sunglasses, singing Joni Mitchell's *'Free Man in Paris'* to myself. I face the exams knowing that I have done *everything* that I possibly can. So, whatever happens, happens. *Que será, será.*

I just hope that God is okay with this and will allow me to get a First. I complete the last exam and head out into the beautiful June sunshine, confident that this time I have done my best.

A few weeks later I get the news, when I telephone the Head of the Chemistry Department on the crucial day. I ask Professor Tebby about my degree result, there is an agonising pause, and then he tells me about my performance. I *do* get a First, I come first in my graduating class and I also win the Royal Society of Chemistry prize. *I did it!* It was an impossible dream, but I did it. I can't believe it.

Thank you, God.

Janice gets a Lower Second Class degree in Biochemistry; there is no prospect of her doing a PhD. She gets a graduate trainee job at a chocolate bar factory in Newcastle (I think it's in Quality Control or something) and buys a flat there.

I attend the ceremony of my school friend Katharine's wedding to William, a guy she met at University. Andrea is there; she looks nice. We exchange small talk. I try to be cool and self-assured.

I'm in occasional contact with friends from Hampton School. There's news of Pyler. He had left school without studying in the Sixth Form and so did not attend college. Apparently, he joined the police. *That's reassuring.* I hope he only kicks bad people.

THE PERFECT GENTLEMAN

Warm

1985-86
Age: 23

I RETURN TO STIRLING UNIVERSITY as a postgraduate student, starting a PhD in Chemistry. It is my dream come true. I left as a failure and return as a brilliant academic success.

I am now better equipped than ever to attract a girlfriend. I am a postgraduate; I have a better room, an Alfa Romeo and my own microwave oven (possibly the only privately owned microwave on campus); I know my way around; I have a laboratory which doubles as an office; I don't have exams or lectures, so my time is completely flexible. I wander around campus, looking for that elusive person to drop into my life.

There are many American girls on campus, thanks not only to the Exchange Programme, but also because Americans are coming to Stirling University directly, without involving the Programme. Apparently they have discovered that, even allowing for the travel costs, it is cheaper than attending some of their own universities (and British universities are very happy to accept their money). They can use Stirling, with its American system of semesters and course units, to obtain some of the credits they need for their own degrees.

I have always found American girls in general to be very attractive and intriguing (although *Charlie's Angels* may have set my expectations rather high). I am willing to accept their broad collection of accents as 'exotic', whereas I struggle to be attracted by the wide range of regional accents on offer in Britain. The great thing about American girls is that they are strangers in a strange land; they don't know anyone to begin with, so it is relatively easy to engage them in conversation and mention a forthcoming drive in the countryside. 'Would you like to come?'

A couple of times I am successful in persuading American girls to come on a drive with me to Loch Lubnaig and the surrounding areas. But it doesn't go quite as I planned.

They always want to ask me questions about myself, my national origin, where does my name come from, and so on. I assume that if I talk about being a Muslim from Pakistan, they will not be interested in me. They will associate me with the taking of American Embassy hostages in Tehran in 1979 (even though it was Shias who did that).

My inner thoughts always follow a different track.

'Look, darling, just appreciate the scenery [Scotland always delivers] *and stop being so interested in my family history. This car is an Alfa Romeo. Just relax and try to be attracted to me ...'*

Because of this difference in expectations, I always put up a communication barrier. Their highly advanced female radar always detects this barrier, and so no relationship ever develops.

The BBC series *Edge of Darkness* is aired, a drama in six parts. I think that it is the best television drama series ever made. I watch each episode, riveted; the television room is always packed for this. It is a dark and complex tapestry about the military-industrial complex, fear-driven corrupt government, nuclear waste and global environmentalism. *But a democratically elected government built on modern Western values wouldn't lie to its own people, would it? What if they thought they were acting for the greatest good? Would that justify telling lies?*

There is a theme introduced of 'Gaia' – the concept that the Earth is somehow alive and will protect herself and life will endure, even if Man wipes himself out. Darius Jedburgh, the rogue CIA agent, doesn't think much of Gaia: 'People who put trees and flowers before people, they're beyond reasoning with. You can never appeal to their humanity, because they don't believe in humanity, except as a form of moral pollution.'

In Islam, we do believe that human life is more important than other forms of life, but we also have an obligation to protect the Earth. The Prophet said that it is a good deed to plant a tree, even if you think the world is going to end tomorrow.

Edge of Darkness even touches very briefly on the subject of Rapture. This mainly American Christian belief seems to free its adherents from having to take any responsibility for the consequences of their selfish and greedy actions – such as environmental pollution and global warming – because they do not expect to be *left behind* with the rest of us, to face the outcome. They will be able to watch our horrible suffering (war, famine, pestilence) from the balconies in Heaven, after they have been miraculously Raptured away. The discussions I had about Rapture – with Auden, Robinson and Magnus – always made me waver between fear (in case they were right) and anger (at their arrogant disinterest in the collective future of humanity).

I have a new friend on campus called Tom Williams; he has come from California on the Exchange Programme. He is a nice guy, gentle and softly spoken, but he seems to have a dark history. He tells me about an experience he had while under the influence of cocaine.

'I felt myself surrounded by this wonderful, brilliant white light, which completely wrapped itself around me and cushioned me with a warm feeling of complete Love. It was the most joyful thing I have ever experienced. If I believed in God, then I would have said, without a shred of doubt, that it was God. But I know it was the cocaine.'

1985-86
Age: 23

I am troubled by this, because Tom is my friend and he is a compassionate and decent person – and yet he was also a hard drug user, something which my Islamic self views with absolute contempt. In some Muslim countries, possession of cocaine could cost him his life. It seems that life is full of difficult dilemmas for me; nothing is simply black and white.

And California seems a mysterious, compelling and powerful place. I've always felt that it changed Janice noticeably (and not just her jeans size).

It is a Saturday afternoon and I am sitting in the campus room of Julian Hamilton-Peach, who has just returned from an exchange year at the University of Illinois.

There is a knock at the door, and Julian calls, 'Come in!'

The door opens and the most beautiful girl on campus walks into the room.

Now, I am not a laggard intellectually. Though my heart leaps initially, it does not take me long to figure out that, since we are in Julian's room, and she does not know me from Adam, that she has come to see Julian, not me.

Bastard! Lucky bastard!

The beautiful girl says, 'Hi, Julian. You mentioned playing squash sometime. I'd like to take you up on that.'

Julian says, 'That would be great. Give me your address and I'll come and arrange it.'

I think that my presence in the room barely registers, although I do mumble something of no significance. I'm not sure that she even remembers me from Karate training two years ago. She gives Julian her campus address and departs.

Bitter, twisted and deeply hurt inside, I turn on Julian.

'How do you know *her*?'

'Oh, we got talking and I found out that she liked squash and I said that we should play some time. I gave her my room number. I never really thought she'd take me up on it. This must mean that she likes me.' He looks intolerably pleased with himself.

'What's her name?' I ask him.

'It's Wendy Bramham,' he replies. 'She was particularly impressed that I took in her last name, when she only said it once. I even spelled it correctly to her.'

'I could have done that,' I think. *'All I had to do was chat with her.'*

I visit Janice a couple of times in Newcastle, taking the train down there. I always visit on a Saturday and never stay the night (although longingly I imagine doing so). She collects me from the station in her Honda Accord. She has a new boyfriend, to whom she introduces me. He seems a pleasant enough fellow; *does he know he's only temporary?*

It does bother me that I'm still a student and she has started her exciting career in the world of business. She has money and attends important meetings. I live frugally and do intellectual stuff with test tubes in a laboratory. I know which is sexier.

At the university, someone is giving an introductory talk on Transcendental Meditation, so I go along to find out about it. It's in a relatively small lecture hall, with about thirty people in the audience. The presenter is a nurse, and she describes how meditation helps her to relax, to unwind from the stress of the day. She makes us perform a breathing exercise, in which we picture a hand going around a clock. We breathe in and out, smoothly and evenly. The presenter tells us that sometimes you may get a peace-inducing effect by repeatedly chanting a calming phrase, known as a *mantra*.

There is a restless young man in the audience. When it's time for questions, he suddenly makes his move. He calls out confrontationally, with wooden words that have clearly been prepared in advance: 'Is it not true that when you meditate, you recite mantras which are the names of Hindu gods?' It's not a question – it's an accusation.

The presenter tries to explain that meditation is not a religion, that no specific belief is attached to it, but that it is a way of achieving peace in the mind.

The young man swings around again with the accusation about using the names of Hindu gods, implying clearly *false* gods. His position becomes obvious. He is an evangelical Christian and he is attacking this heathen practice.

Once I understand what is going on, I observe from a position of quiet, Islamic detachment. I have no sympathy for the young man at all; he is, after all, another of these arrogant fundamentalists who would assert that my family and I are going to Hell, for not accepting the blood sacrifice of his mythical man-God.

I have a great deal of sympathy for the nurse, who seems like a decent and well-intentioned person. But there is a problem. If meditation really *does* involve chanting the names of Hindu gods, then I am running a mile in the other direction. My own One and only true God would not be amused if I dabble in anything like this. He is, after all, a jealous God.

The subject of my PhD thesis is '*The Solvolysis of Acetals in Highly Ionising Non-Nucleophilic Solvents*', which is riveting. I spend a lot of time in the Sufi section of the university library, researching this subject, but apparently the Sufis didn't know a lot about it. The Sufis focus on God as Love, as a wonderful brilliance into which they seek to totally lose themselves and their sense of separate identity. This is strange, though; it sounds a lot like Buddhism.

Whilst there is Chemistry research to do, the question of religious truth is still foremost on my mind. When we choose a religion, we have an intellectual obligation to explain the phenomena, the miracles and events of *other* religions, within the framework of our chosen belief

1985-86
Age: 23

system. To not do so, to simply ignore other faiths, means we are not secure in our own beliefs, that these beliefs are not solid enough to face any challenges.

The possibility that Islam is a satanic conspiracy still troubles me, and I have to deal with the Christian evangelists' mysterious Holy Spirit phenomenon. And of course, all fields like astrology, numerology, Tarot, portent reading, channelling and so on are forbidden. They are all satanic distractions and deceits. This is both the Islamic *and* Christian view of these practices. All of these phenomena are meant to deceive people and divert them from worship of the One, true, omnipotent God. It's amazing how closely aligned strict Muslims and Christians actually are.

But was it an angel or a demon in that cave, speaking to Muhammad? Magnus and company say it was a demon. Muslims believe it was an angel. This is the ultimate question.

I have a mysterious dream. It is a long time ago, in a place that seems to be Atlantis. It is a peaceful, civilised time, advanced in philosophy and science.

I am in Atlantis with some old friends. We are wearing white robes, and there is architecture reminiscent of ancient Greece. There is at least one man and one woman, in addition to myself. We are very close, and there are *warm* feelings of friendship and love. This is the most poignant, lingering aspect of the dream – the *warmth* of the friendship (even though I cannot identify who my friends are).

But there is also a bittersweet aspect. We are saying goodbye, but it is understood that we will meet again for sure, in another, later life.

I awake and it is a bright Saturday morning. I am in my sparse student room, in the wooden bed that is so narrow, one wonders if it is really true that some students have sex sometimes.

I lie here, looking towards the window. Well, this dream doesn't make any sense at all. I have never given Atlantis a thought (outside of that crass television series *The Man From Atlantis*), and as for meeting again in a later life, what kind of nonsense is that? It sounds like Hindu reincarnation theology. We have only one life. Only Islam or Christianity can be the true religion, and I'm sure that it's Islam.

But the warmth of the feelings of friendship lingers on. I can still feel it. It is tangible.

I am still young and in my life I have not experienced the depth of friendship which the dream conveyed. Such friendships would take a very long time to grow, a lot of shared experience.

Later in the day, I see Julian Hamilton-Peach in his room. I tell him all about this strange dream with its alien concepts. Julian, in his characteristic way, does not perform any obvious analysis, but instead focuses on my use of the word 'warm', and what a good word that is for conveying certain emotional feelings. *Warm.* Yes, it's a good word; it does convey the feelings.

I study Islam some more. So many Islamic rules are clearly for our own good.

The prohibition against alcohol is an obvious one, and is also adopted by some Christian churches. Alcohol is an addictive drug – I have seen the harm that it does. The effects are both direct and indirect: drunkenness, violence, unwanted pregnancy, road-accident deaths. The list is endless. People say that they should have freedom of choice – but what choice do the children have whose lives are torn apart by fear, nightly witnessing their drunken fathers abusing and beating their terrified mothers? What choice do those killed by drunk drivers have?

1985-86
Age: 23

The prohibition against gambling is common sense. Gambling is addictive and destroys the lives of the gambler and his family. It serves no higher purpose and brings with it all manner of other evils.

Eating pork is bad for you. In Third World environments, pigs transmit tapeworms into human hosts. But, more significantly in the Western world, pigs are omnivores and the material that they eat, some of it endlessly recycled, has higher levels of cancer-causing toxins than the grass eaten by cows and sheep. Some Christian churches, especially American ones, also prohibit the eating of pork, in accordance with the Bible.

Smoking is un-Islamic, although many Muslims do not realise this. The Qur'an prohibits you from doing anything that you know to be harmful to your body, so that clearly includes smoking. If cigarettes had been around at the time of the Prophet, they would have been mentioned specifically.

Usury is forbidden in Islam. Whether this means charging *high* interest on a loan, or *any* interest, is a matter of debate, but the fact is that interest-based economics creates theoretical wealth (money making money) that has no basis in any tangible creation of value, as well as enslaving people (individuals and nations) to debt from which they can never escape. People who devote themselves to using money and pieces of paper to 'make money' become obscenely wealthy and powerful, but people who actually do useful things (growing food, digging-up minerals, driving buses, teaching children) get left behind. The practice of bonded labour exists in some Third World and Muslim countries, whereby people are literally enslaved by a debt that they neither understand nor can control, and must work forever for their creditor masters. This is totally un-Islamic, and yet Muslims are the worst offenders in this in supposedly Islamic countries like Pakistan.

1985-86
Age: 23

It's clear that so many of the rules of Islam are there for the protection and well-being of both individuals and societies. God would only want to help and guide us. I am convinced that *Islam is the way!*

But what happens to people who don't follow these rules? I am troubled, because most of my friends drink alcohol, and one or two of them even have sex without being married. Should I even associate with such people? Does it compromise my chances of getting into Heaven? And what about them? Will they go to Hell for such things? Should I be trying to 'save' them?

Christians and Muslims have one big thing in common; we all want to go to Heaven and avoid being sent to Hell. But we can't seem to agree on the way and we are each forced to make a choice. The consequences of getting it wrong are too horrible to dwell upon.

And what about animals? Do they have souls? Do they also get sent to Heaven or Hell? It doesn't make sense that they would be judged and then sent to one place or the other, based on their behaviour. There's no point in judging a shark for killing a human – because that is what sharks do. I think this through very carefully and the conclusion I come to, based on the application of absolute logic to my religious beliefs, is that animals have no soul. They are biological machines which merely respond to stimuli in a programmed way which mimics consciousness.

The month of Ramadan comes and I decide that I have no excuse for not keeping the fasts. In the past, I have done this intermittently, but this time I decide that I will keep all thirty of the fasts. This is the worst time (May–June) for Ramadan to occur, and virtually the worst place (Scotland) to keep the fasts. The days are so long; the fast runs from about 4 a.m. to about 10 p.m. each day. Only in Scandinavian countries and near the North Pole could it be worse; these places have few or no night-time hours in June.

1985-86
Age: 23

This raises interesting questions about the universal practicality of Islam. Did God not intend that Eskimos could follow Islam, if they chose to do so? If they followed the fasting rules absolutely strictly, Eskimos would die. I learn about this in discussion with some of my Muslim brothers on campus. Apparently, Islam allows for such extreme circumstances. If you are in a place where fasting according to actual sunrise and sunset is not practical, then you adopt the timing of the nearest population centre where it *is* practical. So, Eskimos would look to one of the Scandinavian cities where there is a Muslim population keeping the fasts according to the daylight hours, and keep those same hours.

But even in such population centres the timing can be extreme – perhaps only a couple of hours of darkness. How do we judge what is reasonable and what is not? Would it not make sense for the whole world to keep the fast according to the timing in Mecca, the centre of the Islamic world? Being near the equator, in Mecca the length of the day and night is more or less even, all year around. So if the fast runs from 7 a.m. to 7 p.m. in Mecca, you could fast from 7 a.m. to 7 p.m. in your own time zone, wherever on the globe you are. This would be rational and practical, in my personal opinion. In this modern age of computers and communication, we can all have access to the necessary information.

This Ramadan, the days are extremely sunny, hot and slow. The afternoons in my laboratory are long and arduous, almost an ordeal. It's not food that I miss; it's coffee! I wonder what it must be like for smokers; they have to abstain from cigarettes. We are each denied our vice, whatever it is, perhaps something as innocent as chocolate. There is no temptation to break the fast during the day. Once you make the commitment at the beginning of the fast, you have no interest in cheating; you know that God is watching, even if no one else is. The temptation is not to *start* the fast; to find some valid reason why you can opt out one day, such as travel or illness.

One day I go with Susan Ellison, a fellow Chemistry postgraduate, to the coffee bar for afternoon tea, as we often do. I've always liked Susan – who is from Glasgow and has the accent to match – but we've never been particularly close. I've always found her warm and pleasant, easy to talk to and to be with. She knows that I am a Muslim and that I am fasting; I don't have to hide anything or pretend to be someone I'm not. I can relax and be myself, and it is a real pleasure to be in her company.

We sit outside in the brilliant sunshine. She has coffee and a pastry. I smell the coffee, but I don't eat or drink anything, of course. I also notice, as I often do, how incredibly beautiful, elegant and desirable Susan is. I want to make love to her so much, it hurts. But this is Ramadan and these are thoughts I should not be harbouring. I feel very guilty.

When Ramadan began, I was determined to keep all thirty fasts but, about halfway through the month, I begin to think about taking 'a day off'. There are so many little pleasures that I miss during the day; apple pastries with coffee at mid-morning, for example. It seems unbearable to go another two weeks like this.

Julian Hamilton-Peach has graduated and left Stirling, but he happens to be visiting the campus. I mention to him that I am fasting, but planning to take a day off. He cautions me to think about this very carefully. 'If you take a day off, you'll have a day's guilty pleasure, which won't last long. But if you keep all thirty fasts, imagine how happy you will feel. What an achievement that will be.'

He is right. I imagine the joy and satisfaction of completing all thirty fasts. I don't take a day off.

1985-86
Age: 23

Most days I *break fast* in my room, preparing a rather self-indulgent meal of everything that I have craved during the day. It is a mistake to go shopping in the fasting state. Every item that I see, I crave and place in the Tesco shopping trolley, with the intention of eating them all that night. Coffee and chocolate always complete the meal.

Some evenings, the Muslim students have a gathering to *break fast* and some wonderful Malaysian or other exotic food is provided. After the meal, the smokers gather to light up. Even though I hate smoking, I feel sorry for them: what an ordeal it must be. Why don't they just give up? Surely Ramadan is a great opportunity to do so? (*Yeah, and I should give up coffee and chocolate.*)

Unlike Christmas, which appears to be a festival of excessive self-indulgence in all things material and sensual, the process of fasting during Ramadan cultivates a feeling of gratitude and deep appreciation for all the routine things that we take for granted, which many people in the world are never able to enjoy.

I go to the Eid celebration on campus at the end of Ramadan, and I am overwhelmed by the brotherhood of all the different nationalities. This is the first time that Islam gives me an emotional high, like that which I associate with Christianity. After the prayer, we eat delicious food and we watch videos in which Ahmed Deedat, an articulate Muslim scholar, demonstrates that the blood-redemption doctrine of Christianity, the Trinity, the divinity of Jesus and so on, were all synthesised by Paul and his adherents – they have no foundation in the teachings of Jesus. He proves this by referencing the Bible and demonstrating contradictions in the texts.

Deedat presents an Islamic view of what happened at the Crucifixion – quoting the Bible, not the Qur'an. Jesus, Joseph of Arimathea, Nicodemus and the centurion (whose

1985-86
Age: 23

servant Jesus had earlier healed) were all in on it. Roman crucifixion usually took at least three days (often much longer) to kill the victim, unless his legs were broken to accelerate the process (because then he could no longer push himself back onto the little seat). But the Gospels make it absolutely clear that Jesus' legs were *not* broken. About three hours after the crucifixion began, Jesus' companions gave him something pungent to drink. Immediately after this, he gave a '*loud cry*' and appeared to die. But a man genuinely on the verge of death from asphyxiation is incapable of emitting even the faintest whisper – his muscles are too exhausted to move any air in and out of the lungs. Joseph went immediately to Pilate and requested Jesus' body. Pilate (who was very experienced in these matters) was *surprised that he was dead already*, and asked the centurion, who confirmed it. Joseph and Nicodemus took away Jesus' body and applied a huge amount of healing herbs, which Nicodemus had brought in advance. They wrapped Jesus in a linen cloth and placed him in the tomb. Two days later, the tomb was found to be empty. (The Gospel of Peter, banned by the Church, describes three men being seen walking away from the tomb – two of them supporting the third.)

Jesus made a few appearances to his closest followers, but these were always discreet, because he did not want to be captured and crucified again. People heard that he'd been seen alive, even though everyone believed that he'd been crucified, and rumours spread that something miraculous had happened.

Paul took this story of inferred Resurrection and merged it with his own belief system that entailed buying divine redemption through blood sacrifice. There were many early Christian groups, with widely varying beliefs, but Pauline Christianity became dominant due to its adoption by the Roman Empire. The 25th of December was the birthday of the Roman Sun god.

1985-86
Age: 23

Oh my God! This is incredible. Auden, Robinson, Magnus – they never told me any of this!

This is exactly what the Qur'an says: that Jesus was not really killed on the cross, but it seemed that way. If Christianity has got it wrong, then Islam is true. My doubts are suppressed, and from now on I voluntarily attend Friday prayers on campus with my fellow Muslims. I also start performing *all* of the five daily Islamic prayers, but not always on time. (Some of them are regularly done late, in catch-up mode, especially the pre-sunrise one.) But campus life is quite flexible and there is a room designated as a mosque, so it's easy enough to do most of them at the right time. Ablutions take place in the nearby men's room; the floor around the washbasins is always wet.

There's news of Willy Johnson; my parents know someone who knows someone who works at the Department of Health and Social Security. Willy Johnson telephoned to say that he could not make it to the appointment to discuss his on-going need for unemployment benefits, because his bicycle had been stolen.

Escalator

1986-87

Age: 24

MILTON COMES BACK to Stirling University to do a master's degree. His room is just as untidy as it ever was; we talk there often. We explore Scotland in my Alfa Romeo. It's just like old times! (No success with women either, just like old times.)

There's a girl with whom I've become acquainted, purely as a friend. Julian Hamilton-Peach introduced me to Jennifer last year. He practically forced me to go to visit her in her room, to overcome my shyness problem. I see Jenny around campus a lot, and this evening I drop in on her again. She is attractive, but she smokes, which is somewhat off-putting.

We have a good time, chatting in her room. Jenny teaches me backgammon and, astonishingly, I win three games in a row. We have a great conversation about old advertising slogans and compete to see how many each of us can remember, like *'Beanz Meanz Heinz'* and *'A Mars a day helps you work, rest and play.'* Of course, I have a head start with *'Lifebuoy kills the bacteria that cause BO.'*

In a moment of reckless abandon, I tell her about the difficult time I had in school, when I was the first boy in my class to develop BO and how Lifebuoy soap practically saved my life. She listens intently and sympathetically.

Jenny decides to start guessing things about me. She deduces what type of underpants I wear (plain Y-fronts) and that I am circumcised. She also says, curiously, that she is always afraid to make the first move, because she is afraid of 'rejection'.

I think she wants to go to bed with me! But I'm not sure. *Rejection from what?*

If it's *recreational sex?* No problem. *Being my girlfriend?* Maybe. *Getting married?* Not likely; she really isn't the one.

I'm reasonably sure that Jenny is giving me a green light; that if I initiate something, she will not reject me. I am excited and terrified. I start to think this through logically. I will have to sleep in my contact lenses. *(Not good, but do-able.)* Where do I put my clothes? *(Neatly folded on the plastic chair?)* At what point do I remove my socks? *(Don't know.)* Do I need to wash my feet, in case she wants to suck my toes? *(I've heard of such things.)* Will she smoke in bed? *(I won't like that.)* What about condoms? *(Does she have one? Will it be the right size?)*

What about Islam? This isn't allowed. At least it's not adultery, which is really bad. It's only fornication, a lesser misdemeanour. I think the penalty is seventy lashes … or is it one hundred? It's not worth it for one hundred. Anyway, I won't get any lashes, obviously, because we are not in an Islamic state. (Anyway, in an Islamic state I would never be alone with a single woman in her place, late at night.) I think God will probably let me off, or maybe I'll get one hundred lashes' worth of bad luck?

Although I feel a stirring in my Y-fronts, my body sabotages the whole process. My stomach starts to make noises and I feel flatulent. I have to get out of here. I hastily say that it's late and I should be going. From out in the corridor I see her face looking disappointed, maybe rejected, as I close the door.

I stand outside the door for a moment, trying to figure out how I feel. I'm really not sure. Then I head out of the hall into the cold, dark night. It is late.

I think about this incident over the next few days and what I have learned from it. It seems that in order to get a girl to

1986-87
Age: 24

like me, to want to go to bed with me even, all I have to do is communicate with her, to talk to her naturally, to just be myself and not pretend to be some mythical (and unsustainable) 'Mr Cool'. This is completely bizarre. It is the exact opposite of my strategy all these years. It seems too good to be true.

I enjoy and appreciate performing the five daily Islamic prayers, the *salaat*. I try not to rush them. They help me to slip into a sense of calm and detachment, and to feel close to God. *Salaat* is not a chore, it's a form of ritualised meditation that takes you away from the worries of the world. (It's true that as a postgraduate student, I really don't have a lot of worries beyond whether my Alfa Romeo will need any expensive repairs and how I will survive until I get my next grant cheque.)

Usually I pray alone, but if a group of Muslims are gathered together at prayer time, typically in the mosque, then the custom is for them to pray together in a coordinated way, with one person leading. It's traditional for the Friday noon prayer to be a community gathering, and for these the Islamic students on campus always procure a lecture hall. I usually attend. Sunnis and Shias pray together here, since it really isn't practical to arrange two separate prayer meetings on campus. You can tell who is Sunni and who is Shia, of course, by watching how they position their arms during the standing part of the prayer.

On one occasion, I'm slightly late as, just before the prayer time, I run into a beautiful blonde girl named Dawn Humphries, whom I met at the beginning of semester, and she is just going to lunch and (not knowing anything about Friday prayers) she asks me if I am going to lunch too, which of course I say that I am. After a hurried lunch at the MacRobert cafeteria, I arrive at the hall gasping for breath, having run across campus; I had gone to the usual place, the Logie Lecture Theatre – only to find a sign there that the prayer had been moved to Andrew Stewart Hall, all the way across campus.

There is a Muslim called Hakim, who is also a postgraduate student in the Chemistry Department. He's from Dewsbury in Yorkshire, although his ethnic origin is obviously the Indian subcontinent. Hakim starts dominating the Friday prayers; he's always giving the sermon. And what he keeps saying does not strike me as Islamic at all. He never bothers to talk about love, peace, forgiveness and tolerance; he prefers to lecture on the hellish Afterlife that awaits those who don't believe and act as he does. Rather than being uplifting (like Mr Campbell's talks), Hakim's sermons leave one with a sense of fear and dread. (I don't remember Mr Campbell *ever* mentioning Hell, but he still made you want to be good, for its own sake.)

In one sermon Hakim gives a whole speech about the Islamic version of the Antichrist, who is called *Dajjal*. He lays out all the complex and detailed prophecies about *Dajjal* and what he's going to do and how he's going to mislead people with amazing miracles – thus gaining influence over the whole world. Then Jesus is going to return (descending from Heaven), defeat *Dajjal*, and embarrass and humiliate all the Christians by declaring that he *never* said he was the 'Son of God'. The Muslims will get to say: 'We told you so!' It's an Islamic version of the Revelations prophecies about the end of the world, Armageddon, the ultimate fight between the forces of Good and Evil, and so on. It's *exactly* like the dark predictions made by Auden and Robinson back in Hampton School – but it's the other way around, of course; in this version, true Muslims represent the forces of Good, and everyone else is working for Satan.

None of this is in the Qur'an. This is all from the '*Hadith*' – the alleged 'sayings of the Prophet'. But there are *so many* volumes of these, and some of them were compiled hundreds of years after his death, that they can't possibly *all* be authentic. And some *Hadith* are so bizarre and awful, that no reasonable Muslim would *want* them to be authentic.

This is all a lot of superstition and prejudice and stupidity that has wrapped itself around Islam like a cancer. I feel very uncomfortable sitting here, listening to this nonsense.

In another sermon, he expounds that men and women should not mix socially, and he berates those present here today (*and they know who they are!*) who have been mixing with girls, having coffee with them and so on. I feel very uncomfortable. I have coffee with girls all the time. In fact, I'd have more coffee with more girls if only more girls would agree to have coffee with me. This is not Islamic, it is all Arab Wahhabi* cultural baggage; it is not in the Qur'an and it is his personal prejudice, which he is abusing his position to preach. I am so angry, I imagine standing up and walking out. But I don't do it.

Of course, Hakim has very definite views on how women should dress. I disagree. Where in the Qur'an does it say that women must be covered from head to foot? *It does not!* It requires women to '*veil their bosoms*' and to '*guard their modesty*'. The Qur'an asks both men and women not to overtly flaunt their bodies purely for the attention of others; what great advice that is in today's world, where so many people suffer from deep insecurity about their

---

* The Wahhabis are the most puritan of all Islamic schools of thought, believing in very strict rules of personal conduct, segregation of men and women, severe codes of dress, and opposing 'frivolous' pleasures such as music and anything else which might bring sinful joy. The Taliban of Afghanistan were heavily influenced by the Wahhabis, who have been encouraging Muslims around the world to study Arabic as a second language, instead of English.

1986-87

Age: 24

appearance. There is plenty of flexibility to allow for culture and context.

Hakim has a very simple view of Life and Afterlife. Whoever lives an absolutely moral and puritan life, defined by Hakim's standards, will be rewarded with a wonderful eternity in Paradise. Whoever spends their life in the ways of wickedness (i.e. doing anything fun), will face the unbearable flames of Hellfire.

Despite all of Hakim's nonsense, I feel more confident about Islam than ever. Whatever seems repulsive about Islam, on objective examination turns out *not* to be Islamic, but cultural contamination.

As a postgraduate student, I get paid to assist undergraduates in their laboratory classes. In practice, this means that I wander around the lab chatting with them, hoping no one will notice the demographic bias in the students I spend the most time with.

One afternoon, I'm speaking with a young woman who turns out to be very much into 'animal rights'. She expounds on how outrageous it is that rabbits are used to test products destined for human use. This immediately sparks my interest. It is obvious that animals can't have souls like humans do. Nowhere in the Bible or the Qur'an does God worry about sending animals to Heaven or Hell – He's already got His work cut out dealing with all the billions of humans. Animals are just machines; they respond to stimuli with conditioned responses which some foolish people mistake for consciousness, even love. What really pushes my buttons is the amount of concern that some people show for animals, when there are so many people suffering and in need of help. Money donated to an animal charity could always be better spent on a human cause.

I explain to the young woman that it makes absolute sense for rabbits to be used for medical experimentation,

1986-87
Age: 24

because only humans really matter, and rabbits are not really conscious beings. It's a just cause. I'm not saying that we should be deliberately or frivolously cruel to animals – only that they are there to serve humans. (I don't tell her that I believe it's divinely ordained. How else can you explain the amazing gifts of milk, eggs, honey, wool, silk and so on – before you even get to the slaughter products of meat and leather?)

She becomes visibly outraged by my reasoning. This amuses me, and I deliberately state my case even more coldly and dispassionately, which makes her angrier. She is seething with rage about my opinion. What makes *me* so angry is that she puts rabbits before people, and I enjoy getting her worked up with my cold logic.

I didn't really want a date with her, anyway.

One of Milton's MSc classmates is a chap named Alan, with whom I develop a passing acquaintance. One November evening on campus, I run into Alan and he suggests that we go for a drink in the student bar. Since my social life is not exactly a frenzy of activity, I happily agree.

Once we are settled down with our drinks, Alan steers the conversation in a very definite direction: *Christianity.* I realise immediately that he is an evangelist and wants to preach to me, to help me to see the Light. I am delighted; I relish this opportunity. When I had my discussions with Magnus a few years ago, I understood little about Christian and Islamic theology, the Bible and the Qur'an. It was easy for him to confuse and scare me. Now that I have a solid understanding, it will be fun to debate with a Christian.

Alan tries to convince me that Jesus is God and died to pay the price for our sins, but I quote the Bible back at him, pointing out inconsistencies in this argument. I really enjoy this. It seems to throw him; I don't think that he has ever had a debate with a Muslim who can use the Bible to argue against him.

1986-87
Age: 24

I move on to my favourite case; the issue of Isaac and Ishmael – *which* son did God ask Abraham to sacrifice (as a test of faith)? The Bible says it was Isaac, whereas Muslims believe it was Ishmael. The real reason this is so important is that Isaac is the father of the Jews, whereas Ishmael is described as the father of the Arabs – so this has become a matter of tribal ego. But I'm not an Arab or a Jew – I'm only interested in the accuracy of the account.

I point out the facts to Alan, systematically and articulately. The Bible says that Ishmael was the firstborn son of Abraham (by his slave girl, Hagar), and Isaac was born later (of his wife, Sarah). *Agreed.*

When it comes to the sacrifice request, God asks Abraham to kill his 'only son'. You don't have to be a genius at analytical logic or verbal reasoning to understand that this can only have been the *firstborn* son. Since both sons outlived their father, there was *never* a time when the second-born son (i.e. Isaac) could have been the 'only son'.

Even though the Bible states Isaac's name in this context, I tell Alan you can see how the name has been inserted into the text – it doesn't fit the logic or the rhythm of the language: '… *thy son, thine only son, Isaac* …'

This is a perfect example of insertions and changes being made to ancient stories to suit the agendas of those recording them – history being rewritten, even as it's written. That's why the Bible is inherently unreliable, and can't be taken as the absolute Word of God.

Soundly defeated on this, Alan unexpectedly changes his approach altogether. He starts talking not about scripture and theology, but about miracles and his direct communications with God. This is where it gets a little weird. He tells me that he regularly has two-way conversations with God. He is not joking; he is absolutely sincere. He tells me about various miracles and manifestations that he has directly experienced.

I find this very troubling. I am well equipped to argue scripture, but the Holy Spirit and miracles I've always been uncomfortable with, finding them harder to explain away. Alan is telling me about miracles and making the case for Christianity compelling, on this basis. He is urging me to accept the sacrifice of Jesus, to invite Him into my life, and I will experience the same abundance of miracles and manifestations of God. But I have to *believe* first.

I tell him that for me to make such a step is not acceptable from an Islamic perspective. It would be betraying the absolutely singular God of Islam and thus losing His protection, opening my life to Satan's deceptions and confusion. I say that I have to see the miracle *first*, not afterwards.

Alan is persistent, but eventually accepts that I am not going to budge on this issue. For me it must be *miracle first, belief afterwards*. He says that he will have a word with God to see what can be arranged.

At the end of the evening, I head back across campus towards my room. It is late, and I am deeply troubled by this conversation with Alan. Just when I think that I've made (Islamic) sense of the world, something comes along to throw everything into doubt again. And this time it wasn't about scripture, it was about miracles and supernatural phenomena – concepts which still bother me.

Magnus always made me afraid and now Alan has done the same. What if, after I die, I discover that Jesus really is the Son of God, that he really did die for my sins, that I was wrong in refusing to believe this, and now it's too late to do anything about it, and the fire of Hell awaits?

There is something weird about this evening. It is near midnight, campus is deserted and the wind is howling around me in an eerie way. A shiver runs down my back as I walk along the covered walkways to my own hall of residence, all the time with the wind screaming and gusting. I am a little scared; my rational faith creaks a little in the wind.

During the night, the phenomenon arranged between Alan and his 'God' takes place. I am awoken from my sleep by a presence entering my room through the window. I can feel the entity as a tangible thickness in the air, a heaviness over me. I am not frightened; my emotions appear to be suppressed; my body is frozen. It's as if Time has stopped. I can feel that my guard is up and my heart is firmly closed. I am wearing a mask of cynicism, not willing to betray God/Allah by readily accepting the Christian theology of a three-part god and redemption through blood sacrifice.

The entity hovers above me and a slightly distant voice, which sounds as if it's coming over an old wireless in the early days of radio, says slowly and authoritatively, *This is Jesus Christ.'*

I maintain my barrier. This isn't good enough. I won't open-up and accept. I firmly believe that many supposedly religious phenomena are actually deceiving Jinn, and there is no reason to think that this is not the case here.

The entity retreats back through the window and the room returns to normal. I return to sleep.

The phenomenon was real; I'm sure it was not a dream.

Although this experience does not swing me over to Christianity, I am somewhat disturbed by it. There is a Sudanese Muslim in the corridor of my campus residence. I meet him in the kitchen one day and, without going into the specifics of what has happened, I mention that the Christians are trying to convert me. He disappears back to his room and returns with an audiotape.

'Listen to this, brother,' he says. 'You won't have any more worries.'

The tape is of a lecture by Dr Gary Miller, a Canadian and a former Catholic priest turned Muslim. He conducts a very intellectual discussion about Islamic and Christian theology. He points out that the idea of a god-figure being sacrificed to save the world is not unique to Christianity; it

1986-87
Age: 24

predates the New Testament by thousands of years. Drawing on this material, he makes it blatantly obvious that the theology of redemption by the blood sacrifice of an innocent has been superimposed on events in the life of Jesus, by individuals influenced by those earlier belief systems.

Dr Miller makes an important point, which I realise has always been true. *'An explanation is not a proof.'* When you debate with a fundamentalist, they keep telling you *what* they believe, but they can't be drawn into explaining *why* they believe it. Belief by itself is meaningless; it needs to have a rational foundation. Otherwise, how do you decide which faith to subscribe to? There's no shortage of belief systems in the world. They all have stories and explanations.

Also, Dr Miller emphasises the importance of not being drawn into beliefs by feelings and emotions, but to maintain a strong sense of rational evaluation. This invariably brings the open-minded seeker of truth to Islam, which is the only theology that sits comfortably with the assumption of a single all-powerful God.

'An explanation is not a proof.' This is a great mantra to keep in mind.

The tape has a wonderfully reassuring and positive effect on me. It helps to dispel the essentially emotional influences of Christianity, in favour of rational evaluation, which always leads me back to Islam.

It is a beautiful, bright winter's day. The sky is blue, the sun is shining and the air is crisp and cool. It is still light but, this being Scotland, it will get dark soon.

I am heading into town in my Alfa Romeo Alfasud coupé. I am wearing a trench coat – the right colour for a Burberry, but it's actually from C&A. I start the car and I pull away onto the quiet perimeter road that runs around campus.

1986-87
Age: 24

283

The most desirable place to live on campus is the chalets, a group of about a dozen wooden Swedish-style detached houses, each one with five bedrooms, two bathrooms and a kitchen. These are spaced out between the road and the edge of the hill forest that borders the campus, in a little community of their own.

As I approach the chalets, Wendy Bramham emerges from amongst them. I am driving very slowly, and she is waiting to cross the road. I look at her as I drive past, and she looks at me.

She is beautiful, as always. The sunshine of the day seems to make her face and hair more radiant than ever. Her eyes are sparkling and there is a cheerful, upbeat look about her. She even seems to smile warmly at me. She is dressed smartly against the winter cold, in an elegant coat.

How I long to reach out and talk to her, to give her a lift into town, to be friends with her, *anything* but this distant, remote recognition.

I wonder what she sees, from her perspective. An awkward, shy young Asian man, unable to communicate in an inspiring, self-confident way, wearing a Burberry-like coat and aviator sunglasses, and driving an orange car. Isn't this the same guy who held her feet over three years ago at Karate training and didn't say a word?

One Friday, at the prayer meeting on campus, there is a certain buzz of excitement. An Arab man called Faisal is visiting, and apparently he is a renowned and well-known Islamic scholar of some sort. I've never heard of him, but he seems to represent some kind of international brotherhood of Muslims. He is in his early thirties and wearing casual Western clothes, with a neat hairstyle and no beard. He doesn't lead the prayer, but his presence is clearly felt; those who know him seem to project an aura of respect and admiration for him.

1986-87
Age: 24

Afterwards, a couple of my fellow Muslims say that they are going to visit Faisal tonight at someone's home in Stirling, and ask if I would like to come. I am intrigued, so I agree.

Hakim looks on with ill-disguised hostility; it is clear as day that he disapproves of Faisal and feels that he has been upstaged in some way.

After the sunset prayer, we drive to town in someone's car, park in front of a modest-looking council block, and ascend an outside staircase to a flat. There are many Arab men in the apartment, sitting around Faisal, and the smell of cigarette smoke hangs in the air.

It seems that he is going to lead a discussion, but first he must perform the sunset prayer, which apparently he has not yet done. I find this very strange. It's now nearly an hour since sunset, and the sunset prayer is the one which traditionally is performed at a very specific time, *immediately* after the sun has gone down. We wait quietly while Faisal and his associates perform the sunset prayer (three *rakahs*, plus an optional two).

The discussion which he then leads is very interesting. He talks about many apparent Islamic beliefs and practices which have no true basis in Islam; they are actually local cultural traditions, which cause confusion about Islam. He talks about the sound scientific basis for many Qur'anic statements. This is very close to my heart, as I've always felt that you should be able to reason your way to the true religion.

Snacks and tea appear, brought out from the kitchen on trays by one of the men. I get the impression that there are women in the kitchen and bedrooms, but I never see any.

The next part of the discussion is the most fascinating. Apparently there is an old Islamic belief, attributed to the Prophet himself, that '*when the sun rises in the West*' the light of Islam will illuminate the whole world. Faisal explains the true meaning of this: it is not to be taken literally. What it

1986-87
Age: 24

conveys is that when people in the West realise the truth of Islam, they will embrace it willingly, and then Islam will once again have a Golden Age, this time one that lasts forever. There will be true peace and justice in the whole world, because everyone will be united in universal brotherhood. He says that this is beginning to happen even now; everyone knows of Westerners who have converted to Islam. (It's true; on campus there is a gentle, softly spoken, bespectacled Irishman named Victor, who has become Muslim.)

The idea of forcing people to convert is nonsensical. The Qur'an says clearly: '*There is no compulsion in religion.*' It has to be a free choice, based on genuine belief. If someone converts because a sword or a gun is being held to their head, they aren't really 'embracing Islam', they are exercising self-preservation. Such an act of violent coercion is a betrayal of Islamic values.

Faisal says that the cultural baggage and negative propaganda that have distorted Islam are the cause of the West's suspicion and frequent hostility; much of this is the fault of Muslims themselves, for not representing their religion accurately. We have a duty to be ambassadors of true Islam to non-Believers – by our words, attitudes and deeds – and thereby invite them to examine Islam with an open mind and with accurate information. Such an examination always compels the open-minded person to '*see the light*' and embrace Islam gladly.

Faisal puffs a cigarette during this intense dialogue, as do many of the others. The air is thick with both elation and smoke.

It does sound exciting: the idea that one day everyone will be united in a peaceful and just, global Islamic state.

But it doesn't ring true that Muslims always put their universal brotherhood first. What about all the tensions and hostility in the so-called Islamic world: Sunnis and Shias; Arabs and Persians; Arabs and Turks; Arabs and Africans;

1986-87
Age: 24

people who were natives of Pakistan and those who migrated from India; West Pakistani soldiers and their barbaric, state-endorsed mass rape of East Pakistani women during Bangladesh's war of independence; the tribe of Al-This vs the tribe of Al-That ... the list is endless. *Where's the universal brotherhood?*

But also, I have a deeper feeling and it makes me feel ashamed; I should not be having such rebellious thoughts. Although it does not always seem compatible with Islam, I love the heady freedom and excitement of the Western world, just as it is. The Islamic world always seems stern and afraid. People should pray and fast because they genuinely *want* to, not because someone orders them that they *must* do. I wouldn't want there to be people like Hakim in every corner of every public place in every country, pointing and shouting: 'You can't do that! You will go to Hell!'

If everyone on Earth becomes Muslim, the world might turn into a very sombre place.

The Chemistry research is not going well. In fact, I hate spending all day in a laboratory in a white coat, doing experiments that nobody will ever care about. I stare out of the window at the distant hills and the occasional car that goes by, and imagine being out in the world, doing something interesting. My research supervisor, Dr Howard Maskill, is a Quaker, which means that he is a Man of Peace. This is a good thing, because a regular supervisor would have killed me by now.

I go many times to the University Careers Office and start reading graduate recruitment brochures. I see pictures of young graduates in suits, sitting in meetings, or traveling somewhere, often overseas. I'm not sure what they actually do, but it looks like fun. I also learn that most of these big companies recruit graduates of any discipline into their business functions, providing them with comprehensive training programmes.

I buy an Amstrad computer from Dixons in Stirling and start learning to programme it, which involves a language called Amstrad BASIC. I put the computer to work in my laboratory and use it as an integral part of my experiments. I find that the computer is able instantly to analyse the data from the experiments, replacing laborious calculations that have previously taken me hours. I buy a printer and integrate it into the arrangement. I become more interested in developing the process of using the computer to streamline my work, and less interested in the actual results of the work, the Chemistry itself. I become interested in a career in computer systems.

There is one brochure that really appeals to me. It is for Unilever, an Anglo-Dutch multinational that most people have never heard of, but which owns many famous brands (such as Lever Brothers) in household consumer goods, including detergents, toiletries and packaged foods. I learn that Lifebuoy soap and Brooke Bond PG Tips tea are made by Unilever, and the company immediately earns my respect. This brochure shows how graduates who succeed in entering the 'Unilever Companies Management Development Scheme' (UCMDS) will have a series of assignments at different companies and develop a really exciting international career.

In the brochure there are illustrations of young men and women in suits, carrying attaché cases and ascending an escalator that symbolises their successful careers. I picture myself on that escalator.

It really is the *best* opportunity. It's international, and it is not tied down to one particular industry. I decide that I want to work in Business Systems in the Finance function of Unilever.

But the UCMDS form is eight pages long. Apart from the standard questions about education and experience, it

1986-87
Age: 24

asks searching questions about motives, ambitions, interests and so on, leaving half-page spaces for the answers. There is a whole page for a summary of my life, including the key events that have been most influential.

Apparently, submitting the form gives me a one-in-three chance of a campus interview. The campus interview gives me a one-in-three chance of being called to a Selection Board (a one-day process). Attending the Selection Board gives me a one-in-five chance of being chosen. So, combining the probabilities at each stage, I have a one-in-forty-five chance of being offered a job with Unilever, if I apply. That's about 2 percent.

I go to the library to research Unilever. I find books on the (almost romantic) history of Unilever and also discover that it currently owns hundreds of companies and legal entities around the world. (There is also a thick report entitled *Unilever's World* by 'Counter Information Services', which has a cover graphic depicting suited white men with briefcases trampling all over the globe in an exploitative capitalist way – but conveniently it is over ten years old, so I choose to ignore it.)

It will be very hard to get into Unilever, but it really is the opportunity that I want the most. I intend to write the perfect answer in each section of the application form, using all of the available space. I develop an innovative solution. Obtaining several copies of the form, I un-staple the pages and establish the precise location and format of every section on every page, in terms of printer instructions. I then create individual print files for each answer and work meticulously, using my word processing software, to develop the perfect answer to each question, including that challenging one-page life summary. In every case, my final answer fits the space perfectly. (Personal computers, word processing software and printers are not at all common, so this is a most unusual thing to achieve.)

This activity takes all my spare time over three months. I think about little else but Unilever; I pray to God to give me the opportunity and constantly *visualise* being successful, being one of those suit-wearing graduates on the escalator to an exciting international career – although it is hard to imagine that Unilever would recruit *me*. (I am a little worried that Unilever's many businesses include packaged food products containing pork and also some involvement with alcoholic drinks – but this is a drop in the ocean and I hope that God won't mind.)

The application form is due to be submitted to the Careers Office by noon on a certain day in February. However, I still have not successfully printed out the different files for each answer, together on the *same* form. Something always goes wrong with one of the print files. This will take some careful, dedicated effort.

I wake up on the morning of the day that the form is due in. If I *really want* to work for Unilever, I *must* go straight to my laboratory, where the computer and printer are, lock the door, and work meticulously to get these answers all printed onto one copy of the application form. Lying in bed, I think about it and I can't be bothered. *Who am I kidding? Unilever is never going to hire me. They have the brightest and the best applying to them. I am wasting my time with this foolish dream.*

Miraculously, inexplicably, suddenly I find the energy to get up and complete the task. In my laboratory, it takes me many attempts and many copies of the form to get one version together which has all of the answers in the right place. There is one line that will not print correctly; it's the bottom line of the life summary. Finally, with barely minutes left before noon, I write that particular line by hand and then run over to the Careers Office to submit the form, breathless, just before the deadline.

1986-87
Age: 24

I return to my laboratory, but I have lost interest in Chemistry forever.

Two weeks later, the letter comes, with the big 'U' logo on the envelope. I am invited to attend an interview on campus, when the representative from Unilever will be spending a day at Stirling University. My interview is near the end of the day.

Interestingly, the room allocated for the interview is the one which is normally assigned as the campus 'mosque' or prayer room for Muslim students. (During this recruitment season, a different room has been assigned to us.) I am very familiar with this room and I almost remove my shoes as I enter, from force of habit.

The interviewer is an attractive woman, Nicola Moulden, with a PhD in Chemistry. She works in the Internal Audit department. I recognise her from the Unilever recruitment brochure and mention this. She says that I am the first person today to have noticed this fact – as if I'm the only one who has actually studied the brochure. The interview goes brilliantly well. Unusually for me, I am confident of making it through this stage.

I am correct. In another envelope bearing the big 'U', I receive an invitation to one of the Selection Boards. I am to come to the Waldorf Hotel in central London, one Thursday evening, where the candidates will be briefed and will have dinner with recent recruits. The next day will be spent at Unilever House, facing the Selection Board.

I travel down to my parents' house in London and prepare for the Selection Board. Into my attaché case I carefully pack a fresh shirt, Y-fronts, socks, pyjamas, toiletries. I can't get a prayer mat to fit in there, so I decide that I will just use a fresh towel in the hotel room for this purpose. I also pack a second tie; I don't want anyone to notice me wearing the same tie on both days. With my grey

1986-87
Age: 24

suit, I will wear a blue shirt on arrival and a white shirt the next day, so it will be obvious that these are different.

I take a train to Waterloo station and walk over to the Waldorf Hotel. At the front desk, they have my name on a list, so I don't have to pay them anything. This night in the Waldorf is a new experience for me – staying in a luxury hotel. The room is smaller than hotel rooms on television (but much bigger than a student room), the bed seems narrow, and it is hot and stuffy – but it is exciting nonetheless. I feel very apprehensive as well: will I be lucky enough to get through this? I take a shower to freshen up before heading down at the appointed time.

The evening is both exciting and a little tense, because of what is at stake. There are ten candidates; three are women, and I am the only darkie. Two recent recruits are hosting the dinner for the prospective candidates. There is a Marketing person from Lever Brothers, whose job is to persuade consumers that Persil is better than Ariel (which comes from rival company Proctor & Gamble) or some other similar critical responsibility. The other host is Daniel King, a Finance person from Internal Audit.

Curiously, the Marketing guy is wearing jeans and a checked shirt, whereas all of the candidates and Daniel King are wearing suits. His manner of dress does not go down well with the Waldorf restaurant manager. He berates the young man about compromising the standard of the restaurant but, due to the sheer number of us in the group, there is nothing that he can do except to express his disapproval.

I sit next to Daniel King at dinner. He seems a nice guy and I like him. He studied science at university before joining Unilever. He is down-to-earth and friendly. Being in this position of success does not seem to have gone to his head. We have a long discussion about what a great opportunity this is to build a successful global corporate career.

1986-87
Age: 24

During the night I sleep with the window open and awake in the early hours, quite hungry. I get up and look in the mini-bar, also a novelty for me. There are small bottles of alcohol and soft drinks, and some snacks. I bear in mind that Unilever has paid for the room, but we are each liable for any additional charges that we incur. I look at the price list; it is all horribly expensive. A jar of peanuts looks appealing. I examine it closely; *the seal has been broken!* A previous occupant has already had some peanuts. I carefully unscrew the lid, tip a few peanuts into my palm and screw the lid back on, taking care to make the tear in the seal as discreet as possible. Irrationally, I shake the jar gently, to spread the remaining peanuts out a bit more.

The next morning we gather in the hotel lobby and we walk over to Unilever House as a group. It is a fresh, sunny, spring day and it is exciting to be in the City of London at such an early hour. Unilever House is a daunting grey building from the 1930s, with columns and stone statues. It seems amazing to be going inside; a privilege.

The Selection Board is an intense series of group exercises, written tests and individual interviews. During the first half of the day, we ten candidates sit around a circular table. The six selectors sit against the walls of the room, forming a bigger circle, so that we candidates are in a little world of our own, being watched impassively by seemingly invisible observers. The first group exercise is a discussion; the selected topic is 'The North–South Divide'.

The challenge is obvious: everyone needs to speak in order to make an impression, but what one says also needs to be of some value in the discussion. We are all in competition with each other to be noticed by the selectors, but at the same time we must ensure a meaningful and creative discussion. It would be lame to say something worthless, just for the sake of speaking. There is no format to this discussion; no assigned turn to speak.

Every time that I wait for a natural pause in the conversation, to make my profound contribution, someone else lurches in, before I can speak, and takes the stage. A few agonising minutes pass, and now I am the only one who has not spoken. I feel this global career opportunity slipping away. If I really want this, I have to do something *now*.

I see a perspective that no one else has addressed. The debate launched right into the so-called North–South Divide in England: the perception that London and the South East are more prosperous than the North of England; house prices are much higher in the South; jobs are more readily available and so on. But an assumption has been made, completely unstated, that this discussion is to be about the North–South Divide *in England*, and not the global North–South Divide – the observation that economists and others make that the majority of people in the Third World live to the south of people in the developed world. This raises issues of the role of climate and so on, in the relative prosperity of nations.

This will be my valuable contribution. I hesitate for just a moment, then I go for it. Using my experience from the auditions for the Turkish Knight, I take a deep breath and suddenly interrupt the proceedings by stating in a loud, forceful voice: 'I'm becoming increasingly irritated at all the assumptions being made here.' I make sure that the words come out slowly, in a measured way.

There is a sudden silence in the room. I notice one of the selectors sit upright and lean to one side to observe me better. Everyone is looking at me. I have the stage.

I continue with as much authority as I can muster, articulating the words carefully, holding myself together to appear calm, confident, intelligent and authoritative, with fifteen pairs of eyes upon me. I explain very carefully that it

1986-87
Age: 24

is *okay* for us to decide that the North–South Divide of the debate is the English one, and not the global one, but this is an assumption that we must identify and agree upon first. We have carelessly launched into the discussion, assuming what it is about and assuming that we all see it the same way.

I finish speaking, there is a moment's silence, and then someone else jumps into the gap to say what a valid point I have made. The focus moves away from me and I breathe again discreetly and let my tense body relax a little. I have established my presence.

The rest of the day seems to go well and I feel good about it. (Even the interview with the psychologist seems positive – he doesn't appear to find anything wrong with me.) We are told that the members of the Selection Board will not leave the building this evening until they have reached a consensus decision about each candidate. If we call Human Resources on Tuesday morning, we can find out our results (Monday being a holiday).

On Tuesday morning, I am very nervous. I can think only of the failures in my life: not getting into medical school; not going to America on the Exchange Programme; not passing the Honours Qualifying exam. Again, I doubt whether God will let me be so lucky as to receive such a prestigious and valuable opportunity.

I dial the number. The woman in Human Resources recognises my name, pauses a moment while she consults a list, and then tells me, 'Yes.' I can't believe it. *Thank you, God.*

Unilever sends me an offer letter. I will get my specific job assignment later, but it is certain that I will start work by September.

At last, I will no longer be a student; I will be in a prestigious graduate job, with excellent prospects. This will

1986-87
Age: 24

make me a more viable romantic candidate for Janice, who could not have envisaged anything between us while I was still a student and she had already embarked on her corporate career. (*Let's just hope our children grow up to enjoy things like this.*)

There's news from Janice. Her career is going well, and they are sending her on an assignment to Australia for a couple of years. *Oh well.* It's not forever, and I will still marry her one day. But she is selling her Honda Accord. *Would I like to buy it?*

She wants £1600 for it. This is a rather high price for an eight-year-old Honda Accord, but I know that this is a brilliant car; it's been maintained fastidiously and its low mileage (26,000 miles) is completely genuine. I can't let it get away. (And, it's Janice's car.) I like my Alfa Romeo, so I decide that I will buy the Honda as a surprise present for my mother. I can easily get a bank loan for it.

I make only one condition. I will send Janice the money in advance, she will give me the car just before she leaves for Australia (in about a month), but I want it with a new MOT certificate.[13] She is absolutely unconcerned about the MOT test. 'Oh, it will pass easily!' *We have a deal!*

I have had an account with the Bank of Scotland on campus since the time of my first arrival at Stirling, nearly six years ago. I have only been overdrawn without authorisation once, when I withdrew £5 from a cash machine, but only had £4.90 in the account. This made me ten pence overdrawn, but I rectified the situation immediately by transferring money from my savings account. It happened three years ago.

Now, I expect no problem with this loan application for £1600, since I have a job offer from Unilever. I complete the form, write a detailed covering letter, and attach a photocopy of my prestigious Unilever offer letter. I drop the application directly into the bank's postbox.

1986-87
Age: 24

I am slightly uncomfortable about applying for this loan, because Islam prohibits usury. The problem is: *what is usury?* Is it charging *high* interest, or is it *any* interest at all? Hakim gave a whole sermon on the sinfulness of usury, and he was very clear that it was hideously wicked to be involved with *any* amount of interest, in *any* way at all: charging it, paying it, even recording it as an accountant. This is very difficult for me. I don't see how I can live a normal, independent, successful life in the West without ever paying or receiving at least some interest. (By these criteria, I should not even have a savings account.) I don't believe that arranging this car loan will be wicked, since I'm the one who will be paying the interest; I am not exploiting or oppressing some poor farmer or labourer in the Third World, who is at the very end of the long lender–borrower chain.

The next day, the bank manager telephones me at my laboratory and asks me if I can come over to his office. I rush over there, excited. He is a white-haired Scottish man, nearing retirement. He tells me that he does not wish to give me the loan, but he can't seem to give me a reason. I show him the Unilever offer letter. He makes excuses.

'The job doesn't start until September.'

I demonstrate that I've got the money to make the payments easily until then.

'The job is contingent on you passing a medical examination.'

I say that I'm in good health, I'm only twenty-four years old, I don't smoke at all and I'm very fit. There is no reason to believe that I won't pass the medical.

I don't tell him that I plan to give the car to my mother; I tell him that I need it for my new job and it's a very good car.

He doesn't want to give me the loan, but he doesn't seem to have a valid reason. As soon as I mention that I intend to pay it off early in any case, he says they don't approve of such intentions.

1986-87
Age: 24

'You can't do that.'

Conveniently, I just gave him a reason to decline the loan.

I leave the meeting in a state of anger and disappointment. I really can't believe that after all these years with the Bank of Scotland, and with a very prestigious job offer, that he wouldn't loan me £1600 for a car to drive to work. *Surely it can't be racism? After all these years, surely not?*

My father is much more helpful. When I tell him that I would like to buy this car for my mother, he agrees it's a great idea and loans me the money. We agree the repayment terms; £100 per month, interest-free. He sends me a secret cheque.

Unilever assigns me to its Internal Audit function, based in London. This department sends teams of people around all of the Unilever businesses, performing internal audits of the records and systems in each company. Each of these audits typically lasts for a few weeks. It will involve lots of travel, learning about businesses and qualifying as a Chartered Management Accountant, which involves study and exams (*oh no!*).

I tell my supervisor that I'm going to quit my PhD; the research really hasn't been going very well and I've been offered an exciting job. Dr Maskill, a very decent man, has cut me a lot of slack, but I just couldn't make the Chemistry work successfully. I'm sure that he's breathing a sigh of relief; I think that I'm probably his worst postgraduate researcher ever.

In the last few days, I'm wrapping up my research notes and spending as much time as possible with Milton and other friends. One of my closest friends is Isobel Galloway, who is in the same research group as me, but there's also Susan Ellison. I've always been attracted to Susan, despite her Glasgow accent. (Perhaps these things don't bother me so much anymore.) She dresses very elegantly and has a certain class, which is unusual for the ragtag assortment of graduate students in the Chemistry department. Milton, Isobel, Susan and I go out to dinner; it is warm and wonderful – good conversation, laughter, friends at ease with one another. These are halcyon days.

On the last day of May, I pack all of my worldly goods into my Alfa Romeo, say goodbye to Stirling for the last time (as a student) and head back to my parents' house in London; I am due to start work in September.

Janice does a double-cross. She's already cashed the cheque but, as the time approaches for me to collect the car (in early June), she calls me to say that the car has failed its MOT test. It needs a new exhaust and this will cost £130. She suggests that we split this cost. I retort that we had a deal (£1600 in advance from me and a new MOT certificate from her), but she replies darkly that her father can easily arrange to sell the car to a dealer for more money, and reminds me that she's doing me a favour selling it to me. I agree to pay her another £65 on collection.

I take a train to Leicester and Janice picks me up from the station and drives me to her parents' house in Melton Mowbray. There we chat for a while over coffee, just like the old days, and then it's time to say goodbye. She is leaving for Australia in the next couple of days. I get into the car and start the engine. Janice approaches the driver's window and leans towards it. I turn the handle quickly to wind the window down. She kisses me lightly on the lips. I drive off, wave, and watch her in the rear-view mirror as I head towards the entrance of the cul-de-sac, in the process of which I nearly crash the Honda into Dr Singh's oncoming £28,000 Mercedes 500 SEC. I don't know when I will see her again, but I'm sure that we will get married when she returns from Australia. I have faith that Janice and I are meant to be together.

The drive home to London is a joy. My mother is surprised and delighted by the car. It is immaculate and it's hardly been used. She gives me her blue Renault 5 to sell and lets me keep the money. (She doesn't know that my father loaned me the money to buy this car for her.)

The Honda has a big UCSD (University of San Diego) sticker on the rear windscreen. I leave it there always, as a reminder of Janice, Stirling and old times.

With about three months to go before I start work, I particularly seem to be missing Susan Ellison. I don't know what to do about this. (I seem to be confused between Susan, who represents honest, unpretentious friendship, and Janice, who represents perfect, unattainable desire.) Four weeks after leaving, I drive back to Stirling to stay for a few days, sleeping on the floor in Milton's room. I love being here and, since this is my last summer vacation before I start work, I might as well spend some of it in my beloved Scotland and with my friends.

It's a wonderful summer. Immediately upon my arrival, Milton and I play a round of golf on the University's course. My mind is on Susan, but I don't really have a goal in mind or a strategy for getting there. Over the next few days, I hang around the Chemistry department and the coffee bar, and spend a little precious time with her, but nothing develops. It's clear that she sees me as a friend, but has no interest in me beyond this. There is no point in inundating her with gifts, songs and flowers. If the personal chemistry isn't there, it just isn't there. I am sad about this, but not sullen, and I will always respect her, not resent her.

One evening I drive up to Stirling Castle, with Milton and Isobel. I park the Alfa Romeo in the large cobbled car park at the top of the hill. We walk around for a while, enjoying the magnificent views, and then find ourselves on the road down from the castle. Obviously, the car needs to be retrieved and Milton offers to go to get it for me.

This is a joke on his part. Everyone is acutely aware that I am extremely possessive about my car, treating it with the utmost care as if the slightest mishandling will break it. In part this is due to my experiences with my Renault 5, and my lack of money to pay for repairs, but also because there really are some unique characteristics about the Alfa Romeo. It is very hard to put into first gear, if you are not familiar with it, and the handbrake is virtually useless, requiring the development of some special driving skills, especially when starting on a hill.

However, I am also sensitive to the fact that people think that I am very uptight and a control freak. In a moment of forced easygoingness, I hand him the key and say, 'Sure.' (Although I almost choke on the word.) But I warn him about making certain that the car really is in first gear when moving off, and ask him only to drive to the bottom of the hill and to wait for us there; I am painfully aware that he will not have the experience to manage a hill start in this unique car without a working handbrake. *I really shouldn't be letting him do this, but he's only going to drive the car a short distance down a hill. What could possibly go wrong?*

Milton cannot believe that I am allowing him to do this, but he takes the key and walks back up to the car park. Isobel and I are walking further down the hill when Milton drives past us in my beloved Alfa Romeo. I am immediately aware that the engine is being revved much higher than it would be if I was driving it, but I let it go; he soon reaches the bottom of the hill. Isobel and I are still walking down when Milton does something unexpected. He turns the car around and tries to bring it back up the hill, stalling in the middle of the junction.

Suddenly, there seem to be other cars all around him. I watch in horror and start running madly – that which I most feared is happening. Milton is revving the engine like crazy, but the car won't move. I know this is because he is in third gear, not first gear – he hasn't paid attention to my instructions. It gets worse in a most horrifying, heart-stopping way. Smoke starts to billow from under the bonnet as Milton's excessive revving causes the clutch plates to start melting.

I am running and frantically yelling 'Stop! Stop!' for what seems like an eternity, but he doesn't stop; he keeps trying to get the car clear of the junction, which can never happen in third gear on a hill, from a stationary start. The cloud of smoke gets thicker and larger.

I reach his window and order him to stop the engine, and to keep his foot on the brake. I go behind the car and order Isobel to join me, to push against it to stop it rolling back. Then I tell Milton to join us. Once he is with us behind the car, pushing against it, I run around and slide into the driver's seat. I take control, start the engine, put her in first gear and do that special trick that allows me to do a hill start without a working handbrake. I drive the car clear of the junction, turn her around and then bring her to rest in a safe place, out of harm's way.

Milton and Isobel walk over to my window. I rant and scream at Milton, calling him a stupid idiot. He says he can't understand why the car wouldn't move. I yell, 'Because you were in bloody third gear!' A few American tourists are watching this debacle; Isobel is trying not to laugh at my uncharacteristic and inexperienced attempt at fury. I rev the engine gently and drive off.

I'm not sure where I'm going. I want to make sure that the car hasn't been damaged by this nightmarish abuse. I want to drive her and *feel* that she is just fine. I handle her sensitively, tenderly, work through the gears, watch the rev counter and listen to the engine. I drive out of Stirling and onto the motorway, ease up to 70 miles per hour, then exit at Bridge of Allan and come back past campus. She seems to be fine.

1986-87
Age: 24

I cannot remain angry with Milton. *One*, because he is my best friend, and *two*, because all my stuff is in his room and I am sleeping on his floor – I have nowhere else to go. I drive back into town and find Milton at the bus station. I stop the car and he gets in. We are both subdued; never has such an event occurred between us. He apologises and I explain that I was angry because he had not listened to my instructions; he had assumed that he was right and that I was too neurotic about my car – but what I had told him about it had in fact been true.

I do remain concerned in case any permanent damage has been done to the car, but none materialises.

A couple of days later, Milton decides he needs a haircut and I decide to have one too. I go along with him to my usual barbers in Stirling; it's probably the last time that I will have my hair cut here. The barber finishes my perfect trim and now it's Milton's turn. Milton decides, on a whim, to have a 'number one'.

'Are you *sure*?' exclaims the barber.

'Yes,' says Milton. He is sure. He would like to try the comfort and convenience of very short hair.

In a matter of a couple of minutes, the barber shaves off Milton's hair. I think that, as he sees in the mirror the first swathes being cut, Milton realises that he's made a mistake, but it's too late to do anything about it now. My best friend has inadvertently become a skinhead.

It is embarrassing to be seen with him. As we walk in the shopping centre, where I'm looking at suits, people seem to do a double take now and then – are they really witnessing a skinhead walking with a Pakistani?

Milton, Isobel, Susan and I have dinner again. A few days later, I leave Stirling yet again. I'm getting used to this. If you do it enough times, you know it can never be the last time.

I have to buy suits for my new job. On Hounslow High Street, I buy the cheapest business suits that I can find; a blue one from British Home Stores and a grey double-breasted one from Dunn & Co.

There is further news from Unilever. Internal Audit is glad that I am available early and would now like me to start in July, ahead of the graduate training which starts in September. I have arrived in the world of business!

I open a new bank account, with the Midland Bank, and withdraw all of my money from the Bank of Scotland, except for ten pence. (For years to come, they are obliged to send me a monthly statement for the ten pence.)

My start at Unilever coincides with Milton coming down to London to visit. He would like to stay with me one night at my parents' house. This is fine, but I will be in Unilever House (my first day there) at the time of his arrival in London. We make an arrangement to meet outside the building at about 5:30 p.m.

I spend Monday at Unilever House as planned. In the morning, I can't believe that I'm going inside as an employee. The process of being photographed and issued with an ID card is almost surreal; it shows my face in a tie and jacket, and the big 'U' logo (it makes me think of *The Man from U.N.C.L.E.*). I love the idea of presenting this card to the uniformed security guard to gain admission to the building; it means that I belong. I meet various important people and I am briefed on my first assignment. I am to travel to Liverpool tomorrow morning to work on a company audit for a number of weeks. For this purpose, I am to meet a manager (Cathy Potter) at King's Cross station for the 8 a.m. train to Liverpool. Achieving this rendezvous will be my first independent task.

1986-87
Age: 24

I emerge from Unilever House, with all the smart professionals streaming out at the end of the working day. I am carrying an attaché case and wearing a suit, of course. A skinhead dressed in casual clothes is standing near the entrance. I appear not to notice the skinhead, but a shrewd observer would see that I give him a barely perceptible nod. I walk towards Waterloo station and the skinhead follows me.

Only when we are well away from Unilever House do I acknowledge my best friend. Well, I don't want people at Unilever to think that I'm friendly with skinheads.

At 6:15 a.m. the next morning, my brother Rehan kindly gives me a lift to the station in the Honda Accord. Because he's still a student, I give him £20, saying, 'Thank you, Luigi.' He replies, 'Thank you, Señor Templar.' (It's an old joke between us, from the 1970s.)

I stand on the platform, awaiting the 6:35 a.m. train, which will get me to Waterloo station in good time to take the Tube to King's Cross station. I am wearing one of my new suits and carrying my attaché case and a new Samsonite garment bag from Selfridges. There are many emotionless, professional men in grey suits, waiting on the platform, and I am one of them now. *I'm on the escalator!* This is so exciting.

The 6:35 a.m. train is cancelled. The next train is at 7:05 a.m. and it means that I cannot possibly make my rendezvous with Cathy for the Liverpool train. I have failed my first task. I imagine my reputation dissolving into ruins; I've stumbled on the escalator. This is a disastrous start to my career.

I take a later train to Liverpool, by myself, Cathy doubtless having gone ahead without me. From a phone booth in King's Cross station I call ahead to the company, asking them to give Cathy a message that I am coming on

the later train and that my local train was cancelled –
emphasis on *cancelled*, not *missed*.

When I emerge at Liverpool station, it is lunchtime and
Cathy is waiting for me, along with Daniel King. He is also
on this audit and will be my trainer. It is good to see him
again; he is a pleasant person and I like him. I frantically
explain that my local train was *cancelled* and they just laugh;
it's no big deal.

We have lunch at the Cavern, named after the club
where The Beatles originated. It is the first of thousands of
business meals that I will have in my career. Afterwards we
go to John West, the Unilever company that we are
auditing, and I begin to gain my first insight into UK office
life. (It doesn't seem quite as exciting as the brochure made
out, which is slightly perturbing.)

In the evening I check into the Adelphi hotel in the
centre of Liverpool. It is a posh business and leisure hotel.
My hotel room seems luxurious. *(Bond strode across the hotel
room, turned off the air conditioner and flung open the French
windows.)* I still can't believe it. I am *so lucky* to have this job.

These weeks in Liverpool are a whirl of meetings; learning
about the process of auditing and actually doing it; business
breakfasts, business lunches, business dinners; checking in
and out of the hotel; making sure that I keep all of my
receipts. I return to my parents' house every Friday night,
hot and tired, glad to get out of the suit and relax. But I am
loving it. Career-wise, I think that I have really made it.

Daniel King and I have dinner quite a few times and we
also play squash one evening, in the hotel. I let him win,
partly because that is better for my career and partly
because he is much better than me at squash.

There is a problem with the heat of summer and my new
suits. I find them very uncomfortable against my sensitive
skin, which becomes inflamed, and I have to resort to my

childhood trick of wearing cotton pyjamas underneath. There is no way around this. What I later realise is that buying cheap suits is a big mistake. I should wear only cool, light, pure wool suits, which are more expensive but infinitely more comfortable.

Of course, now that I'm working, I can't perform Islamic prayer during the weekdays, as I used to on campus. I do much of my *salaat* in catch-up mode, when I get back home or in the hotel room after work.

The only downside to this corporate life is the need to be up extremely early on Monday mornings to get that damned 6:35 a.m. train.

Shoes

1987-88

Age: 25

I HAVE A DREAM. I see a group of French cabaret dancers prancing in a line across the stage in their characteristic way, kicking their legs in the air, and they are singing, 'Are we angels or are we demons?' This is the spectre which continues to haunt me. *How am I supposed to know? And do I go to Hell for all eternity, for making the wrong judgment?*

I tell Milton about it. He says that it's quite obvious that my biggest concern in life is whether it was an angel or a demon that delivered the Qur'an to Muhammad. This doubt, which has been implanted in me, never seems to go away, no matter how much I discover the truth of Islam. Perhaps it is impossible to rationalise a religion completely, and you can't avoid having to make a leap of faith. *Wouldn't it be better if the theology you believe in is not as crucial as how it makes you feel and behave towards others? Surely that's the most important thing?*

My contemporaries join Unilever Internal Audit and we have our two-week induction course, which includes the theory and practice of auditing. I feel superior to them, because I've already done four weeks of auditing, and because I'm older, having done two-thirds of a PhD. This is a mistaken attitude on my part; they are bright, ambitious and determined, and they soon catch up.

On Friday evening, we are required to gather in a pub for drinks. I sip Diet Coke and try to mingle. The talk is of football teams and the different kinds of beer, subjects about which I know nothing. I wait patiently for the discussions to veer towards Comparative Theology; then I will be able to participate very knowledgeably.

One of my new female colleagues says something slightly provocative and fingers my tie with both hands. This is disappointing, because she is not the one to whom I am attracted; like all the men there, I fancy the other new girl, Geraldine, the one with the long blonde hair. Alas, I am invisible to her; we barely ever exchange a word.

Eventually, I slip away from the gathering discreetly, which turns out to be very fortunate. I learn later that, after everyone had had a few drinks, the girls went around pulling up the trouser legs of the men, to see which ones had hairy legs. In my case, they would not have been able to examine my legs, and would not have been able to determine that they are indeed hairy. The cotton pyjama bottoms would have blocked their view.

I shudder to think of the consequences to my reputation had I stayed.

Katharine and her husband William invite me to afternoon tea at their house in Harrow. Andrea and her boyfriend are there too. Andrea still looks beautiful; I can recognise what I saw in her, but the feelings have gone now. Her boyfriend seems like a nice guy and I'm happy for her. At last we are able to converse without a shred of tension. She is training to be an accountant, just as I am.

On Saturday afternoons, I attend the Islamic Circle at the magnificent Central London Mosque in Regent's Park. The Islamic Circle is a discussion group, hosted by Yusuf Islam (formerly the singer Cat Stevens). A large group of Muslims from many countries, including white Englishmen, sit together on the floor in a big circle and have a discussion about pertinent topics. We call each other 'Brother': 'Brother Brian', 'Brother Yusuf' and so on.

1987-88
Age: 25

There are two circles; one is for men, and behind a partition there is a smaller one for the few women who attend. Microphones on the men's side are connected to loudspeakers on the women's side, so that they can hear what is being said. There appear to be no microphones in the women's circle (I assume this to be the case, because I never hear a woman speak). I'm not happy about this, but it is a battle beyond my ability to fight.

In general, this communal gathering reinforces my Islamic beliefs and sense of universal brotherhood, although I am uncomfortable about these creeping elements of Wahhabism.

One Saturday, there is an old Englishman who tells his story. He had gone to Israel as an ardent Zionist, who wanted to see the Palestinians completely kicked out of the Holy Land. He hated the Palestinians and treated them with contempt, as subhumans. One evening, he was literally 'lost in the wilderness' as darkness was falling. Some Palestinians came upon him and provided him with shelter for the night in their home, giving him their only bed. He stayed in the village for a few days and was totally overcome by their hospitality. He had previously dehumanised them, but now, by spending time with them, he came to see the Palestinians as human beings. He was overwhelmed by their humanity and subsequently converted to Islam. He is in tears as he tells this story. His account is very touching and greatly reinforces my belief. Islam, sadly, usually lacks such emotional stories (whereas Christianity has plenty of them).

One of the Englishmen is Brother Jollian. We chat occasionally. He works for a scientific research company in Cambridge. He tells me about when he decided that he was going to start performing his prayers at the correct time during weekdays, in other words, *at work*. This would entail performing the preparatory ablution, including the washing of the feet. He was in the men's toilets and was very tense about it, hoping no one would come in. He had just placed one of his feet in the basin, and he nearly jumped with surprise as the door opened. He wasn't sure what to do as a colleague came in and saw him washing his feet. He decided to just carry on as if it was nothing out of the ordinary, and his colleague just went about his business. Apparently everyone knew he had become a Muslim and therefore readily understood that his unusual behaviour was due to this.

House prices in London have gone crazy. Most people cannot buy a home with just one income. My parents help me out, as there seems to be a certain urgency that I must get settled down. A brash, extrovert Indian mortgage-broker gives me some forms to fill out. He has the smallest mobile phone that I have ever seen: instead of occupying an entire attaché case, it is no larger than a brick. The broker takes a substantial fee and arranges a very big non-status mortgage, which requires no proof of income. My parents provide the deposit that I need to buy a house around the corner from them – a two-bedroom terraced house, with a large combined lounge/dining room and a separate garage in a nearby block. It costs £67,000. The mortgage, endowment policy payments and bills swallow virtually my entire monthly income. This is not quite as dire as it sounds: I can live very frugally; I eat at my parents; the utility bills are very low; by saving some of my travel allowances, I can have a little money to spend. The important thing is that I have bought a house (and will be better able to afford it as my salary rises). My colleagues are amazed and unduly interested in how I achieved this.

I am very grateful to my parents for helping me to buy a house. Out of a sense of gratitude and obligation, I agree to let them find me some marriage candidates – to at least give the process a chance. (My mother in particular is anxious, lest I be 'trapped by some secretary' at Unilever.) The truth

1987-88
Age: 25

is, I really haven't had much success in this department by myself, and the love of my life is now on the other side of the planet. In any case, that kind of marriage (with a non-Muslim, non-Pakistani woman) was always going to cause a family upheaval; I've never really been prepared to deal with it. So I can show some respect to my parents, and make them happy, by at least having an open mind about this.

The arranged-marriage process is mainly one of introduction and facilitation (usually). The word gets out that such and such a family has a nice, eligible boy (or girl) and everyone bends over backwards to find a nice girl (or boy) from a good family, to create the perfect match. There is usually a lot of exaggeration and distortion from both sides about each candidate's qualities, education and current job. (A medical technician would be a 'consultant doctor'. A classroom assistant would be a 'head teacher'. A solicitor's clerk would be a 'top lawyer'. Somewhere along the communication chain, my status would probably be twisted into a 'big executive'.) Any embarrassing personal history is always covered up. The two families meet, at the house of one or the other or that of a mutual friend, and everyone chats away, while pretending not to watch as the boy and girl eye each other discreetly. Then, after the meeting, feedback is elicited and the fixers – the middlewomen – determine whether there is to be another meeting between these candidates. Family members are always present and the candidates become fiancé and fiancée without ever being boyfriend and girlfriend.

I allow this process to begin and dutifully go with my parents to a number of such initial viewings; the food is always delicious.

I watch a video of a debate between Jimmy Swaggart, the famous American evangelical preacher, and Ahmed Deedat, the South African Muslim preacher of Indian

1987-88
Age: 25   313

origin. This takes place at the University of Baton Rouge, in Louisiana. The subject of the debate is: 'Is the Bible God's Word?'

Apparently Swaggart has been bashing Islam a lot in Baton Rouge, his headquarters, and some Muslim students at the University of Louisiana have invited Deedat to come over to Baton Rouge and organised the debate with Swaggart.

This is more fun to me than watching a football or boxing match on television. What could be more exciting than a theological debate? *Islam or Christianity? Angel or demon?*

Swaggart doesn't know anything about the Qur'an, whereas Deedat is an expert on the Bible. The debate is focused mainly on apparent biblical contradictions and errors. Deedat's approach is to demonstrate these and thus prove that the Bible *cannot* be the infallible Word of God. I am excited to see how Swaggart will deal with this.

The amazing thing is that Swaggart completely ignores every biblical contradiction or implausibility that is pointed out. Once again, I am taken aback by the *absolute certainty* of the evangelical Christian.

Swaggart asserts that there is only one version of the Bible, with many translations; he infers that the Qur'an has had more than one version. This is the exact opposite of the truth. Whilst the Qur'an has many translations, there is only one source version: the original Qur'an in Arabic has remained intact and unaltered throughout the centuries. The Bible, on the other hand, has many versions: the King James Version, the Revised Standard Version, the New International Version and so on. These are not just different translations; they differ in what is included from the source material. They have different content and are definitely different versions. Which one can be God's Word?

1987-88
Age: 25

The debate drifts towards the relative moral righteousness of the two religions. Deedat makes a big thing of Islam's prohibition on alcohol, which is a debilitating drug that hurts people and families.

Swaggart declares, 'True Christians don't drink either!'

The mainly Christian American audience applauds in support. (American society clearly does not have a problem with sobriety, unlike British society which, judging by the behaviour of many people after work and at weekends, seems to consider heavy alcohol consumption to be mandatory.)

The debate turns to Islamic rules and regulations – intended to create a safe, fair, moral and just society – and whether these have any merit. Swaggart declares that rules and punishments are not necessary, because for Christians who have surrendered to Jesus, 'the nature of sin is broken!' The hall explodes into uproarious applause.

I shake my head throughout the debate. I never cease to be impressed by this absolute faith, which no amount of logic, rationality and factual evidence seem to be able to shake.

In another video debate, Deedat asks an evangelical preacher (who also asserts that true Christians do not drink alcohol) about the fact that the Bible says that Jesus turned 'water into wine'. (Muslims do not believe this really happened – because it would be a frivolous use of the divine power which Jesus was allowed to channel – but his point is to challenge the reliability of the Bible.) The evangelist replies that it was 'fruit juice' that Jesus created from water (still a miracle) and the Bible is referring to it allegorically as 'wine'.

I understand the reason why one cannot argue rationally with an evangelical Christian. I have found that Auden, Magnus, Alan, Swaggart and others have always been consistent on one point: the blood of Jesus *guarantees* the Believer a place in Heaven. Failure to hold this belief

1987-88
Age: 25

guarantees a place in Hell. In Islam, there are no guarantees. The ultimate decision on every individual's final destination lies with God. We can assume nothing; we can only hope for the best and hope to be treated mercifully by the Almighty. That's why we say '*insh'Allah*' a lot, 'God-willing'. It's an acknowledgement that every decision, every outcome, is in the control of God.

Milton finishes his MSc and moves to Edinburgh again, where he gets a job. I take the train up there to stay with him for the night, and then the two of us head for Aberdeen, where we are attending Isobel's wedding. The reception is in the Amatola Hotel, where Milton and I share a double room to save money (*two beds!*). It's a very traditional Scottish wedding; it's absolutely wonderful. I wear my grey double-breasted suit from Dunn & Co. Susan is here, as a bridesmaid, and I end up doing Scottish country dancing with her. She *is* beautiful, but there's nothing between us except a friendship we both know will fade with separation.

I take the train back to my corporate life down south (and imminent Accountancy exams), with bittersweet feelings. Life is moving fast, everyone is moving on, many are getting married. The carefree times, when the future really was completely unwritten, are over. Some people I will perhaps never see again.

There's a letter from Janice. She's met a very nice Australian man; they have decided to get married; she will settle in Australia permanently. This isn't quite what I expected. *Is it really over? Was I wrong all this time? I really thought God had ordained the convergence of our paths for a purpose. Isn't that His job?*

I am very proud to be at Unilever, as one of their high-potential UCMDS graduates, and I want to do well, but it's

1987-88
Age: 25

not going quite as I hoped. There are some areas in which I am awkward and don't fit in with the crowd.

I'm too quiet and reserved. I have a lot going on inside my head. I am judgmental and analyse everything in terms of theology and what God must be thinking about it.

For example, there is one aspect of the Internal Audit culture with which I am very uncomfortable: *alcohol*. This is the great forbidden fruit of Islam. (I remember Hakim giving a particularly sobering exposition on the sinfulness of alcohol: drinking it, supplying it, carrying it, buying it for others to drink, being associated with it in any way.) Every Friday, whether we are returning to London or have been in Unilever House, there is an expectation of meeting at the pub for drinks. I don't drink and I hate pubs, more because of the cigarette smoke than the alcohol. At the end of a hard week of long hours and travel, wearing uncomfortable suits, all I want to do is get home, shower, put on casual clothes and collapse in front of the television, read a book or listen to music. I have no interest in prolonging the week by socialising further with the same people whom I've been with all week; I hate this. Unfortunately, the relationship-building and posturing over alcohol seem to be an integral part of one's credibility and career progression. If someone is leaving the department, then the Friday-evening gathering becomes their 'leaving do', and attendance is virtually mandatory.

Some of the jokes told by some of the men are both lewd and un-amusing. I am very uncomfortable about this; these jokes feel wrong. It's hard for me to pretend to laugh when I view the narrator with absolute contempt. This happens a lot during the weekdays, when we are away from London in teams, and meet for dinner in restaurants in the towns that we are visiting. There is one individual in particular whose jokes are vulgar, tasteless and completely unfunny. 'Smiffy' is a manager (as he keeps reminding us) and his subordinates laugh at his jokes to safeguard their careers, but he sees the poorly disguised disrespect in my face and knows what I think of him.

One afternoon, I'm traveling on a train with one of the nicest managers, a woman named Christianne Le Pla. We have quite a frank conversation. She tells me about a 'leaving do' that took place a couple of years ago, before I joined. Everyone had gathered at the pub, as required, and a 'strippergram' arrived. She quickly disrobed and went around the room thrusting her bare breasts in front of everyone's faces. They all thought this was hilarious – except for Christianne, who was outraged and gave a speech denouncing this vulgar exploitation of women. Everyone thought Christianne's outburst was even more hilarious, including the strippergram herself, and Christianne left in disgust.

I am greatly disturbed by this account. I am uneasy that I am in a corporate culture where strippergrams are considered appropriate, but I am even more troubled about something else. I know that Christianne did the morally correct thing in speaking out against this and leaving overtly. But I know deep in my heart that if I had been there, I would not have had such courage, and would have just tried to stay low-key. Christianne says that this is what most of the women did. Regardless of what they were thinking, they did not make a fuss about it.

I'm not the only one who has rebellious thoughts; I'm just not very good at hiding them. I cannot separate the contempt that I feel for certain individuals from the need to be perceived as absolutely dedicated to the job. I am becoming unmotivated and quietly aloof. This profile is making me stand out as *not* one of the crowd.

Furthermore, I have a special characteristic that is quite unique amongst my colleagues. I always wear slip-on shoes and, when I am sitting at a desk for any period of time, I like to discreetly slip them off under the table. To me this is entirely logical and consistent with all the world's most

1987-88
Age: 25

noble cultural traditions. It is comfortable and helps to keep the feet fresh. Being a Muslim, I have grown used to the pleasure of having fresh feet. I see no purpose in keeping them stifled inside hot, tight shoes all day long. However, this habit of mine is noticed and my colleagues all consider it to be bizarre. This earns me the not-altogether-friendly nickname of 'Shoes Off'.

I have seen a number of marriage candidates, but none of them is Teresa di Vincenzo. I need a woman to be intelligent, independent, career-minded and, of course, beautiful. It goes without saying that she will be a graduate and enjoy driving. Her having a good job is particularly important, as I need help to pay the mortgage. Although I am managing to do this, living with absolutely zero disposable income is beginning to wear me down.

Despite the lack of compelling candidates, I've caved in on this issue of a facilitated marriage. Why have I accepted it so readily? Since I was a child, all I wanted was to experience romantic Love – the forbidden Love of Western culture. The Love they sing about all the time.

All you need is Love …

I was desperate for such Love, but I always believed that I could never have it, because I'm not good-looking enough and I'm foreign-born and, most embarrassingly, I'm Muslim – we're so boring, we make the Amish look like swingers. And my practical experience confirmed it – I've been a complete failure at this.

But most obviously, the reason it can't happen is that it would cause too much anguish in my family. I don't want to hurt my parents – I love them so much and I owe them so much. I have an absolute duty to make them happy.

Western people marry *only* for Love, and we marry for *anything except* Love.

1987-88
Age: 25

There is no Love in Pakistani culture, except for family Love, and that comes with strings attached. It's only there if you keep within the rules and don't go off pursuing your selfish desires like a vulgar white person. There is no other Love at all. Romantic Love is completely forbidden, and all other kinds of Love are brutally absent – 'love they neighbour' (*why bother?*), 'love thy enemy' (*not a chance!*). From what I have observed, everyone in Pakistani society hates everyone else, based on religious sect, region of origin, native language, class, gender and so on. This is the great failure of the British masterplan of Partition, and the great failure of our Islam. It seems that all being Muslims hasn't been enough for us to love and respect one another. The only time that Pakistan functions as a coherent nation is when it's at war with India.

From this angle, Christianity seems to win hands down. Even though Islam is superior in its logical approach to the historic facts of Jesus' life, the Christian ethos of unconditional love is so compelling. Christian theology is so irrational, but the practice is so much more joyful. It doesn't make sense.

And the other issue is that I've never successfully had a romantic relationship anyway. I was *sure* that Janice and I were supposed to be together, that this was the work of an omnipotent God who made our paths cross – but it hasn't happened. It is well and truly over. She is as far away as she can possibly be on this planet (apart from New Zealand) and she's getting married.

I might as well have an arranged marriage. It's so much less trouble. I don't have to tell Janice that it was arranged, and she will be surprised to hear that I was successful in getting hitched (and will perhaps feel a twinge of regret). And I need the money.

Isn't Love all you need …?

1987-88
Age: 25

On the news I hear that Jimmy Swaggart has been caught consorting with a prostitute and is humiliated. I don't understand. He said that, through Jesus, 'the nature of sin is broken!' His whole argument rested on that. But apparently in his case, it *isn't* broken.

However, he makes a lavishly orchestrated televised public apology and carries on preaching. I am grateful to him. He has really helped me with my 'angel-or-demon' dilemma. Jimmy Swaggart is the best proof that Islam is true!

One Friday afternoon, after a week's auditing in Liverpool, I have the misfortune of sitting on the train to London with Mark Timson, one of my newest colleagues. He has already earned my contempt by earlier referring to one of the staff at John West as 'Big Tits'.

On the train he says to me, 'Last week me and my mates got completely smashed. It was great! I'm going to get completely drunk out of my mind again this weekend!' He notices that I have slipped my shoes off under the table and he exclaims, 'I hope your feet don't stink!'

I mumble some non-committal response to him. *Dear God. This is torture. Did this person really complete the same eight-page application form that I did? No wonder I was able to get through the whole process so easily!*

Despite my discomforts, I am proud to be a fast-track graduate recruit at Unilever and I *do* appreciate the opportunity. Unilever Internal Audit does not feel at all racist to me in any way – quite the reverse; it has an inclusive global outlook. (The attitude to women is ambiguous; they are treated as capable and equal, but strippergrams are okay. It's probably just a growing pain.) If there is any way in which I am an outsider, it is because I am a believing and practising Muslim, but this is my personal choice. They are not excluding me in any way; I am choosing to exclude myself to some extent.

I consider myself a very fortunate person. I have had great opportunities and choices. My parents have never been frightened, ignorant, fundamentalist puritans. My father has always been clean-shaven and my mother has never worn a *hijab*. (The presence or absence of a beard or a headscarf has no bearing on whether one is a good Muslim or not.) It's true that I have faced some racism in my life, but it's nothing compared to what my parents had to endure. They just got on with life; they didn't have time for self-pity. Given what they experienced in the 1960s, the possibility that their children would be able to integrate successfully into Western society – with equal rights and opportunities to pursue their own success – was unimagined.

There has been, and there still is, racism amongst the indigenous society, it's undeniable, but this is a feeble excuse to disparage the West in comparison to all the so-called Islamic countries, where tribalism is endemic, using anything as an excuse for discrimination, hatred and mistreatment: village, clan, family, sect, province, class, money, gender, occupation, even shade of skin. And in these countries, people just accept this as *normal*. At least the West is committed to implement the highest ideals – personal freedom, social equality, human rights, justice – and is willing to struggle with the consequences of these. The extent of social progress in Western society over the last few decades has been breathtaking.

But my parents don't represent *all* Muslims originating from the Indian subcontinent. Too many of 'our people' are confused by what Islam is, assuming that it must be the most puritan Arab way of life – an absolute Islamic *non sequitur*.

True Islam is culture-neutral. It really doesn't matter that the Prophet was an Arab; he could have been a Native American, or a Chinese man. What matters is the core

1987-88
Age: 25

message of Islam, which is universal brother(and sister)hood, peace, tolerance, forgiveness, justice, human rights, compassion, charity, humility, self-discipline, good deeds, freedom of religion, and care of the environment. But there is no focus on any of these ideals in the so-called Islamic world, and thus Westerners *never* associate Islam with these core values. (In fact, they associate Islam with the *opposite* of all of these – *whose fault is that?*)

Instead, the emphasis amongst many Muslims is on how stereotypically 'Arab' one can become: Arab clothing, Arab beards, Arab marriage process, even Arab names for converts. At the Islamic school, I was a failure; not because I didn't want to learn about Islam (*I did!*), but because I couldn't bring myself to learn to read and recite (without understanding) Qur'anic verses in Arabic. This was unnecessary to me, since I could read the Qur'an in English. I wanted to discuss Islamic thought and theology, in an intelligent, informed, unrestricted and un-intimidated way. So-called 'Islamic' schools in many countries suck the energy out of their pupils by forcing them to read and memorise Qur'anic verses in Arabic, which neither the pupil nor the teacher understand. If there is any discussion about Islam, the imam is free to define Islam how he sees fit, and who can argue?

Some sinister elements (*and they know who they are!*) are deliberately trying to drive a wedge between Muslims and their comfortable integration into Western society, by pushing extreme and absurd ideas of what is required by Islam – such as totally 'modest' dress, gender segregation, and the banning of music – creating rules which have no Qur'anic basis.

Arab traditions are not the only ones that have contaminated Islam. In many regions, local customs have been retained under the guise of Islam, with their followers ignorant as to their legitimacy. Many of these may be harmless, but some are not. At the very least, they rob

1987-88
Age: 25   323

people of freedom of choice in how to conduct their lives, because 'God' cannot be argued with.

Most hideous amongst these practices are female genital mutilation (mostly an African practice) and stoning to death for adultery (of Old Testament origin), neither of which has *any* basis in the Qur'an whatsoever. These are just a manifestation of man's inherent distrust, fear and subjugation of women, and Islam (like Christianity in Mediaeval times) is used callously as a vehicle for their propagation. This makes Islam appear barbaric to Westerners – and yet most Muslims are too ignorant, too complacent, or too afraid to challenge these abominations.

One Saturday, at the Islamic Circle, there is a rather disturbing incident. During the break, one of my 'brothers', an Arab man in a shabby grey suit and open-necked shirt, starts ranting and raving in the lobby of the mosque. What is the cause of his distress?

A Pakistani wedding is taking place in one of the mosque's large basement halls, which has been rented for this purpose. Guests are arriving in little groups. They enter the spacious lobby of the mosque (which leads to all areas, including the large prayer hall) and from the lobby they take the stairs down into the basement area. Some of these guests are loitering in the lobby, waiting for friends and relatives. This isn't just a mosque; it's also a major cultural, educational and community centre.

What has ignited the rage of the Arab man is that these Pakistani women are dressed *inappropriately*. I see nothing unusual or un-Islamic about it. They are all wearing brightly coloured and loosely flowing *shalwar kameez*, with matching scarves and rather a lot of make-up and jewellery. There are no breasts, buttocks, navels, arms or legs on display at all. This is not good enough for the Arab man, who does not yet seem to have adjusted to life in London. Being an Arab, his cultural preferences supersede those of the Pakistani

1987-88
Age: 25

324

women – he is empowered to define Islam however he sees fit. Even though these women are not going anywhere near the prayer hall, he is ranting that they should not even be in the lobby of the mosque dressed so *provocatively*. He takes his rage out on a younger man, whom he says should go up to these women and tell them what they are doing wrong (it being inappropriate for the older Arab man to engage in such direct conversation with young women). Unsurprisingly, the younger man is reluctant to do any such thing.

This incident is both disturbing and educational for me. It is a manifestation of the problems of the Islamic world: pathetic, tragic and funny. But it also painfully reinforces how far we all have yet to evolve.

My youngest brother, Rizwan, is a great intellectual. He is studying Anthropology at University College in London. One day, he tells me something very interesting and slightly perturbing. There's some writer called Salman Rushdie, and he's publishing a novel in which it's obvious that two of the characters are based on the Prophet Muhammad and the Angel Gabriel. There have been some stirrings of concern about this, apparently, as Muslims don't take kindly to their sacred figures (including Jesus) being used in any fictional way for the purposes of literature or entertainment.

I've never heard of Salman Rushdie and this book sounds as if it is bound to be somewhat obscure. I don't think it's going to be of any consequence.

The Iran-Iraq war is still going on. America continues to support Saddam Hussein, by constantly harassing the Iranians ... but one day things go too far. The *USS Vincennes*, lurking off the Iranian coast, shoots down Iran Air 655 – an Airbus A300 heading for Dubai – with the loss of all 290 passengers and crew (including 66 children). Apparently, they saw it on the radar and thought it was one

1987-88
Age: 25   325

of those F-14 Tomcats which America had supplied to the Shah. This tragedy was obviously a mistake; America would *never* deliberately commit such an evil act. The Iranians really need to understand this, and to forgive and forget.

Unilever Internal Audit department is having a day of paintball war games one Saturday, at a wooded site in Surrey. It's a cold, damp, grey morning as I pull into the muddy field which serves as a casual car park (dotted with much more expensive cars than mine) and I observe my colleagues and managers as they gather for this unique event. There is an upbeat air of excitement, but I can also smell that ugly undercurrent of competitiveness and alpha-male hostility. This will not be a game. Unilever Internal Audit is a place where only the aggressive and strong survive, and the slightest scent of compassion, of humanity, of weakness, would see one being stampeded upon by the herd.

We pull on military camouflage suits over our clothes; wear Perspex masks to protect our eyes; try out the vicious guns, which deliver red paintballs with a deadly sharp crack of exploding gas. As I observe the various personalities, I see they assume that their managerial ranks translate unquestioningly into military ones. I am the lowest rank in Audit department, therefore I must be a mere foot soldier, under the command of great leaders like Manager 'Smiffy'.

I laugh inwardly, and view this egotistical posturing with absolute contempt. In their arrogance, they have overlooked something. It hasn't occurred to them that some of us might actually have military experience. Not one of them knows about my career in the RAF cadets in Hampton School, when I learned to shoot a rifle with unflinching accuracy, to survive and to kill if brought down behind enemy lines – undergoing gruelling training in the school fields and nearby Bushy Park. They all think that you *pull* the trigger, whereas in fact you *squeeze* the trigger,

1987-88
Age: 25

while exhaling steadily. They just think I'm mild-mannered Imran, who's a bit quiet. The fools.

We are divided into two teams, with red or blue bandanas, and proceed to our two camps. I am relieved to see that Smiffy is in the red team, whereas I am a blue. (I'm not sure if the rules would allow me to shoot one of my own team deliberately.) The blue camp is to the west, the red camp to the east, and perhaps two hundred metres of dense woodland separate them. Each camp is defined by a circle of sandbags and has its own flag. The objective is quite clear. The first team which captures the other team's flag and successfully brings it back to their own camp is the winner. *Got that?* Capture enemy flag; return to own camp.

The self-appointed leaders are already strategising and giving orders, the foot soldiers being required to gather around and follow them unquestioningly to their deaths. But I have no interest in this. I have my own strategy to win this 'game' and it requires only myself. *('Imran needs to develop his team skills.')*

I discreetly slip out of the camp (no one pays any attention to quiet, mild-mannered Imran), disappear into the jungle, run due south for a short distance, and then drop to my knees and start *crawling* eastwards. (I suppose, as a Muslim, prostrating myself in an easterly direction comes easily.) That's what I do – I crawl.

My strategy is to move east past the other camp, and then north, and then west again, coming up *behind* it. No one will expect this. And no one will do what I am willing to do – to crawl this enormous distance on hands and knees, completely invisible, listening out for any sign of the enemy.

It hurts and it's tiring. The ground is wet and muddy, and my hands and camouflage suit become filthy. Carrying the gun is a real pain, keeping it out of the mud. But I know that this is the only effective way to cover the distance without being detected, and no one else will do this. They are too busy parading their egos into each other's gunsights. I just keep moving, picturing the kudos I'm going to receive when I bring back the red flag single-handed. *They just won't believe it.*

I hear a sound and drop nearly flat, looking out for where it came from. There in the distance is Smiffy, leading a team of three westwards – he's definitely in charge, it's in his body language and his attitude. He's the brave commander, courageously leading his men into battle. He thinks that walking in a crouch with your head lowered slightly makes you invisible! I would so love to come up behind this group and eliminate them, starting with Smiffy – but it's implausible that they would be so inept as to allow me to terminate all four of them before one of them managed to shoot me. And besides, that's not important. *Capture enemy flag; return to own camp.* That's the mission.

I wait for them to pass, and then I carry on, crawling foot by muddy, painful foot to the east. It takes a while, but eventually I see the red flag to the north of me. There's no sign of activity. I continue on for a short distance, then make the left turn to come up behind the enemy camp. There is absolutely no one around; there's no reason why anyone would be where I am – so far behind the red camp.

As I approach, I consciously slow down, control my breathing, keep even lower and take a moment to survey the situation. There is only one 'red' left to guard their camp. From her long blonde hair and perfect figure, I know it is Geraldine. She is crouching inside the circle of sandbags, looking west, pointing her gun vaguely at the jungle. I am directly behind her, and she is going to get the shock of her life.

I'm not going to spoil this with a moment's carelessness. I have invested so much in crawling the huge distance to be here, and now I just need to execute carefully the final part of my strategy. I crawl more slowly, more quietly, until I'm about seven yards behind her, just outside the sandbags, then carefully I draw myself to my feet. Silent as a shadow, poised as a ninja, I lift the gun and point it precisely (and somewhat mischievously) at her backside. *I'm sorry Gerry, this will only hurt for a second.*

My heart is pounding with the excitement of this. I'm going to return to the blue camp the same way I came, single-handedly bringing in the red flag. This is unbelievable – it's too good to be true. They will be amazed that Imran did this, and they will see me in a new light – never again will they underestimate me.

From this distance, it is impossible to miss (especially for a marksman like me). I exhale in a steady, measured way and slowly *squeeze* the trigger.

It doesn't go quite as I expected.

Instead of the sharp, cruel crack which launches a paintball with painful velocity into soft flesh, there is a gentle, steady hiss of escaping gas and no deadly projectile. I pull the trigger again and nothing happens. I look at the gun in my hand in disbelief.

Hearing noises, Geraldine spins around, is shocked to see me, but not too shocked to raise her gun and fire right at me. I am too close to miss. There is that sharp explosion I was denied, and then a vicious, breathtaking jab into my chest. My numb fingers go there and come back wet with a sticky red fluid, and I know it is the end for me. Time stands still a moment. I feel shock and tearful grief at the loss of the glory which should have been mine, and because no one will believe what I almost achieved.

I walk away, back to the waiting area, a broken man. I'm just mild-mannered, unremarkable Imran after all.[*]

The injustice of this is compounded on Monday, back in the office.

---

[*] Over thirty years later, I am still angry about this malfunctioning paintball gun.

1987-88
Age: 25

THE PERFECT GENTLEMAN

At the paintball event, we had each been issued with one cartridge of ten paintballs, free of charge. Additional cartridges were £1-50 each, and you were supposed to sign a sheet at the armoury every time you took one – so that it could be worked out how much you owed. Being desperately short of money (and being able, as an RAF-trained marksman, to make *every* shot count), I took only *one* extra cartridge, and signed the flimsy, damp, crumpled sheet clearly with my unpretentious and legible signature. I had noticed that many people were taking cartridges with gay abandon. Duncan Owen, the Senior Group Manager with a very upmarket house in Surbiton, had filled *all* the ammunition loops in his belt with cartridges. *Oh, how it must be to have money.*

Smiffy the Manager is the one assigned to work out how much we each owe. He passes me in the hallway and asks me for *ten pounds and fifty pence*!

'What?!' I exclaim. 'But I only took *one* cartridge.'

'Oh, I couldn't be bovvered to work it out for each person, so I just divided it evenly among everyone,' he replies with complete indifference.

My hand is shaking as, fuming with suppressed rage, I write him a cheque.

The search for a perfect wife for me hasn't been going well, as I keep rejecting the candidates for not meeting my criteria (especially not being attractive enough). To bring matters to a close, my father comes up with a brilliant idea. I will see *two* candidates on the *same* evening; it will be easy to make a comparison; one of them must obviously be better than the other; so that will be the one we pursue.

A couple who are friends of my parents are the fixers – they accompany us as we travel in my father's Honda Accord to the viewings. I know that some young men wear a suit for such occasions, but to me, a suit means 'work'. I am dressed in smart, casual Marks & Spencer clothes.

1987-88
Age: 25   330

The first meeting is in Hounslow – a typical semi-detached Pakistani house. The girl is short and seems rather timid as she serves the tea, and she never once looks at me. Apparently, she has a job in Pan Am. She seems a bit plain to me. The adults talk and I field the occasional question. (Wait, I think I'm an adult too, now – unless Unilever employs child labour.) As we are leaving, I make a point of saying 'bye' directly to the girl, and her face jerks away to look elsewhere.

The second meeting is in Hounslow – a typical semi-detached Pakistani house. This girl is reasonably tall, slim, possibly attractive, but her unimaginatively long and straight hair doesn't do anything for her. She has a degree in History – from a local college, she lived at home throughout – but she isn't working. We do exchange glances, make cautious eye contact.

In the car on the way home, my father thinks I should go for the first girl, because she's earning good money, but my inclination is for the second. At least she has a degree and can surely find a job. Plus, she was vaguely attractive. (It does not seem to occur to me that I could decline *both*. There is too much pressure now – both from my parents and from my constrained financial situation.)

Phone calls are exchanged and it seems that the second lot liked me too. Her name is Farzah. We are all set for another meeting.

There is a festive, expectant energy at the second event – everyone seems to know that this is going to happen. I manage to exchange a few words with Farzah, and she seems quite articulate. Her younger brother is also called Imran. There's a lot of laughter and chatter amongst the elders, and the outcome of the second meeting is that : *'It's a Go!'*

So, I'm all set. I have a house; I have a fiancée, soon to be wife (and thus able to help pay the mortgage); I have a great career ahead; soon I will have disposable income and

1987-88
Age: 25

sex three times a week as well (I think I read in *Reader's Digest* that's the norm). *Perfect!* All is well.

I have three weeks of study leave for the first stage of my Accounting exams. About halfway through, I travel to Edinburgh by train (reading about Business Law most of the way), and set-off for Milton's flat in Chester Street. It's dark and cold, and I'm carrying my Samsonite suit carrier. (Fortunately, a career in Unilever Internal Audit has taught me how to pack efficiently.)

An attractive young woman approaches me, and asks for directions. We end up walking together for a while. She is Australian, a doctor *(!)*, and she works in London *(!)* at Great Ormond Street Hospital for Children *(!)*. We have a wonderful conversation – she is such a nice person and we seem to 'click'. She asks me what I do for a living and what I'm doing in Edinburgh. (I don't say 'Auditor' of course, but 'graduate management trainee'.) She is impressed that I'm willing to travel so far to visit a friend. We come to where we must part ways and this would be where I ask her for her phone number and how about we meet in London after work some time for a pizza or something and I'm so excited that such an opportunity has finally come my way and … but wait … I can't – *I'm engaged.* Reluctantly, I say 'goodbye'.

In the last days of study leave, there is a dramatic change in the situation. My parents and her parents can't seem to agree on some things. There are implications or inferences that perhaps someone's son isn't good enough for someone's daughter. This is typical of people from *that* village. *Who do they think they are?* Tension begins to build in the negotiating phone calls, egos are offended, and the wedding is called off. I am no longer engaged. I feel like a yo-yo, the past few weeks have been a roller coaster, and now it's time for the exams …

1987-88
Age: 25

The Monday of the Stage 1 exams, I awake with a dark foreboding. It's a miserable, grey day, which seems to reflect my inner mood. I know that I haven't done what is necessary – that I have allowed a generous three weeks of study leave to slip by without becoming fully acquainted and comfortable with all the material. Quantitative Techniques – I understand that, it's like O-level Mathematics. Economics – I can get by through intelligence and watching the news. Business Law – that's reasoned waffling, and I won't forget to cite 'Salomon vs Salomon 1897' ('a company is a separate entity from its owners'). It's the Financial Accounting which troubles me – I seem to have developed an aversion to it. I don't really care about debits and credits and Fixed Assets and Balance Sheets. It all seems meaningless and artificial to me. The sun will still shine and the moon will still wax and wane – no matter what accountants do.

My assigned exam hall is in East London, which is a long trek. It seems an additional burden to take the train and then the Tube to a place I've never been, and then trudge around looking for the exam hall. The crowd of young people standing outside, some still reading accounting texts, gives it away. There's no one I recognise from Unilever here, which is just as well – I think I want to be alone. I have an old, old feeling. I shouldn't be in this position. After all the effort I made to get recruited by Unilever onto its prestigious graduate scheme, after all the time I've had to prepare for these exams, a person of my intellect shouldn't be so unprepared for a relatively straightforward test in something which hundreds of thousands, perhaps millions, of people understand and do for a living. It's pathetic.

The Financial Accounting exam is a nightmare. I have to produce a Profit & Loss statement and a Balance Sheet using partial records (some were destroyed in a warehouse fire, according to the question) and the profit figure I come up with looks ridiculous. This isn't difficult; the trouble is that I haven't practised enough so that interpreting the numbers becomes second nature.

The other exams go okay. There's an interesting question in Business Law. You meet your accountant at a party; over drinks, he enthuses about a 'great company' he's just bought shares in; you buy shares in the same company; the company fails and the share price collapses. Can you sue him for giving you bad professional advice? It's a perfect question for someone who can waffle ...

Back at Unilever House on Wednesday, it's as if we're back at school, with everyone talking about the questions and their answers. Cathy Potter assures me not to worry. I'm probably being too hard on myself – it's much easier to pass these exams than most people realise. She has no idea how badly I did.

Negotiations resume on the phone, there is a cautious, conciliatory meeting at their house on Saturday evening, the atmosphere turns celebratory, and we are engaged again. The next evening, I head for my BEP ...

My first Business Education Programme is at an extremely upmarket hotel in Wembley. It's a two-week residential course, with the weekend in the middle free. It's like being a student again, except in an unimagined way. We have lectures, group sessions, assignments to prepare and presentations to give. But instead of spartan student rooms, we have spacious hotel rooms with luxurious en-suite bathrooms; instead of beans on toast, we have sumptuous hot and cold buffets in the elegant restaurant; instead of being good-for-nothings, we are the *crème de la crème* of students, smart young adults with responsible and prestigious jobs and decent incomes.

The sexual energy hangs in the air like an electric charge.

1987-88
Age: 25

On the first evening, we have the introductory session from our course managers. We are seated at long conference tables arranged to form a giant square. Bottles of water (still and sparkling), glasses, and bowls of sweets are laid out at regular intervals on the pristine white table cloths.

One of the course managers is Charlotta Geen. She is of Scandinavian origin: tall, blonde, with green eyes. As she paces around the conference table, addressing us, I cannot take my eyes off her. I think she is literally the most beautiful woman I have ever been in the same room with. Her voice is a melody from the garden of Paradise. Whatever she has to say, she has my attention.

During the many evening social gatherings, I am able to find myself conversing freely and naturally with the many attractive young women on the course. Being a Unilever graduate recruit means that I have a degree of *de facto* credibility, and this seems to make me more confident (so much more so than when I was a reluctant and not very good Chemistry student). I actually dare to consider that some of the women may possibly find me to be possibly attractive.

Here's Sarah Reed again. She's chatting with me quite amiably. Tall and slim, with dark hair, she's in production management at one of our Manchester facilities – which is an incredibly responsible position. I wonder if she'll agree to have dinner with me this weekend?

Oh, but wait … I can't – *I'm engaged.*

At one of the social gatherings at a nearby pub, I am seated next to my Audit colleague Andy Whitfield. I feel like sharing my good news, so I tell him that, at the weekend, I got engaged.

'Congratulations!' he exclaims, with genuine warmth. He then proceeds to ask me questions about my 'girlfriend', which I field as best I can, but I'm very uncomfortable with

1987-88
Age: 25

the term 'girlfriend'. She's my fiancée – I don't think she was ever my girlfriend.

My other Audit colleague Jon Watts is also on this course. I tell him about it the next day. This news gives me a feeling of importance, of self-worth.

The BEP ends and we all go our separate ways. I don't ask for any phone numbers.

Officially a fiancé, I pay visits to Farzah's house by myself at the weekend. Things begin to happen which make me uncomfortable.

I'm sitting on the sofa in the living room, and I'm given coffee in a cup and saucer. There is nowhere to place this, so I rest it on the arm of the sofa.

'Don't put it there!' exclaims her mother. 'That sofa cost £700.'

'If I spill it, I'll pay you the £700,' I reply recklessly, but I obey. I consider – evaluating the tastefulness of the sofa – that they were ripped off.

On another occasion, there is a more disturbing development. Her father announces that they have decided to change my name. It's much too confusing to have two Imrans in the family, and Farzah is particularly uncomfortable that I have the same name as her brother. So, they've looked at my name and decided, by making minor adjustments to the vowels and consonants, that it can become 'Umar' – a respectable Muslim name. (Umar, or Omar, was a dangerously hostile enemy of the Prophet, who ultimately became one of the most loyal of the Believers.) From now on, they will all refer to me as 'Umar'.

When I was at Stirling University, doing my PhD in Physical Organic Chemistry, I used to doodle a lot of boxes. My colleague, Isobel Galloway, told me that this meant that I felt trapped. That made sense. I felt

1987-88
Age: 25

completely useless at Chemistry, my research wasn't going anywhere – but with nothing else to do, I felt powerless, a victim of my circumstances. The interesting thing was, it was impossible for me to draw an *open* box. If I drew the base and sides of a box, I felt an absolute *compulsion* to complete it with the lid.

This all changed when I joined Unilever: a fresh start; an exciting career; nothing to do with Chemistry; no prior knowledge required; just my natural talent being applied; a world of possibilities. I found that I could draw *open* boxes and feel no urge to close them. I felt liberated, excited, happy.

Now, this has again changed. Once again, I find myself compulsively doodling *closed* boxes. I am on the phone with my future mother-in-law – she has called me at the office. She is doing most of the speaking and I am listening – forced to do so by the need for respect and politeness. She is very concerned about her daughter's future life with me; in particular, she is adamant that her daughter should not have to work. *How much you earn? How much is mortgage? You wear suit at office?* I have already been briefed by my mother that *under no circumstances* am I to give *any* monetary answers to any such questions – so I am evasive, saying that all is comfortable and manageable. This is a downright lie. The entire purpose of me getting married is so that I can have a second income to pay the mortgage (and also so that I can have sex without breaking Islamic, Christian and Jewish law).

Now she's saying something about giving us a dishwasher, so that her daughter won't have to wash dishes. Well, I don't see how that can be possible. There is absolutely no place in my compact kitchen where a dishwasher could be fitted – unless we remove the fridge or the washing machine or the central heating boiler.

This is an ordeal, listening to her going on and on and on ... I'm not so sure this marriage is going to be a good

1987-88
Age: 25

idea. The top page of my writing pad is now a landscape of boxes.

I tell my parents about all this, and ask them to call it off. I can't bear the thought of having these people manipulating my life. They've already changed my name, and we haven't even started yet.

Gillian Blackhurst mentions something about my engagement, and I have to tell her that I'm not engaged.

'But that's what you told people on your BEP!'

'I know I did. I was engaged then, but I'm not now.'

At the Audit Department Christmas party, I'm standing around, nursing a Diet Coke, when Charlotta Geen comes up to me and starts chatting. It's inconceivable that she could find me attractive, but she is very personable and enchanting. How I would love to leave here with her, but that's not going to happen. Even if she wanted to (completely implausible), everyone would see. I think she's had too much to drink – that's why she's talking to me.

I leave Unilever House to head home on the 9:00 p.m. train, in a melancholy mood. I'm looking forward to the Christmas break, but where is my life going? Will there ever be sex?

My next audit assignment is an absolute disaster. It's a tea trading company in Stratford, East London, and it means I must commute there every day – getting no travel allowances (i.e. some extra money) and the pleasure of staying in nice hotels. So, future prospects aside, daily life is still miserable: no money, no exotic travel, no evenings out – and just more accounting exams to look forward to.

The journey to Stratford is a nightmare. I live to the west of London, and I have to travel to this grim place in the east. It requires that I take a very early train from Hampton every

1987-88
Age: 25

morning, change at Twickenham to get to Richmond, then take something called the North London Link, which trundles around to Stratford in its own leisurely time. The journey takes close to two hours door-to-door, and the North London Link is the longest part of it.

But there is something exciting about this journey. I always sit in the same carriage of the North London Link, which isn't very busy, and I always observe my habit of sitting at the back of the carriage, so that I can have the window open without causing discomfort to other passengers. There is a really attractive woman who always gets into the same carriage at the next stop. She has shoulder length wavy brown hair, a luscious figure, and she's a few years older than me. She tends to wear smart jeans and a tweed jacket, and she reads the *Guardian*. From these observations I deduce that she's a centre-Left liberal intellectual with an interesting job, and she would positively discriminate in my favour (as an oppressed minority) – even though I'm a man. I imagine that she and I could be fantastic friends and breathless lovers. *(I wonder where this assignation might take place. It can't be at my house, because that's just around the corner from my parents, and they sometimes drop in to visit. If it's at her place, then my mother will wonder why I haven't come home for dinner.)*

But the woman has no clue about our potential together, for we have never exchanged a word – so she has no idea that I am well-spoken, intelligent, educated, sensitive and a generally nice person. If only that communication barrier could be breached, she and I could have the joy of discovering each other and of pleasures unimagined.

One day, an amazing thing happens. For the first time ever, she sits directly opposite me. I sit outwardly impassive, inwardly excited, straining not to breathe too loudly, wondering if she can hear my heart beating. This is my chance to make first contact, to make an impression, to begin a fabulous relationship.

1987-88
Age: 25

Unfortunately, I am reading a trashy *Star Trek* paperback, which probably doesn't create the best first impression. If only it was *Catcher in the Rye*, or *The Grapes of Wrath*, or *A Portrait of the Artist as a Young Man* – something intellectual which would impress her. Maybe I'm underestimating her – maybe she loves *Star Trek* (this would be a first, admittedly, a beautiful woman who likes *Star Trek*; Janice expressed disdain for *Star Trek* at its first mention, so I never discussed it with her ever again).

While I'm pondering how to make first contact, the liberal intellectual woman takes the initiative. She leans towards me, reaches for the small, sliding window, and closes it.

Outraged, I react instinctively in the only way I know how.

'I'd prefer it open!' I exclaim, at the same time sliding the window open again.

'That's very antisocial of you,' she retorts, in a delicious, reproachful voice, with an accent delightful for its clear perfection.

She takes no further action and returns to her *Guardian*. I appear to be engrossed in, and intellectually engaged by, my *Star Trek* paperback. *Idiot, idiot, idiot.*

She never sits near me again.

My parents have continued their search for my perfect mortgage-sharing wife. We hear of one girl and there is an attribute of this particular candidate which is unique. Apparently, her father is a multi-millionaire! This is not to influence my decision, of course, but it is an interesting piece of peripheral information. The candidate is a computer programmer, which is a good thing; she will be intelligent, educated, methodical and organised.

We go to the house in Harrow, along with our fixer (middlewoman) and her husband, and at the house their fixer is present. These two women know each other, and each of them knows one of our respective families – so everyone can be vouched for.

The house is detached and big, but a little shabby. (I learn later that it is rented.)

Her father is quite an old man and her mother is much younger. He is described to me as having been, amongst other things, the Chairman and CEO of Coca Cola in Pakistan. (Many years later, I come to understand that Coca Cola operates around the world using independent bottling franchises, and this is what he actually was – a bottler.) Apparently, his business activities made him a leading millionaire industrialist. Apparently, he had to hurriedly leave Pakistan for England, when one of the Bhutto family was threatening to have him imprisoned if he didn't sell one of his companies to them.

They seem very posh and privileged. Her younger brother, Tahir, chats with me first. He's a student at the London School of Economics, which would be called a 'redbrick' in Britain, an 'Ivy League' in America (whereas my university is built of slightly mildewed concrete blocks). The girl enters the room and walks across it, barely glancing at me, and busies herself playing with someone's child. *Oh, she's gorgeous!* She's tall and slim and has lovely shoulder length hair that's been professionally styled. There is a beautiful energy about her. Her name is Sabrina.

Her father is interesting to talk to, and mentions that he is in the process of acquiring some gas wells in New Jersey. *Oh my God, it's like 'Dallas'!* He also tells me a little about his past experiences. He had sent a consignment of goods to the government of the Shah of Iran, worth nearly a million dollars. Then the Iranian Revolution took place suddenly, the Shah was overthrown, and he never received payment. Along with some other business people, he's still involved in proceedings to recover his money from the Iranians. He was Chief Protocol Officer when the Queen visited Pakistan. He founded and was Chairman of a major bank.

1987-88
Age: 25

He introduced Coca Cola to Pakistan; in the first year he made a loss, because some mullahs spread rumours that there was alcohol in the secret formula.

The girl is beautiful, she must be intelligent and sophisticated, and there is a doorway here to a life I never dreamed of.

Back at home in the evening, I make it very clear to our fixer that I really liked this girl. This message is conveyed to the other family, and follow-on meetings are arranged.

In subsequent meetings, I do talk with Sabrina, and there are a few disturbing revelations. She did not go to university; she went to a private and independent school of computer studies in London, above some stores on Oxford Street (I don't think it's officially accredited in any way). She is not really a computer programmer; she works in the support and use of office software in her company. She hates driving; although she passed her test, she gave it up completely after a couple of accidents. She clearly does not meet some of my key criteria.

Apparently, Sabrina had *always* wanted to do interior design, and passed the highly competitive entrance exam to one of Europe's leading and most prestigious design schools but, a few days before the fee was due to be paid, her father showed her a brochure for this computer school and suggested to her that she should learn about computers instead – because computers were becoming very big, and *what use does anyone have for an interior designer?* Her mother did not interfere in this discussion. Sabrina's dream of being a designer was squashed flat.

She has been told that I am highly intelligent, always got A's for everything and have a PhD. (Well, I only did two out of the three years required, so that would be a Ph, but no D.)

Despite her deficiencies, I am keen to proceed with this candidate and, at the fourth meeting in April, we become engaged. I receive a Gucci watch. The wedding will be in September.

The next day, at the tea company in Stratford, I tell my fellow auditor Richard Kingsbury that I just got engaged last night. He congratulates me, but then I can tell from his face that he's confused as to whether this is a new person I've committed to spend the rest of my life with, or is it the same person I was committed to before Christmas, on-and-off. It's funny that, during all these days on the audit, Imran never once mentioned his girlfriend.

The wedding will be at the Porchester Hall in Bayswater. The tradition is that the bride's family hosts the wedding; the follow-on reception, a couple of days later, is organised by the groom's family. There will be other events before the wedding too, celebrations with singing and dancing, and much Pakistani chaos.

I plan the honeymoon. The Greek islands look beautiful in the brochures (and cheap), so that's what I'm thinking of. Then I watch a television documentary about the drunken and obscene behaviour of young English people at Mediterranean holiday resorts, so I decide to look elsewhere. *What about Disney World? That was the best holiday I ever had when I was a kid, and with sex it would be even better.*

I book a trip to Orlando, with Virgin Airlines. I secure a big overdraft to pay for this, but it doesn't matter. Soon I will have a second income which will eliminate all my financial worries. I arrange a total of three weeks of vacation time in September; we will leave on our honeymoon a few days after the reception.

One day I'm asked a question from the bride's family. *What car would I like?* I convey the answer back. That's easy – a Honda Prelude. That's a quality car which is sporty, without being too flashy. I imagine it being parked outside

1987-88
Age: 25   343

my terraced house, and driving to Internal Audit assignments in it. People will be so impressed. It will always start, it won't take an eternity to warm up, and it will be flawlessly reliable and wonderfully comfortable. The handbrake will work, just as it's supposed to. I will have to sell the Alfa Romeo – it has served me well, but one must move on, not maintaining attachment to material things.

This new car must be part of my wedding gift package, which includes suits, ties and countless shirts. I have really made it!

I am so looking forward to being married. I think.

One day when I arrive at her house, Sabrina tells me that there's a hi-fi system which has been delivered for us as a wedding present. One of her father's friends is very big in the electronics business apparently, and he has sent us an Akai system, which comes in several boxes. She thinks one of them is a CD player.

I'm familiar with these systems – I've seen them in showrooms. The CD player will be multi-disk, there will be surround sound speakers, a remote control, graphic equaliser, digital display on the radio tuner and many flashing lights. Excitedly, I load the boxes into my soon-to-be-made-redundant Alfa Romeo.

It's not quite as I expected.

When I open the boxes back at home, the reality is somewhat different – surprisingly so. There is no CD player, one of the boxes turns out to hold a record deck (I haven't bought a record in years), there's no remote control or surround sound speakers, and the radio has one of those old sliding needle tuners. This Akai is some aged, obsolete model which no one was ever going to buy, so it's been dumped on us.

This doesn't make any sense.

One week before the wedding, at one of the celebratory events, I feel a deep foreboding that I am not doing the right thing. I may not be marrying the right girl, or for the right reasons. There isn't that spark I need; perhaps my enthusiasm is really because her father is a multi-millionaire?

But, it's too late. Over four hundred people are coming to the wedding (not including the ones without an invitation – a typical Pakistani habit), and my entire department from Unilever is coming to the reception, which my parents have arranged at great expense. For me to change my mind now would cause great heartache, pain, humiliation and embarrassment. I don't have any choice.

What would Mr Campbell (my old Headmaster, who taught me about Jesus) say, if I asked his advice? He would ask me if I love her. White people, Christians, Westerners – whatever we call them – they marry 'only for Love'. We marry for anything *except* Love. They seem really happy; we seem always stern and serious. The traditional Asian bride is required to keep her gaze lowered and look sad. That's probably because she really *is* sad. She has not one iota of freedom or free choice in her life. Nobody asked her what *she* wants out of life. She probably doesn't even know herself – she never had a chance to think about it, to try things out. She's adorned with hideous jewellery, plastered in heavy make-up, and weighed down with garishly bright clothing. Her natural beauty is buried under this vulgarity. And her first duty is to reproduce, and it had better be a boy.

But my family, we're not like that, are we? We are modern, liberal, forward-thinking. We follow traditions only to provide some décor to life. We believe in the education of women and social justice and planned parenthood. But marrying 'only for Love' – that's going too far. It's irresponsible. It's not practical. And to fall in love requires a degree of interpersonal intimacy which is verging on immorality.

1987-88
Age: 25

The Western happiness – it's an illusion, isn't it? Their divorce rates are terrible, they suffer from so much stress, they become alcoholic. It's all false, isn't it? This obsession with Love instead of practicality – it doesn't work, it doesn't pay the bills.

Love.

I used to think that Christianity is easy, because all you have to do is sing hymns and there isn't the heavy burden of rituals and practices which define Islam. But rituals are easy, compared to 'Love thy enemy'. That's really hard. And it's not rational – it will get you killed.

Islam is logical, Christianity is illogical. That's why there's so much emphasis on 'faith' in Christianity – you need that to fill the holes.

It's compelling – but in an irresponsible, exuberant, undisciplined kind of way.

I'm just getting cold feet, because I'm nervous about getting married. The facts are:

- o   I'm sure that I love her.
- o   She is beautiful.
- o   She and her family are acceptable to my parents.
- o   Her father is rich (this is purely incidental). (But there's no sign of the promised car.)

I think this is going to work out just fine.

It doesn't go quite as I expected.

To be continued …

Imran Ahmad will return in

The Imperfect Gentleman

1987-88
Age: 25

Tapestry

Glimpses of the Future

Dreams

2000 Age: 37

GENERAL ELECTRIC IS ORGANISING my relocation from Minneapolis to London, for my new European position. London will be the best location for my interactions between the US, Europe and India. I've loved living in America, and I'm sorry to be leaving, but I consider that this will be merely a long-distance relationship, not a divorce. America will always be a part of my life now.

I begin the transition by making a series of transatlantic business trips, which means that my Platinum frequent-flyer status with Northwest Airlines looks to remain secure. In London, I stay at my parents' house instead of a hotel, to save the company money (because I care so much about the shareholders). It's also fun to be staying at *home* again.

GE is providing me with a rental car temporarily, but I do need to get a personal car sorted out. In America, I always had a brand new car, but I cannot afford such an extravagance back in England, because house prices have gone crazy and I need to save every dollar I can for a deposit on a house. (Also, I'm not as wealthy as I was supposed to be, after my shares in my previous employer fell from $81 to about three cents.) I decide to buy a cheap, old car, and discuss it with Milton on the phone. 'How about a Jaguar XJ-S?' he suggests. *That's ridiculous; an XJ-S is an unattainable dream car.*

Two weeks later, I drive out of the posh dealership in my Jaguar XJS (a later model than XJ-S). The smile on my face is as wide as the Grand Canyon. It has two previous owners, a full service history and a new MOT. It's an old car and a relatively inexpensive one, but it really gives me pleasure. The interior is grey leather with walnut panelling, and there's a huge walnut and leather centre console with shiny controls. There are switches on the console which control the *electric* windows. These are a bit rickety, so it's best not to operate them too often.

It's a childhood dream come true. When I pull into my parents' driveway, my father looks out and is surprised to see me in the Jaguar. I tell him it's mine and he thinks that I am joking. For some reason, he finds it easier to believe that this week Hertz has given me a Jaguar XJS.

The next morning, a Saturday, I set off to visit Milton in Edinburgh. I'm driving to Scotland in a Jaguar XJS; *what could be better than that?* As I cross the border, my heart leaps with joy, as it always does when I enter Scotland.

I call Milton on my mobile phone as I'm about to park beneath the window of his flat. He looks out and shouts something about me 'trying to park an ocean liner'. We travel to Stirling this evening, for dinner at *Qismat*. Of course, I don't let him drive it.

How lucky I am! A Jaguar XJS is my car. My car is a Jaguar XJS.

It doesn't go quite as I expected.

The Jaguar XJS turns out to be a triumph of marketing over quality. Its build is inferior to the very cheapest Honda or Toyota, and it suffers endless problems. I drive it to important meetings of General Electric and the damned thing breaks down on me. The car is a money vacuum; no matter how much I spend fastidiously on its repair and maintenance, it always sucks up more money.

I learn later, through Internet research, that when *Return of the Saint* was being filmed, the XJ-S was always giving them problems, even though the production crew had a dedicated Jaguar engineer assigned to them full-time. When

2000
Age: 37

the Saint (or rather Ian Ogilvy, the actor) was driving the car back to England from Italy, it broke down just outside Rome – the gearbox totally disintegrated.

On another website, I read that I should consider the money I spent on buying the XJS as 'merely a down payment'.

I have a theory that the men who assembled these cars hated the 'rich bastards' that they were destined for, and so deliberately put them together in a slipshod way. The car is such a disappointment to me; it has no integrity or reliability.

It is beautiful, though.

———————

Soulmate?
2004 Age: 42

Thanks to bad weather this afternoon, my flight is two hours late getting out of Richmond, Virginia. At Newark Airport, before I can board the overnight flight to London, I must go to the outbound INS office to answer their questions (to ensure I haven't been engaged in terrorism-related activities) and to register my departure from the United States. These are the rules of Alien Special Registration and, if I neglect to do this, Homeland Security will never let me enter the US again (which would be really career-limiting in my American company).

The office is poorly signposted, discreet and small – regular people do not have to come here, only 'special' people like me. There's only one INS officer and one aged Pakistani man being questioned. I interrupt, ask forgiveness, and explain that my flight out of the US is leaving in just a few minutes, and I have to register my departure urgently. Sometimes INS officers act uncaringly and strictly by the rules, but this guy is quite decent and lets me cut in; he hurries through my departure registration; I thank them both; I sprint for it.

A kind and friendly Indian couple let me cut in front of them at the security screening – everyone can see that I am literally running for a flight. As I approach the gate, I can see the aircraft is just beginning to back away. Even with my optimistic outlook and positive visualisation, I know this means it *really* is too late.

I immediately make a decision, thanks to all those books I've been reading. This is not a disaster or an adversity – it's merely an experience, and I am going to live, breathe and appreciate every moment of it. The Indian couple look shocked as I pass them walking back the other way. I smile.

At the Continental ticket desk, they reschedule me for a flight tomorrow night, so it means I'll be spending Thanksgiving Day here. Fortunately, there is a Sheraton Hotel at Newark Airport, so I'll get some frequent guest points out of this – and dinner, breakfast and lunch on the company too.

Despite my Platinum membership card, the attitude at the Four Points Sheraton Newark Airport hotel is appalling. The sullen (and possibly hostile) man behind the counter says that they don't have any Club level rooms, to which my Platinum membership card entitles me. (On the night before Thanksgiving, they *can't* be busy with business travellers, so he *must* be lying.) He won't even let me have a bathrobe – despite the fact that I have no luggage, so no change of clothes. He claims they don't have bathrobes!

The ordinary room is badly lit and without any elegance, and I can hear traffic and police sirens when I open the window. I take the elevator up to the top floor and confirm that it *is* a Club Level, with superior rooms. I walk up and down the corridor, feeling the thicker carpet beneath my shoes, and knowing with absolute certainty that each of these rooms has a pair of luxurious Sheraton logo bathrobes hanging in the closet (with accompanying slippers). I can't tell if these rooms are all occupied, but it seems completely implausible that this floor could be full on *this* night of the year. I am entitled to a room on this floor, but the miserable, obstructive man downstairs won't allow it.

The hotel restaurant is closed and the only dining facility in the immediate vicinity is a strip club – which would not look good on my GE expense claim. I order a pizza to be delivered and eat it with no clothes on (I have hung them up near the window to freshen them as much as possible).

I'm really struggling to see anything positive in this experience.

The next morning, I return to the special INS office to explain that I didn't actually leave the United States last night, even though they think I did, because I missed the flight. She looks at me with exasperation (as if to say, 'Get outta here!'), examines my passport, and tells me not to worry about it – as long as I *do* leave tonight. (This system seems seriously flawed – if I *was* a terrorist, I wouldn't be following their rules.)

I have to pass Thanksgiving Day at Newark Airport, which is exciting. I get some breakfast, and then decide to ride the AirTrain up and down, and observe the goings-on.

I'm standing on the platform at Terminal A, when I am strangely compelled to become aware of two women walking towards me – a youngish white woman and an older black woman. They stop near me, and are engrossed in conversation. When the AirTrain arrives, they get on at the back of a carriage – and on a whim I follow and stand beside them.

The white woman is perhaps in her mid-thirties. She is a brunette, with an attractive face, shoulder-length hair, lively eyes, and an excellent figure. She is dressed casually in jeans and has no luggage. There is a vivacious quality about her as she speaks, and I find myself captivated.

The African-American woman is perhaps in her early sixties, but could be older or younger – it's hard to tell, because she is in very good shape. She is simply dressed, with a distinct elegance; her smart luggage is functional and limited, indicating a lack of ostentation; she has an aura of absolute dignity. The airline label on her suitcase handle indicates that she has just arrived from Minneapolis-St. Paul, and clearly the younger woman came to Newark Airport to meet her. She listens to the younger woman, giving her full attention, but saying little; when she does speak, her voice is soft but authoritative. There is something mysterious about her and it sparks a subtle awe and respect in me. I *feel* that she is a Wise Woman.

I casually listen to their conversation, and learn that the younger woman moved to the East Coast in April 1995 – nearly ten years ago. Also (in another random snippet), that the younger woman likes outdoor activities, and once had her sunglasses stolen from an outside pocket of her backpack, while she was wearing it, by a youth she describes as a 'little shit'. I think that's a good term – it's as strong as you can get to convey deep contempt, without verging into unacceptable profanity. (This term might be useful if I ever do get around to writing a book, but want to keep the language within acceptable parameters.)

I like this mention of a backpack – it means that she would love Scotland. *Is it possible that I might take her one day?*

But what is their relationship? To meet someone at the airport on Thanksgiving Day indicates a very close, possibly *family* connection. Given their different races, could it be that the older woman is the mother-in-law? In which case, this encounter is going nowhere. But I check the younger woman's left hand and there is no ring. Married American women *always* wear wedding rings.

The AirTrain leaves the Terminals, and is now heading for the Newark Airport rail station – crossing a large area of open land. It's not brilliantly sunny, but there is a high level of ambient light – certainly enough for me to be uncomfortable and to justify putting on my sunglasses, which I always like to do. But I'm conscious that I don't want to appear creepy or odd in front of these two. Regular people would not wear sunglasses in these conditions – it's not *that* bright.

The younger woman reaches into her handbag and puts on a pair of smart sunglasses.

Thank you!

I casually reach into the pocket of my smart, navy blue blazer (which I bought when I first joined GE and have

2004
Age: 42

worn on every business flight since) and extract my elegant Serengeti sunglasses. I put them on and busy myself looking intently out of the window at the unfamiliar landscape.

There's a pause in their conversation – an almost expectant silence.

There is no one else left in our part of the AirTrain. Given the label on the luggage, it's the easiest thing in the world for me (despite my shyness and reserve) to initiate a conversation.

'Have you just come from Minneapolis?' *(Casual.)*

'Yes.' *(Friendly.)*

'I lived there for five years.' *(Justifying intrusion by establishing mutual connection.)*

They quickly establish my credentials by asking about the places where I lived in Minneapolis, and then the Wise Woman says to me, indicating the younger woman: 'She's from Saint Paul.'

Now we are conversing freely. I put myself in the role of stranded passenger, wondering how to pass Thanksgiving Day, before taking my flight back to London tonight. The younger woman tells me that the station in New York City which I would access from Newark Airport rail station isn't very centrally positioned, and that if I am time-constrained and worried about missing my flight, travelling into the city probably isn't the best idea.

We arrive at the rail station, and the Wise Woman strangely detaches herself from us and goes to make some inquiry of the station staff, leaving us alone to talk. We both remove our sunglasses.

There are so many questions I can ask, so much to establish, but somehow *I feel* that I will have time later. I don't even ask her name, or give her mine. Instead, I tell her that I'm a writer and hand her the business card for my website, which has my assorted writings on it (so much easier than writing a whole book and waiting for it to get

2004

published). Although this website has an e-mail address on it, nowhere does it give my name. For some reason, I judge that I don't need to give her my proper business card, with all of my employment and contact information on it, because the writing website will suffice.

I say goodbye to them, as they head into the rail station, and I take the AirTrain back towards Newark Airport.

As the train crosses the vast tract of open land, I reflect upon what has just happened here, and whether it was significant – *or am I being delusional?* The brunette woman was just perfect: intelligent, vivacious, attractive, fit, articulate, the right height. I *think* we had chemistry between us. And the African-American woman was mysterious and wise – and it seemed like she *wanted* the younger woman and me to talk. But I'm very wary of interpreting things the way I *want* them to be, and I also don't have any expectation of my perfect soul mate ever being delivered to me. That part of my life has been a complete disaster. The 'marriage' was terrible for Sabrina as well, but at least we both learned a lot and are on excellent terms. (I have learned that relationships are hard work – it's not all moonlight and satin sheets. A healthy relationship requires a great deal of patience, sensitivity and compromise, and the courage to be vulnerable. I know all this because I read it in a book.)

At this point, looking out of the AirTrain window, I unexpectedly witness an old friend – the phenomenon known as Epiphany. The bright sun is partially hidden in an isolated cluster of clouds, and its rays are lighting up those clouds into magnificent, brilliant whiteness, and bright, vertical, visible columns of light are coming down, illuminating the countryside below, where they hit the ground, leaving the surrounding areas comparatively grey and dull.

2004
Age: 42

Whenever I see Epiphany, I feel that something significant is happening. But this Epiphany is different – there is something about it which I have *never* seen before.

A beautiful clear rainbow runs over the top of it.

I return to Newark Airport in a state of almost inebriated joy.

I hope she e-mails me. And if she does, I know exactly what to do: *communicate, communicate, communicate!*

Reunification
2006 Age: 43

Because he's a major character in my book, it's only fair that I tell Auden about it. He was one of the Christian fundamentalists in school, who kept trying to convert me and were convinced that the Qur'an came from Satan, in order to deceive people away from Christianity. Ironically, it was that kind of constant haranguing which drove me to be absolutely certain about Islam – effectively becoming a fundamentalist myself.

I get in touch by e-mail and he reads an early version of the narrative. He tells me that he really enjoyed it, and we agree to meet. I drive over to his place one afternoon.

That such a day would come was to me, for many years, unimagined. It is good to see him again and we talk for hours.

He tells me about his own spell of fundamentalism.

He had been a member of an evangelical Christian fellowship while at University, but he never completely lost his sense of intellectual honesty, which Hampton Grammar School encouraged in us. Sometimes he would ask searching questions and others would look at him with unease, as if his faith was severely deficient. Eventually, he could not reconcile certain attitudes and beliefs with the need to be true to himself. He left the Fellowship, as a matter of conscience. Later, freed from the dragging weight of the intellectual and spiritual constraints it imposed, he started re-evaluating many things. One of these was his Christian fundamentalist outlook which, after a time, he also abandoned (including the belief in Rapture). The word went around that Satan had managed to get him and his soul was lost.

We have a great conversation. I ask him about the mysterious phenomena which were a significant feature of my dealings with the evangelists. He says that the events do not surprise him, and were not unusual; I was clearly so anxious about a miracle appearing to convince me that the evangelists were right, that my troubled psyche manifested things.

This makes sense to me. Who knows what our minds create, in the petrified, grey netherworld between sleep and wakefulness: demons, ghosts, aliens?

We adjourn to the kitchen, where he makes dinner. *Who would have thought it?* Two fundamentalists, sworn enemies, Crusader and Saracen (Narnian and Calormene), each committed to his own, one *true* God, have stumbled out of the darkness and, each in his own way, has seen a greater Light. Who would have imagined that their deluded, self-imposed Partition would one day be swept away by Reunification?

Now, there's no Rapture or Judgment to worry them, but they have to take full responsibility for the problems of the world. No acquiescent sky-God is going to absolve them of the outcome of their neglect, greed, fear and selfishness, with admittance to a sensual, exclusive paradise. They have to solve the problems, or face the consequences.

In the meantime, they enjoy the finest pasta and microwaved sauce that this life has to offer.

Star

2011 Age: 48

Star has been completely lethargic all Saturday. The vet saw her this morning and said that she hasn't been eating because of her teeth troubling her again. She has lost nearly half-a-pound and is no longer overweight for an old Dutch rabbit of seven-and-a-half years. The vet gave her some nutritional mixture for feeding by syringe and said to bring her back on Monday morning for tooth surgery.

Star normally wanders freely all around the house, but now she's totally immobile. Late in the night, I carry her up to my bedroom and lay her down on the carpet, next to the bed, along with a glass bowl of water and some coriander right in front of her nose. She doesn't even sniff it. I've never seen her like this; she has absolutely no energy.

I leave the bedside lamp on – I don't like the idea of her suffering, weak and unable to move, in the dark.

It's 2:55 a.m. when she wakes me suddenly with a commotion. I'm not sure how she did it – I would swear she cried out to me. She's leaping about – there's water splashed everywhere and even the coriander is scattered all over the place.

I lurch out of bed, exclaiming 'What's the matter, Star?' and then I'm down on my elbows and knees beside her. She's stopped moving about, suddenly. I hear her take two slow, deep, distinct breaths – I've never heard anything like this from her before. I run my hand along her beautiful, soft, shiny black fur; I kiss her gently on the side of the head; I say, 'I love you, Star.'

She stretches out her legs and lays her head down sideways, her deep eyes wide open.

There is something strange and still and sacred and protected about this moment. I swear I hear music – but there's no sound. I swear there's a bright light – but there's only the dim glow of the bedside lamp. I swear I hear Star – but she's silent. I swear she's still here – but she's gone.

She's completely still. I stroke her gently, I kiss her, I tell her that I love her. The tears flow now and I talk to her, thank her for the joy and happiness and laughter and learning that she brought me, and the unconditional love she always gave. Eventually, I cover her and go back to bed.

The July sun wakes me soon after 5 a.m. I know what to do.

There's an area of the back garden I call the Fairy Wood. It's thick with trees, but long ago I cleared all the lower branches to create a heavily sheltered sitting area with a canopy of branches overhead and a deep carpet of soft, dry foliage underfoot.

In the solitude of the early morning, I choose the tree that Star will become part of, and dig a hole beside it, taking care not to hurt the roots. Back in the house, I find a cotton bag that will degrade easily, gently place Star in it – with her head sticking out slightly – and carry her out to the garden. The burial is swift and subdued, and afterwards I wander around the house – which has signs of Star's presence everywhere – and think about whether I should remove everything immediately, or leave it a while.

Star the Rabbit taught me so much, especially about unconditional love, and all she ever asked for was fresh broccoli and coriander. I miss her presence in this physical plane – but I can feel her energy and I know it's not lost. I hope to see her again one day (many, many years in the future).

2011
Age: 48

AFTERWORD

If I speak in the tongues of men and of angels, but have not love, I am but a noisy gong or a clanging cymbal. And if I have prophetic powers, and understand all mysteries and all knowledge, and if I have all faith, so as to remove mountains, but have not love, I am nothing. If I give away all I have, and if I deliver up my body to be burned, but have not love, I gain nothing.

Love is patient and kind; love does not envy or boast; it is not arrogant or rude. It does not insist on its own way; it is not irritable or resentful; it does not rejoice at wrongdoing, but rejoices with the truth. Love bears all things, believes all things, hopes all things, endures all things.

Love never ends ...

So now faith, hope, and love abide, these three; but the greatest of these is love.

1 Corinthians 13: 1-13

I never, *ever*, imagined that I would quote reverently from the writings of Saint Paul in any book of mine. Muslims aren't really comfortable with Paul, because he is the architect of the theological rift between Islam and Christianity.

And yet, these words of Paul are *so right* and so powerful. Without Love – what are we, what have we? Throughout the world, absolute certainty, righteousness and outrage have displaced Love and compassion. So, although we *all* know that we are right, where are we without Love?

It's such a difficult lesson to understand that someone can be wrong in theory and yet right in practice – because we want the world to be black and white, right and wrong, us and *them*.

The Cold War was a happy time for me, a young Muslim boy from Pakistan, growing up in London. America was working with Pakistan and various Muslim countries to drive the godless Communists out of Afghanistan; my home country's historical enemy India was aligned more with Russia; there was no issue of being on the wrong side. No one could confuse me for a godless Communist – I was on the same side as 'the West', the same side as James Bond and The Six Million Dollar Man (that seems pretty cheap now). We, who all believed in one God, were united together.

I was even able to read the description of James Bond in the novels by Ian Fleming ('black hair', 'dark face', 'longish nose') and come to the conclusion that there wasn't much difference between James Bond and myself (apart from the cigarettes, vodka and women). James Bond was the ultimate establishment figure, and because I was like him, I also *belonged*. Belonging was very important to me – I was growing up in a society which was, in parts, inherently racist, and constantly advising me to 'go home'. (The need to belong is very important to human beings. The problem is: we are often careless and unthinking in what we choose to belong to, and on what basis.)

Then, something unexpected happened. The godless Communists became capitalists and joined 'the West'. After that, there was a vacuum. And, as Gore Vidal commented in the late eighties, the military-industrial complex cannot stand a vacuum. There has to be an 'other' – someone to be angry at, to be afraid of, to hate. It gives us a feeling of validation and self-worth.

A few years later, something else completely unexpected happened: 9/11. What a horrible event, a day of rage and inhuman madness – but also of courage and compassion. But beyond the human tragedy of that day, out of the dust and the rubble, a new 'other' began to emerge … and it was me.

It was not unexpected that some people in America would be outraged at Muslims for this barbaric act. We should not be surprised at the abuse and vitriol being hurled around the Internet. It's what people do when they are hurt, angry and afraid of something they don't understand. What is disappointing is those so-called Muslims who immediately fell into a lazy tribal position over this tragedy – saying that it was America's fault, because of its foreign policies. And therein lies the problem: how easily we fall into tribal groups, based on some arbitrary shared attribute, and so easily dehumanise and demonise 'the other'.

But could it be that 'the other' isn't a homogenous group which has one opinion, one motive and one set of values? Could it be that 'the other' is human like us, has a valid point of view – perhaps may even be 'right' sometimes?

I observed in despair as the world descended into an insane, hate-filled tribalism, driven by certain dark forces because it suited their agendas. How they wanted to present everything as black and white, good and evil, us and them. *'America is waging war on Islam and wants to oppress and kill Muslims.' 'All Muslims are crazy hate-filled terrorists who oppress women.'* Everything so simple. A homogenous 'other' you can hate, attack and kill without moral ambiguities.

And this same insanity appeared at home in England on 7th July 2005 with the Tube bombers and I wondered: 'Did these young men not grow up in the same Britain that I did?' The answer, I learned later, was apparently not.

The difference between a civilised person and a barbarian is that a civilised person, although outraged by some unjust act – and if unable to understand and forgive, which is the highest course – will only consider taking action against the actual perpetrator of the crime. But the barbarian is happy to take revenge against *anyone* that he can *associate* with the actual guilty party – even through some arbitrary common attribute, such as race or religion. We've been doing this for thousands of years.

I get angry when some people in the West make hurtful and unfair comments about 'all Muslims'. But we Muslims should refrain from doing the same about America and 'the West'. There is no more 'one West' (or even 'one America') than there is 'one Islam' in the whole world. We Muslims fight each other just as much as we fight non-Muslims.

Islam is the most deliberately misrepresented and most misunderstood religion on the planet – to the extent that even many Muslims don't know what is truly Islamic and what isn't (although some are *sure* that they know). (I am not claiming to be an authority here – but neither should others.) Therefore, whenever you hear something outrageous or barbaric about Islam, please bear in mind the possibility that it may not be authentic – even if an uptight and agitated man with an unkempt beard and wearing something unfashionable on his head says that it is.

Recently in a bookshop, I met a white English man who told me (somewhat loudly and with hostility): 'I know all about Islam!' I just didn't have the time or the energy to present him with the *possibility* that perhaps he did not – it would have taken hours, perhaps days.

The trouble is: an outrage-inducing untruth spreads many times faster and further than a dull, reasonable fact. Sadly, we live in a world where truth is less important than negative emotions, where lies become unchallenged, established 'knowledge'. Outrage is like a drug – and most of us are addicted. The tabloid newspapers have exploited this for decades, and now social media is the dangerously incendiary enabler.

When some people chant *'Death to America!'*, which America do they mean?

The America that intervened to save the Bosnian Muslims from total genocide? Why did America even bother? To my knowledge, there's no oil or strategic value in Bosnia. Could it have been because it was the morally correct thing to do (without consideration of race or religion)?

The America that tries to prevent massacres in Africa, and gets attacked and abused and sees its own fallen soldiers' bodies being mutilated – for having the courage to do the right thing?

The America that arrives quickly with emergency assistance, whenever and wherever there's a catastrophic disaster, anywhere in the world, and without strings attached?

The America that yearned to stop the genocide, rape and murder in Darfur, but could no longer bear the consequence of so-called Muslim countries accusing it of waging a Western imperialist 'war on Islam'? (And yet these so-called Muslim countries did *nothing* about Darfur, because it's only black Africans, and who cares about them, even if they are Muslims?)

The America that put men on the moon, and was gracious enough to say that it was on behalf of 'all mankind'?

From the moment we are born, we are herded into a tribe and compelled to give our affiliations, our loyalty, to some group or other and, in so doing, we cut ourselves off from the greater whole.

How difficult it is to look at another person for the first time and see only a kindred soul, rather than a black person, an Asian, a woman, a Sikh, a Jew, a homeless person, a Mexican, a gay person, a transgender person, a Tamil, a Tutsi, a Shia, an overweight person. When we look at another human being, we focus instantly on their *separation* from ourselves, rather than their *oneness*.

The loyalty that we should have for our collective Oneness is given frivolously: to a country, a political party, a football team, a religion or sect, a gang, a socio-economic group; in fact, to anything other than to where it truly belongs – *to all of us*.

And the logical outcome of this tribalism is Partition, separation, segregation, security barriers, borders and barbed wire.

But Partition does not end inter-tribal conflict. In Pakistan, clashes between Sunnis and Shias continue to the present day. Occasionally, violence breaks out between 'natives' of the region, and those who came because of Partition. What is the ultimate logic of Partition? That we must divide and isolate ourselves in ever-smaller groups, until surrounded only by those who are exactly like us in every way, so that no reason for conflict can arise?

There is some serious growing-up that needs to take place in many quarters. In societies in which individuals have no freedom, no ability to make choices (and face the consequences of their choices), limited information and no right to think or express thoughts, there is little capacity for personal and social growth. Without the Journey, and all it teaches, what purpose does Life have?

There is hope for us all on this beautiful Earth, if we can just remember always our common humanity – without the illusions of race, religion, gender and tribe.

Don't get me started on the subject of women. Okay, I have to say something. I am deeply concerned about women's history, their rights and their current situation. Western women may be free and equal (theoretically), but around the world, most women are not.

Women are generally more intuitive than men, and more emotionally intelligent. Men are afraid of the intuition, and they resent the fact that because they desire women sexually, this gives women some power over them. They react to this by dehumanising women into mere property or sex objects, or both.

Where men have felt threatened by women's greater intuitive abilities and resistance to the empires of institutionalised religion, they have hysterically demonised women, even burning them as witches. What words are there to describe this behaviour? Beyond me, I'm afraid.

Western women have fought their difficult war and have effectively liberated themselves from the status of property to that of human beings, with equal rights. Their sisters throughout the developing and Islamic worlds are still dealing with this struggle. Women in *so-called* Islamic countries are denied the very rights that they are guaranteed under Islam. They would be better off in the West.

Where in the Qur'an does it say that women must be covered from head to foot? It does not. The requirement is only for self-dignity. There is plenty of flexibility to allow for culture and context. We should be mature enough to be able to make such judgments without fear.

The obsession with covering women from head to toe stems from the desire to control women as property and prevent them being sought by other men. This is based on bigotry and deep-seated insecurity, not Islam. The woman's opinion appears to be irrelevant. Unfortunately, some Muslim women also have become convinced that this is pure Islam, it is not negotiable, and they seek to enforce it puritanically on other Muslim women.

If a woman is kept wrapped-up, not allowed to drive, not allowed to play tennis, or jog or swim or do aerobics or pursue academic, social, artistic and intellectual activities, then what becomes of her? Surely she becomes only a *shadow* person, a mere fraction of her true potential as a human being?

I am saddened by what Man has done to Woman. We have denied Her value and dignity; burned as witches our sisters who showed special intuitive gifts; raped and mutilated and sold and enslaved and buried in sand and thrown into rivers the hated, feared other half of ourselves. Truly, this is an abomination.

A quick note to any Asian (i.e. Indian, Pakistani, Bangladeshi) young people reading this. You are *not* responsible for your parents' happiness. Your first priority must be your own happiness (especially in the areas of love, marriage and career). Whether your parents *choose* to be happy or not is *entirely up to them*. But you cannot make your parents happy by making yourself unhappy – that ultimately destroys everyone's happiness.

This is a lesson your parents may still need to learn, despite their advanced years. Life is a great opportunity, and your personal happiness and fulfilment – however these are defined – are both the journey and the destination. Use your brain, but listen to your heart. Once you've balanced the two, you're all set. (I'm still trying to achieve this, but at least I don't deny my intuition anymore.)

If you are a girl and you want to pursue education and a career – of course you must. It is your divinely ordained right! Don't let anyone tell you any different. Those miserable meddling people trying to influence your parents do not have *your* best interests at heart. They just want you to be miserable as well.

Man or woman, if your parents are hassling you into a marriage and it doesn't *feel* right to you – don't do it! You can hear this from me or you can learn it the hard way. Just remember and meditate upon these wise holy words of ancient metaphysical wisdom: '*It is better to be on the shelf than in the wrong cupboard.*' This is more important than anything your anxious parents, their interfering friends, or sullen religious 'teachers' can tell you.

If you live in Europe or America or Australia, under no circumstances be complicit in allowing someone to be imported from the sub-continent to be married to you (especially if you are a woman). This immigration scam has been going on for over half-a-century under the not-so-watchful eye of the authorities, who don't interfere due to 'cultural sensitivity'. That candidate being imported isn't really the 'perfect match' for you. (Remember: everyone involved in the matchmaking process is a liar, exaggerator or reality denier.) This transaction will ruin your life. You have the *right* to a free and happy life *on your own terms*. There is nothing selfish or dishonourable about that. Just say: 'No!' *Break free* if you have to.

On the subject of 'cultural sensitivity', may I now raise a matter which it may be politically incorrect to mention. I am proud and amazed at how much Britain has changed just in my lifetime. Considerable effort and investment has been made by the authorities to persuade white people not to be racist – and it has been largely successful. Racism has been moved from being casually normal to being structurally unacceptable. There are still racists, of course, but they are much less likely to express racism with impunity in a public space than when I was a boy. Well done, Britain – I am proud of this country and proud to be British. (Sometimes though, people we quickly brand 'racist' actually have valid concerns, but are frustrated by the mainstream political parties' reluctance to address genuine 'elephant in the room' issues.)

But, racism is not a one-way street. It is not exclusively something which white people express towards non-white people. It seems not to have occurred to the authorities that non-white people (from the Indian subcontinent, from the Middle East etc) can also be racist, and this endemic racism has remained under the radar screen, completely unchallenged.

I don't have an immediate solution – I am just pointing this out. I am not constrained by 'cultural sensitivity'.

Since the experiences related (with painfully embarrassing honesty) in this book, I have had some profound learning experiences. I finally understand what the Sufi text was conveying – we are all on a journey back to 'God' and there are many converging paths. All are valid – just take the one which works for you. Whether it's the right path *for you* can be determined by how it makes you feel and treat others. If you feel joy, peace and compassion – that's a good sign. If the feelings inside you are fear, contempt, superiority and hatred – I would humbly suggest a reappraisal of your path.

How things turned out for me has been completely unimagined. Now I believe in the moral and spiritual validity of other religions (I understand and respect Hinduism!); I don't believe that God wants me to hate gay people (one of my best friends is gay, although I didn't realise this for years, and I stayed with him and his partner recently – *no, not Milton! I was Best Man at his wedding*); I believe that honest friendship is the most effective approach with women; and *To thine own self be true* is the best approach to life. And a beautiful little rabbit taught me that not only do animals have souls, but they can practise unconditional love more naturally than most humans can.

The greatest threat to our collective future is the 'lazy tribalism' we so easily fall into, the need to belong, and the need for someone else to fear and hate – the 'other' who defines our group by our difference from them.

It's tragic to see that some unscrupulous elements in America (and other places) today are trying to drive a new McCarthyism – using the tried and trusted formula of stoking up fear against a sinister, incomprehensible 'other' (homogenised into a singular entity) to further their own ends. Some in the media are hungry for any 'news' which can outrage people, without any sense of balance or context. There is a complete absence of moral accountability for the impact of such deliberate hate-mongering.

And it seems to work – it always does. But the America I know has surely grown beyond this – America is a country I truly admire, respect, enjoy and love (this is not necessarily referring to all Administrations, but to the nation, its people and its principles).

Twice (in 2009 and 2012) I have driven around mainland America and conducted speaking tours encompassing approximately 40 cities, on the subject of 're-humanisation' of the relationship between America and the Muslim world. These were extraordinary experiences. Despite the image of America projected by the media, I struggled to find any hostility at a personal level (even when the car broke down in South Carolina).

Many of my talks were hosted by Unitarian Universalist churches. The UUs do not have any fixed religious doctrine – they believe that the inherent worth and dignity of every individual are not determined by DNA or belief. Their core values are compassion, humanity, social justice and a commitment to world peace. *That sounds good to me!* It was an honour and a privilege that they would host me – but I also realised that I needed to reach a wider audience. The people coming to my talks were mostly already on-board with peace and compassion!

A little while ago, in the gloomy darkness of a Scottish winter, I was sitting with Milton in front of the log fire of his cottage in the countryside. Outside, the snow was two feet deep and the temperature was like Siberia. We were discussing this book.

'There's a huge gap between where you are now, and where the main part of the book finishes,' says Milton (stating the obvious). 'At the end, you are still pretty narrow-minded and quite unpleasant in many of your views. You haven't explained what happened to make you change so much. How are you going to address that?'

I shift about uncomfortably and nudge the glowing logs with the brass poker. 'I know, I know … I'll have to relate that somehow. I'll have to write another book which describes what happened. When will I ever find the time …?'

What Milton was alluding to is the unimagined changes in my thinking. How the heartless arrogance of absolute certainty has been replaced by the joy and humility brought about by embracing continuous learning and discovery. How every stranger, every situation, every bump in the road can bring precious growth. How I have come to realise that so many things I believed to be absolutely true were fear-driven and deluded.

Fortunately, I am not alone in this. We are all on this journey together and we are making progress. We are going to change everything about our attitudes, fears and behaviours that is not working and we are going to do it in *this* generation, because our time is running out. But we can't force this enlightenment, just as we can't force peace and justice with bombs and tanks and helicopter gunships.

We will have to achieve it *one heart at a time*.

Imran Ahmad

www.unimagined.co.uk
www.unimagined.org
Twitter: @unimagined

BOOK GROUP

Suggested Questions for Discussion

1. To what extent is *The Perfect Gentleman* the story of a Muslim boy, as opposed to that of *any* boy, or of *anybody*?

2. Imran Ahmad has said about the writing of the book: '*The Perfect Gentleman* is not written as a reflection on things past – with the benefit of hindsight and maturity – but as a narrative which takes place in the moment.' Do you agree that the book excludes a perspective derived from 'hindsight and maturity' or do you think it plays off the opposition between a child's and an adult's perspective? What is your evidence?

3. Why does *The Perfect Gentleman* change narrative tense in the fourth chapter?

4. Which events and experiences in the book strike you as most crucial in shaping Imran's identity as both British and a Muslim – as a *British Muslim*?

5. Autobiography does not straightforwardly offer the 'truth' about a life; it always involves the selection and shaping of particular events. What is the logic behind the choice of episodes that Imran has selected?

6. What is the importance of cars in the book?

7. Imran's life is touched at several points by racism, either directly or indirectly. Which incidents in particular stand out? What is Imran's attitude towards these incidents and what techniques does the book use to critique racist attitudes?

8. *The Perfect Gentleman* tackles a potentially highly sensitive topic: what it means to be a Muslim in the West today. How does the book present this topic and how do you respond to its presentation?

9. What is *The Perfect Gentleman's* attitude towards women? Does it change during the course of the story?

10. Why is there no focus on radical Islamism or terrorism in this book?

11. What are the main changes in thinking which Imran undergoes during his life?

Questions courtesy of Professor Ruth Evans – Department of English, Saint Louis University, Saint Louis, MO

ENDNOTES

for non-UK and Younger Readers

This book is written using British English grammar, which differs sometimes from American English grammar in how quotation marks are placed.

———————————————

[1] Infant school is ages 5 to 7 and junior school is ages 8 to 11. In England, the school year runs from September to July. Each chapter of this book (except the last one) represents one school year plus the summer vacation.

[2] 'Doctor Who' is a famous science-fiction television programme which everyone in the UK knows about. The Doctor is a traveller in time and space, who has amazing adventures. His craft is called a TARDIS and is disguised as an old police box (a special telephone booth for contacting the police — now obsolete). It is bigger on the inside than it appears on the outside. Whenever the actor who plays the character is replaced, the Doctor undergoes a 'regeneration', so that his body changes into that of the new actor.

[3] In many parts of Britain, lunch is referred to as 'dinner', and dinner is referred to as 'tea', or possibly 'supper'. But universally, the ladies who served the lunchtime meal in schools were known as 'dinner ladies'.

[4] The main shopping street of every town and district is usually called the 'High Street'.

[5] There were two types of 'dinner lady' – those who served lunch and those who patrolled the playground during the lunch break to keep an eye on the children (while the teaching staff sheltered in the relative safety of their staff room).

[6] A 'pantomime' is a comedy theatrical production with exaggerated characters, traditionally staged in the Christmas season.

[7] The '*Carry On*' films were an iconic and popular series of comedy films with extremely vulgar humour.

[8] The 'building society' was a financial institution specifically for saving money for the long-term and getting a mortgage – not for holding a cheque account as with a bank (in America this would be a savings and loan association). Nowadays the roles of banks and building societies completely overlap.

[9] C&A was a well-known cheap mass-market clothing store in the UK, comparable to Kmart, but now extinct.

[10] 'Ordinary' or O-levels were national exams taken at age 16, typically in about six to eight subjects. Your O-level results would be a good indication of which subjects you were good at. 'Advanced' or A-levels were taken in the Sixth Form at age 18, in about three subjects. Your A-level results would define your eligibility for a university or college place.

[11] In those days, college/university education was free to residents of Britain, and we also received a 'grant cheque' every term, to help with living expenses. The amount of this grant was based on your parents' disposable household income. Students from poorer backgrounds would get 'full grant' – ironically making them more cash-rich at university than middle class students, whose parents rarely made up the difference between their actual grant and the recommended full amount. There was no such thing as 'student loans'.

[12] In the UK, generally we don't track Grade Point Averages. University degrees are classified — through a combination of exams, course work and projects — as a 'First' (outstanding, very hard to get), an 'Upper Second' (very good), a 'Lower Second' (good), a 'Third' (not very good), or a 'Pass' (a disaster).

[13] The MOT is a Ministry of Transport vehicle safety inspection certificate, mandatory on all cars over three years old, and valid for one year from the date of the inspection.